KALLIS' iBT
TOEFL® PATTERN

Reading 1

KALLIS' iBT TOEFL® Pattern Reading 1

KALLIS EDU, INC.
7490 Opportunity Road, Suite 203
San Diego, CA 92111
(858) 277-8600
info@kallisedu.com
www.kallisedu.com

ISBN-10: 1-4953-1751-X
ISBN-13: 978-1-4953-1751-4

iBT TOEFL® Pattern - Reading I is the first
of our three-level iBT TOEFL® Reading Exam
preparation book series.

Our **iBT TOEFL® Pattern Reading** series helps
students understand the *context* of each question
and provides numerous types of *practice* to
master test-taking skills. **Hacking Strategies**
and **Quick Looks** break down each question
type seen on the official exam so that students
have a better understanding of what they are
asked to look for in each question. *Practice*
includes **Warm Up** questions, **Quick Practice**
for focusing on particular question types, and an
Actual Test that combines all question types.

KALLIS

KALLIS'

TOEFL® iBT

PATTERN

READING 1

EXPLORER

Getting Started

A study guide should familiarize the reader with the material found on the test, develop unique methods that can be used to solve various question types, and provide practice questions to challenge future test-takers. *KALLIS' iBT TOEFL® Pattern Series* aims to accomplish all these study tasks by presenting iBT TOEFL® test material in an organized, comprehensive, and easy-to-understand way.

KALLIS' iBT TOEFL® Pattern Reading Series presents the ten different types of questions that you can expect to encounter on the reading component of the iBT TOEFL exam. An entire chapter is devoted to each question type, allowing you to easily discover which question types you find most challenging and then develop an individual strategy for each type of question. Each chapter presents the test material in unique ways in order to make the practice questions as easy to understand as possible.

Putting the Question in Context

▶ The beginning of each chapter provides a definition of the question type that you will learn to master throughout the chapter.

▶ The *Question Model* section located below the definition provides a sample question that is then solved in a step-by-step process called the **Hacking Strategy**.

▶ The *Question Formats* section presents the specific wording used to ask each question.

▶ The *Tips* section provides helpful hints so that you know the features of a correct answer and how to identify incorrect answers.

Hacking Strategy

• **Hacking Strategy** provides a step-by-step visualization of how to approach each question.

• Because dealing with so many different types of questions can be confusing, the **Example Breakdown** that follows the **Hacking Strategy** develops a common process to assist you in properly analyzing the text and selecting the most logical answer.

Quick Look

• **Quick Look** provides essential information on how to solve the practice questions.

• The hints given in **Quick Look** can be utilized to learn new aspects of English grammar, and they can be used to brush up on concepts that may already be familiar to you.

• For the more difficult types of questions that are presented in later chapters, **Quick Look** combines visual representations and written descriptions to illuminate what you need to find in each question.

Enhancing Test-Taking Skills with Numerous Practice Questions

Though understanding test-taking strategies will greatly improve your success on the reading test, the best way to improve your skills is through practice. Thus, *KALLIS' iBT TOEFL® Pattern Reading Series* includes a variety of practice questions with varying levels of difficulty.

Warm Up

- The **Warm Up** provides practice questions that are simplified versions of the problem types that you will encounter on the actual iBT TOEFL exam.

Quick Practice

- Each chapter contains **Quick Practice**, which is composed of ten practice passages with questions that elaborate on the skills developed during the **Quick Look** and **Warm Up**.
- At the end of each chapter, you will be challenged with a **Pop Quiz** that tests your vocabulary skills using words from the passages in the corresponding chapter.

Exercises

- At the end of every second chapter, **Exercises** provides a mini-test that requires you to distinguish one type of question from another and use multiple strategies within the same reading passage.

Actual Practice

- Located in Chapter 11, the **Actual Practice** provides passages with multiple question types that require the reader to combine skills developed throughout the book.
- This section is more challenging and should be attempted only after you understand the types of questions presented in Chapters 1 through 10.

Actual Test

- The **Actual Test** will familiarize you with the format of the official TOEFL reading test and includes types of questions from each chapter.
- A scaled scoring chart is located at the beginning of the test so that you can grade yourself and get an idea of how you might score on the official TOEFL reading test.
- After the **Actual Test**, you will find **Actual TOEFL Vocabulary**, which contains hundreds of the most commonly employed vocabulary words in TOEFL reading tests.

In Case You Need Help

▶ Toward the back of this book, you will find the **Answer Key**, which provides the correct answer to each question and includes explanations.

▶ If you do not want to repeatedly flip to the back of the book for answers, simply cut out the **Simple Answers** at the very back of the book. **Simple Answers** provides a quick reference so you can confirm that all your answers are correct.

Are you ready to explore?

Table of
Contents

I. What Is a Vocabulary Question?

Vocabulary in Context

The vocabulary question asks you to define a vocabulary word or a phrase as it is used in a sentence. Everything surrounding the vocabulary word is called its *context*. Since many English words can have several meanings, the definition of the vocabulary word or the phrase is determined by its context.

A. VOCABULARY QUESTION MODEL

The strong wind **struck** the table, causing it to fall over.

1. The word "**struck**" is closest in meaning to

   (A) held
   (B) touched
   (C) hit
   (D) tapped

B. VOCABULARY QUESTION FORMATS

The word/phrase is closest in meaning to _____.
The word/phrase means _____.
The word/phrase _____ probably means _____.
What does the word/phrase _____ mean?
In stating _____, the author means that _____.

C. TIPS

1. To identify the correct meaning of the word in context, take a close look at sentence and grammatical structures, usage of punctuation marks, and meanings of surrounding words.
2. In some cases, you can figure out the meaning of a word simply based on your understanding of the passage's main idea.
3. On the official TOEFL exam, some unusual or technical terms have hyperlinked definitions. In this book, such terms are defined at the end of the passage. Because the definition is provided, these words will not appear as questions.

II. Hacking Strategy

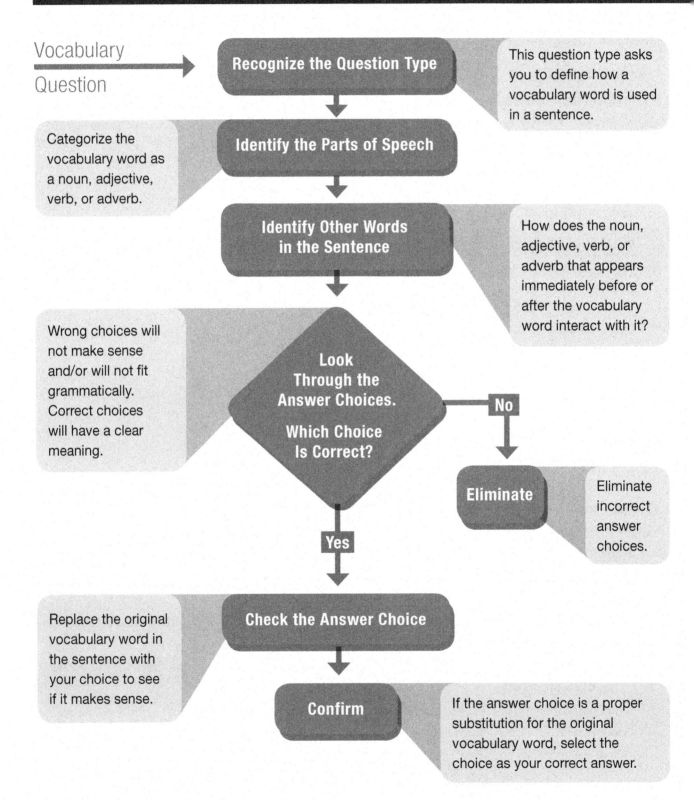

Vocabulary Question → **Recognize the Question Type**

This question type asks you to define how a vocabulary word is used in a sentence.

Identify the Parts of Speech

Categorize the vocabulary word as a noun, adjective, verb, or adverb.

Identify Other Words in the Sentence

How does the noun, adjective, verb, or adverb that appears immediately before or after the vocabulary word interact with it?

Look Through the Answer Choices. Which Choice Is Correct?

Wrong choices will not make sense and/or will not fit grammatically. Correct choices will have a clear meaning.

No → **Eliminate**

Eliminate incorrect answer choices.

Yes ↓

Check the Answer Choice

Replace the original vocabulary word in the sentence with your choice to see if it makes sense.

Confirm

If the answer choice is a proper substitution for the original vocabulary word, select the choice as your correct answer.

(EXAMPLE

| Recognize the Question Type | The strong wind **struck** the table, causing it to fall over. | The word "**struck**" is closest in meaning to
(A) held
(B) touched
(C) hit
(D) tapped |

| Identify the Parts of Speech | **Struck** is a verb describing the wind's action. |

| Identify Other Words in the Sentence | *Strong* is an adjective that describes the *wind*, which is the subject noun. This means that the *strong wind* is what is doing the striking. The *table* is the object noun, meaning that the *table* is the object being **struck** by the *strong wind*. |

| Look Through the Answer Choices. Which Choice Is Correct? | (A) held
(B) touched
(C) hit
(D) tapped | The result of the table being **struck** by the strong wind was that it fell. This information gives us a better idea of what **struck** could mean. |

| Eliminate Incorrect Choices | • Eliminate **Choice A** because *holding* something means keeping something in one's hand or grasping.
• Eliminate **Choice B** because *touching* something means lightly coming into contact.
• Eliminate **Choice D** because *tapping* something means striking something lightly. |

| Check the Answer Choice | The strong wind *hit* the table, causing it to fall over.

This makes sense because *hitting* a table could also cause it to fall over. |

| Confirm | Select the correct answer — **Choice C**. |

II. Hacking Strategy

Word Prefixes, Suffixes, Roots

Prefix, Suffix or Root	Meaning	Example and Definition
ann, anni, annu, enn	yearly	**anni**versary: anni (yearly) + versary (to turn) = *yearly celebration of a special date* per**enni**al: per (throughout) + enni (yearly) + al (additionally) = *everlasting*
ant, anti	against, opposite of	**Ant**arctic: ant (against) + arctic (North) = *South Pole* **anti**social: anti (opposite of) + social = *unsociable*
ation	action, resulting state (noun)	narr**ation**: narrate (to tell a story) + ation (an action) = *storytelling* altern**ation**: alternate (to change) + ion (state) = *successive change*
aut, auto	self	**auto**mobile: auto (self) + mobile (moving) = *self-moving vehicle* **auto**nomous: auto (self) + nomos (law) = *self-governing*
bi, bin	two	**bin**ocular: bin (two) + ocul (eye) = *an optical device* **bi**weekly: bi (two) + weekly = *every two weeks*
co, col	with, together	**col**league: col (with) + league (unity) = *a fellow worker* **co**education: co (with) + education (learning) = *males and females learning together*
de, dif	do the opposite of, reverse, against	**de**stroy: de (down) + stroy (to build) = *to ruin* **de**crease: de (against) + crease (to grow) = *to lessen*
di, dif, dis	not, do the opposite of	**dis**agree: dis (not) + agree = *to oppose* **dis**assemble: dis (not) + assemble = *to undo something that is assembled*
en	make	**en**gage: en (make) + gage (to promise) = *to involve* **en**force: en (make) + force = *to make sure that someone follows a course of action*
ess	female	act**ress**: act (to play) + ress (female) = *a woman who acts* god**dess**: god + ess (female) = *a female god*
ex	out, former	**ex**tract: ex (out) + tract (to draw) = *to pull out* **ex**hale: ex (out) + hale (to breathe) = *to breathe out*

Prefix, Suffix or Root	Meaning	Example and Definition
for, fore	before	**fore**cast: fore (before) + cast (to decide) = *to estimate* **fore**see: fore (before) + see = *to predict*
form, formul	shape	per**form**: per (thoroughly) + form (to shape) = *to accomplish* **formul**ate: formul (to shape) + ate (state of) = *to compose*
hood	state, condition	child**hood**: child + hood (state) = *the state of being a child* parent**hood**: parent + hood (state) = *the state of being a parent*
hyper	over, above, too much	**hyper**active: hyper (above) + active = *overly active* **hyper**sensitive: hyper (above) + sensitive = *excessively sensitive*
il, im, in, ir	not, without	**il**legible: il (not) + legible (easily read) = *hard to read* **im**mortal: im (not) + mortal (dead) = *never-dying*
inter	among, between	**inter**rupt: inter (among) + rupt (to break) = *to stop something* **inter**national: inter (between) + national (countries) = *worldwide*
ism	state, condition, action	hero**ism**: hero (a person of extraordinary courage) + ism (state) = *bravery* critic**ism**: critic (a person who judges) + ism (state) = *judgment*
micro	small, millionth	**micro**scope: micro (small) + scope (viewing instrument) = *an optical instrument used to view small things* **micro**be: micro (small) + be (life) = *an extremely small living thing*
mis	wrong, bad	**mis**conduct: mis (wrong) + conduct (behavior) = *wrongdoing* **mis**inform: mis (wrong) + inform (to instruct) = *to give inaccurate information*
non	not, without	**non**sense: non (without) + sense (feeling, understanding) = *absurdity* **non**fiction: non (not) + fiction (imaginary story) = *real story*
over	excessive, above	**over**work: over (excessive) + work = *to work too much* **over**dose: over (above) + dose (quantity) = *consuming an excessive amount of something*
post	after, later	**post**pone: post (after) + pon (to put) = *to delay* **post**humous: post (after) + humous (the burial) = *happening after a death*
pre	before	**pre**cede: pre (before) + cede (to go) = *to go or come before* **pre**view: pre (before) + view (to look) = *to view in advance*
re	again, back	**re**voke: re (again) + vok (to call) = *to recall* **re**tract: re (back) + tract (to draw) = *to draw something back*
se	without, apart	**se**cure: se (without) + cure (to care) = *to keep something safe* **se**clude: se (apart) + clude (to shut) = *to keep apart, isolate*

Prefix, Suffix or Root	Meaning	Example and Definition
semi	half, partial	**semi**final: semi (half) + final = *the round before the final* **semi**conscious: semi (partial) + conscious (aware) = *not fully conscious*
some	to a considerable degree	quarrel**some**: quarrel (argument) + some (to a degree) = *argumentative* burden**some**: burden (a load, duty) + some (to a degree) = *causing difficulty*
sov, sove, sur	over, above	**sove**reign: sove (over) + reign (to govern) = *a supreme ruler* **sur**vive: sur (over) + vive (to live) = *to continue to live*
trans	across, beyond	**trans**port: trans (across) + port (to carry) = *to physically carry something* **trans**mit: trans (across) + mit (to send) = *to send or forward*
tri	three	**tri**angle: tri (three) + angle = *a figure having three sides and three angles* **tri**athlon: tri (three) + athlon (event) = *an athletic competition with three events*
ultra	beyond, extreme	**ultra**modern: ultra (beyond) + modern = *very advanced* **ultra**sonic: ultra (beyond) + sonic (of sound) = *(sound waves) beyond human hearing*
un	not, opposite of	**un**alterable: un (not) + alter (to change) + able (capable) = *unable to be changed* **un**friendly: un (not) + friend + ly (in what manner) = *not welcoming*
uni	one, single	**uni**ty: uni (one) + ty (state of) = *being united or combined into one* **uni**que: uni (one) + que (suffix) = *being the only one of its kind*

IV. Warm Up

Circle the vocabulary word that correctly completes each sentence.

1. The boy rode to school on his (**bicycle** / **binoculars**).

2. The truck driver had to (**translate** / **transport**) the oranges in his truck across the country.

3. Our legs were so (**overlooked** / **overworked**) during the basketball game that we needed massages.

4. The professor's lecture was (**interrupted** / **interacted**) by loud noises from outside the classroom.

5. These photos are the only things that (**survived** / **surveyed**) the storm.

6. Because it wanted to make its own decisions, the state decided to become (**autonomous** / **automated**).

7. Since her new shirt did not fit, Jessica (**retracted** / **returned**) it to the store.

8. Cindy's favorite type of story to read is (**nonsense** / **nonfiction**).

9. Please be sure that the load on the truck is (**secured** / **selected**) so that it does not fall off.

10. Because Ted was so (**engaged** / **enforced**) in reading, he was late for his soccer practice.

11. The fire completely (**destroyed** / **decreased**) all of the buildings on the street.

12. Tina has been training very hard to compete in the (**triangle** / **triathlon**) this year.

13. He was the only person in the entire party wearing a red sweater, so he looked (**unique** / **unilateral**).

14. We would like to (**preview** / **precede**) the course materials before we enroll in the class.

15. The young boy's parents considered him to be (**hypersensitive** / **hyperactive**) because he could never sit still.

16. The official was fired from her position due to (**misconduct** / **misinterpretation**).

17. Todd had a terrible toothache, so he went to the dentist to get his tooth (**extracted** / **exhaled**).

18. The weather (**forefront** / **forecast**) predicted that there will be snow tonight.

19. The (**Antarctic** / **antisocial**) region of the world is very cold.

20. The (**unity** / **unicycle**) of the group allowed its members to make decisions together.

CHAPTER 1
VOCABULARY QUESTION

V. Quick Practice

Practice #1

Read the passage. Then answer the questions that follow.

New York City has no **parallel** in the United States. Many churches in the city were built in the Gothic **tradition**. There are also many **gleaming**, modern skyscrapers. Most American publishing **houses** are in New York City. Also, **outstanding** orchestras and dance companies **perform** at Lincoln Center.

1) The word "**parallel**" means
   (A) equal
   (B) type
   (C) location
   (D) line

2) The word "**tradition**" means
   (A) belief
   (B) style
   (C) culture
   (D) life

3) The word "**gleaming**" probably means
   (A) enormous
   (B) new
   (C) shiny
   (D) strange

4) The word "**houses**" probably means
   (A) empires
   (B) subjects
   (C) families
   (D) companies

5) The word "**outstanding**" means
   (A) talented
   (B) real
   (C) correct
   (D) loud

6) The word "**perform**" probably means
   (A) put on a show
   (B) stand out
   (C) play a part
   (D) run around

Practice #2

Read the passage. Then answer the questions that follow.

Dolls **help** children in many ways. For example, they **serve** as objects that children can love. They also provide an **outlet** for a child's emotions—how children play with dolls **reveals** their feelings. Children also **rehearse** adult **roles**, such as parent or doctor, by playing with dolls.

7) The word "**help**" means
   (A) teach
   (B) assist
   (C) dislike
   (D) supervise

8) The word "**serve**" is closest in meaning to
   (A) live
   (B) start
   (C) work
   (D) return

9) The word "**outlet**" means
   (A) cause
   (B) method
   (C) memory
   (D) opening

10) The word "**reveals**" means
   (A) shows
   (B) forces
   (C) stops
   (D) raises

11) The word "**rehearse**" is closest in meaning to
   (A) forget
   (B) know
   (C) practice
   (D) find

12) The word "**roles**" means
   (A) styles
   (B) characters
   (C) speeches
   (D) behaviors

Practice #3

Read the passage. Then answer the questions that follow.

African-American musicians may have **absorbed diverse** sources of music as they developed jazz. For instance, music scholars have **detected** Arab Islamic **influences** that may have spread to Africa and been **retained** when enslaved Africans brought their rich music culture to North America. European harmonies and Afro-Latin rhythms from Cuba also became part of the **distinctive** sound of jazz.

13) The word "**absorbed**" means
   (A) taken in
   (B) looked at
   (C) worked with
   (D) referred to

14) The word "**diverse**" means
   (A) appropriate
   (B) similar
   (C) descriptive
   (D) various

15) The word "**detected**" means
   (A) noticed
   (B) taken
   (C) invented
   (D) established

16) The word "**influences**" means
   (A) inventions
   (B) effects
   (C) differences
   (D) activities

17) The word "**retained**" means
   (A) kept
   (B) stolen
   (C) lost
   (D) known

18) The word "**distinctive**" probably means
   (A) famous
   (B) perfect
   (C) official
   (D) unique

Practice #4

Read the passage. Then answer the following questions.

Scientists believe that water **flowed** on Mars billions of years ago. The **evidence consists of** pebbles and valleys that appear to have been smoothed out by streams. Furthermore, scientists have identified liquid water molecules in Martian soil, which may indicate that pools of water exist in **pores** below the surface. A *space probe*—a robotic spacecraft used for research—also has **discovered vast** amounts of frozen water at the planet's poles.

19) The word "**flowed**" means
  (A) flew
  (B) helped
  (C) moved
  (D) relied

20) The word "**evidence**" means
  (A) proof
  (B) work
  (C) appearance
  (D) time

21) The word "**consists of**" probably means
  (A) insists
  (B) includes
  (C) highlights
  (D) realizes

22) The word "**pores**" is closest in meaning to
  (A) drains
  (B) holes
  (C) rocks
  (D) packages

23) The word "**discovered**" means
  (A) used
  (B) explained
  (C) found
  (D) provided

24) The word "**vast**" is closest in meaning to
  (A) thick
  (B) tiny
  (C) frozen
  (D) large

Practice #5

Read the passage. Then answer the questions that follow.

A *library* is a place where resources such as books and newspapers are free to the public. As a result, libraries play a **vital** part in communication and education worldwide. Many **resources** in libraries help people **complete** their work, studies, and networking. Libraries **rank** among society's most **necessary institutions**.

25) The word "**vital**" means
  (A) strange
  (B) lucky
  (C) open
  (D) important

26) The word "**resources**" means
  (A) quiet places
  (B) new ideas
  (C) learning tools
  (D) helpful people

27) The word "**complete**" means
(A) do
(B) create
(C) develop
(D) deliver

28) The word "**rank**" means
(A) start
(B) place
(C) remain
(D) finish

29) The word "**necessary**" means
(A) needed
(B) unique
(C) clever
(D) diverse

30) The word "**institutions**" probably means
(A) malls
(B) businesses
(C) establishments
(D) schools

Practice #6

Read the passage. Then answer the following questions.

People who are **deprived of** sleep cannot **concentrate** because their brains stop working properly. This is **especially** true when performing **routine** tasks. People may be able to carry out these tasks well for short periods, but they may become easily **distracted**. After a while, they become much more **prone** to make mistakes.

31) The expression "**deprived of**" means
(A) desiring
(B) enjoying
(C) forcing
(D) lacking

32) The word "**concentrate**" means
(A) see
(B) focus
(C) survive
(D) concern

33) The word "**especially**" probably means
(A) usually
(B) frankly
(C) particularly
(D) slowly

34) The word "**routine**" means
(A) creative
(B) various
(C) regular
(D) difficult

35) The word "**distracted**" means
(A) anxious
(B) sidetracked
(C) entertained
(D) misunderstood

36) The word "**prone**" probably means
(A) excited
(B) sad
(C) certain
(D) likely

Practice #7

Read the passage. Then answer the questions that follow.

William Shakespeare delights readers for many reasons. His **appeal** is **mostly** due to his **deep** understanding of human **nature**. As a result, his characters are not **conventional**. They are **remarkably** individual human beings.

37) The word "**appeal**" means
   (A) importance
   (B) attraction
   (C) life
   (D) rhythm

38) The word "**mostly**" means
   (A) mainly
   (B) certainly
   (C) slowly
   (D) randomly

39) The word "**deep**" probably means
   (A) strong
   (B) false
   (C) shallow
   (D) general

40) The word "**nature**" is closest in meaning to
   (A) predictions
   (B) services
   (C) characteristics
   (D) supplies

41) The word "**conventional**" probably means
   (A) polite
   (B) old
   (C) typical
   (D) emotional

42) The word "**remarkably**" means
   (A) differently
   (B) variously
   (C) ordinarily
   (D) considerably

Practice #8

Read the passage. Then answer the following questions.

Voting machines provide a fast and **legitimate** way to determine election results. However, these machines must have proper **safeguards** to make it difficult for people to **tamper with** results. Also, good systems must **hinder** the **likelihood** of **erroneous** voting.

43) The word "**legitimate**" means
   (A) cheap
   (B) trustworthy
   (C) original
   (D) professional

44) The word "**safeguards**" probably means
   (A) controls
   (B) alarms
   (C) protections
   (D) parts

45) The expression "**tamper with**" means
(A) change
(B) locate
(C) understand
(D) reject

46) The word "**hinder**" probably means
(A) hide
(B) prevent
(C) increase
(D) provide

47) The word "**likelihood**" means
(A) warning
(B) check
(C) type
(D) possibility

48) The word "**erroneous**" means
(A) necessary
(B) repeated
(C) rushed
(D) mistaken

Practice #9

Read the passage. Then answer the questions that follow.

Sharks sense their **surroundings** in special ways. They have tiny **internal** ears which **contain** cells that can detect vibrations from a great distance away. **In addition**, sharks are able to sense electrical currents. These **traits** help them **maneuver** through the sea.

49) The word "**surroundings**" means
(A) environment
(B) knowledge
(C) experience
(D) strength

50) The word "**internal**" means
(A) thin
(B) inner
(C) powerful
(D) broad

51) The word "**contain**" probably means
(A) share
(B) improve
(C) have
(D) use

52) The expression "**In addition**" means
(A) moreover
(B) next
(C) finally
(D) however

53) The word "**traits**" means
(A) qualities
(B) interests
(C) reasons
(D) quantities

54) The word "**maneuver**" means
(A) support
(B) navigate
(C) maintain
(D) follow

Practice #10

Read the passage. Then answer the following questions.

Opera houses are theaters that are **specifically** designed for opera performances. Most opera houses **seat** more people than do theaters **reserved** only for plays. An opera house also has **equipment** to support the **elaborate** sets **required** by many operas.

55) The word "**specifically**" is closest in meaning to
(A) continually
(B) beautifully
(C) steadily
(D) specially

56) The word "**seat**" is closest in meaning to
(A) hold
(B) attract
(C) make
(D) enjoy

57) The word "**reserved**" means
(A) observed
(B) dedicated
(C) realized
(D) reached

58) The word "**equipment**" is closest in meaning to
(A) devices
(B) advantages
(C) vehicles
(D) effects

59) The word "**elaborate**" is closest in meaning to
(A) complex
(B) valuable
(C) dangerous
(D) old

60) The word "**required**" means
(A) produced
(B) needed
(C) destroyed
(D) employed

POP QUIZ

Select the vocabulary word or phrase that has the closest meaning.

1. **provide**
   A. supply
   B. restrict
   C. reserve
   D. prove

2. **categorize**
   A. classify
   B. decide
   C. concern
   D. involve

3. **make sense**
   A. be reasonable
   B. be capable
   C. be available
   D. be possible

4. **eliminate**
   A. establish
   B. remove
   C. launch
   D. confirm

5. **original**
   A. final
   B. common
   C. obvious
   D. unique

6. **proper**
   A. illegal
   B. simple
   C. proud
   D. suitable

7. **decrease**
   A. defend
   B. improve
   C. lessen
   D. return

8. **disagree**
   A. grant
   B. disappear
   C. oppose
   D. approve

9. **extract**
   A. move in
   B. pull out
   C. make up
   D. start to

10. **forecast**
    A. reflect
    B. judge
    C. think
    D. predict

11. **interrupt**
    A. enter
    B. reduce
    C. disturb
    D. extend

12. **postpone**
    A. delay
    B. continue
    C. maintain
    D. resume

13. **revoke**
    A. remind
    B. cancel
    C. explore
    D. reveal

14. **quarrelsome**
    A. agreeable
    B. friendly
    C. forceful
    D. argumentative

15. **sovereign**
    A. soft
    B. dominant
    C. dismissive
    D. sacred

16. **unique**
    A. distinctive
    B. common
    C. ordinary
    D. abnormal

17. **overlooked**
    A. understood
    B. damaged
    C. unnoticed
    D. handled

18. **play a part**
    A. play a fool
    B. play a scene
    C. play a segment
    D. play a role

19. **raise**
    A. locate
    B. elevate
    C. force
    D. race

20. **appropriate**
    A. amazing
    B. correct
    C. interesting
    D. various

21. **insist**
    A. engage
    B. perform
    C. demand
    D. include

22. **frankly**
    A. recently
    B. seriously
    C. honestly
    D. carefully

23. **polite**
    A. difficult
    B. gracious
    C. informal
    D. pretty

24. **trustworthy**
    A. reliable
    B. awful
    C. typical
    D. superior

25. **reject**
    A. review
    B. decline
    C. determine
    D. attract

1A 2A 3A 4B 5D 6D 7C 8C 9B 10D 11C 12A 13B 14D
15B 16A 17C 18D 19B 20B 21C 22C 23B 24A 25B

I. What Is a Referent Question?

Referent

The referent question asks you to locate a *referent*, which is the noun or noun phrase to which another word, usually a pronoun, refers. A correct referent should be able to replace the pronoun in the paragraph or passage. It must also agree with the pronoun in number and gender (examples: girl → she; dogs → they).

A. REFERENT QUESTION MODEL

California is known as the "Sunshine State." In many parts of the state, especially in the south, sunny weather occurs on most days of the year. **This** is one of the reasons why people like to live in California.

2. The word "**This**" refers to
   - (A) California
   - (B) the "Sunshine State"
   - (C) the south
   - (D) sunny weather

B. REFERENT QUESTION FORMATS

The word/phrase _____ refers to _____.

The word/phrase _____ in the passage refers to _____.

What does the word/phrase _____ refer to?

Which of the following does the word/phrase _____ refer to?

C. TIPS

1. A pronoun's referent usually appears before the pronoun, but can also appear after the pronoun.
2. The referent can show up in the same sentence as the pronoun or in a different sentence.
3. In some cases, you may have to locate the referent for a term or phrase instead of a pronoun.
4. Understanding the meaning of the sentence and the role of the pronoun within the sentence can lead you to the referent.
5. Unless a specific gender is indicated, an animal is usually referred to as "it."

II. Hacking Strategy

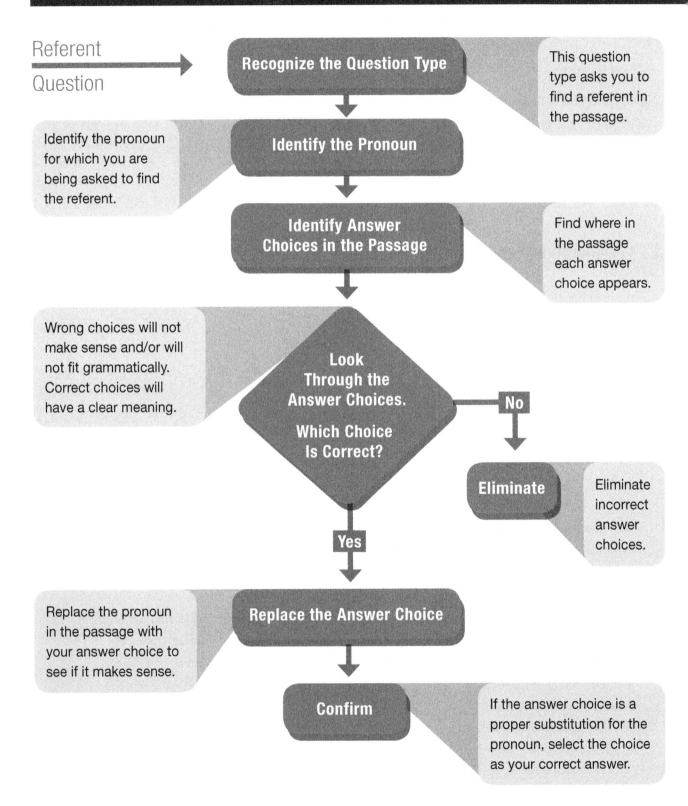

Referent Question → **Recognize the Question Type**

This question type asks you to find a referent in the passage.

Identify the Pronoun

Identify the pronoun for which you are being asked to find the referent.

Identify Answer Choices in the Passage

Find where in the passage each answer choice appears.

Wrong choices will not make sense and/or will not fit grammatically. Correct choices will have a clear meaning.

Look Through the Answer Choices. Which Choice Is Correct?

No → **Eliminate** — Eliminate incorrect answer choices.

Yes

Replace the Answer Choice

Replace the pronoun in the passage with your answer choice to see if it makes sense.

Confirm

If the answer choice is a proper substitution for the pronoun, select the choice as your correct answer.

Recognize the Question Type

California is known as the "Sunshine State." In many parts of the state, especially in the south, sunny weather occurs on most days of the year. **This** is one of the reasons why people like to live in California.

The word "**This**" refers to
(A) California
(B) the "Sunshine State"
(C) the south
(D) sunny weather

Identify the Pronoun

This is the pronoun for which you are asked to identify the referent. Notice that **This** is a singular pronoun.

Identify Answer Choices in the Passage

California is known as the "Sunshine State." In many parts of the state, especially in the south, sunny weather occurs on most days of the year. **This** is one of the reasons why people like to live in California.

Look Through the Answer Choices. Which Choice Is Correct?

(A) California
(B) the "Sunshine State"
(C) the south
(D) sunny weather

Check the choices for grammatical fit and logical meaning.

Eliminate Incorrect Choices

Determine which choices to eliminate by replacing the pronoun with each answer choice:
• Eliminate **Choice A** because "*California* is one of the reasons why people like to live in California" is repetitive and does not make sense.
• Eliminate **Choice B** because "The "*Sunshine State*" is one of the reasons why people like to live in California" is also redundant and does not make sense.
• Eliminate **Choice C** because "The south is one of the reasons why people like to live in California" does not make sense, as *the south* refers to part of the state.

Check the Answer Choice

Replace the pronoun with the answer choice that you think is correct:
• Select **Choice D** because "*Sunny weather* is one of the reasons why people like to live in California" makes sense both grammatically and logically.

Confirm

Select the correct answer — **Choice D**.

III. Quick Look

Pronouns Used in Referent Questions

Subject Pronouns	he	she	you	it	they	we	one
Object Pronouns	him	her	you	it	them	us	one
Possessive Pronouns	his	her	your	its	their	our	one's
Demonstrative Pronouns	this	these	that	those			
Relative Pronouns	who	whom	which/that	whose			

Other Pronouns	some	most	many	any	one(s)	another	(a) few
	the other	(the) others	all	both	none	several	(a) little
	either	neither	each	the first	the last	the former	the latter

Example

one   the other

one   another   the others

one   another   the other

one   another   another   the others

IV. Warm Up

Circle the noun or pronoun that correctly completes each sentence.

1. Rachel liked Ross so much that she asked (**him** / **her**) to go to the movies with her.

2. Some animals pretend that (**these** / **they**) are dead when they are threatened.

3. A peacock is valued for (**her** / **its**) beautiful feathers.

4. The young girls were afraid that their cat would run away if they left (**it** / **them**) alone.

5. Cinnamon is a spice used for (**its** / **their**) fragrant qualities.

6. The boy would often stay awake at night so that (**it** / **he**) could hear the wolves howling.

7. The owl watched the rabbits closely, hoping that (**they** / **it**) would soon be eating them.

8. Many scientists believe that a male giraffe uses (**their** / **his**) long neck to win mating competitions.

9. The mother bird went to catch food for (**their** / **her**) chicks.

10. The professor said that many cultures have different traditions that are based on (**his** / **their**) unique histories.

11. Once Daniel studied the book, (**he** / **it**) always knew how to solve the questions.

12. Bears sleep for a long time during the winter to save (**its** / **their**) energy because there is not much food available.

13. In the animal kingdom, males are typically more beautiful than (**their** / **its**) female counterparts.

14. Jessica ate only (**a few** / **a little**) pieces of chocolate so that she would still be hungry for dinner.

15. Some people do not like to eat dessert, but (**one** / **others**) would say that dessert is delicious.

16. Vegetarians do not include meat in (**their** / **his**) diets.

17. Kayla knitted (**this** / **these**) sweaters for her family members.

18. Please remove (**your** / **one's**) shoes when you enter the house.

19. John decided to take a philosophy class because (**he** / **it**) was quite interested in the subject.

20. The secretary said that somebody called me, but she did not say (**which** / **who**) it was.

V. Quick Practice

Practice #1   **Read the passage. Then answer the questions that follow.**

In 1900, the archaeologist Sir Arthur Evans uncovered a palace in the Cretan city of Knossos that contained many labyrinth-like chambers and passages. Evans suggested that **it** may have been the Cretan Labyrinth described in Greek mythology. He named the inhabitants of the civilization and the civilization itself *Minoan* after the ancient Greek King Minos, **who** supposedly had the labyrinth built to hide a mythical creature called a Minotaur.

1) The word "**it**" refers to
   (A) archaeologist
   (B) a palace
   (C) Cretan city
   (D) Knossos

2) The word "**who**" refers to
   (A) Evans
   (B) *Minoan*
   (C) Minos
   (D) Minotaur

Practice #2   **Read the passage. Then answer the questions that follow.**

Arnold Schoenberg, known as one of the founders of the Second Viennese School, was an important composer in the 1900s. Schoenberg started his career writing in the German Romantic tradition and was known for adopting and further developing the controversial works of Brahms and Wagner. Turning away from German Romantic music in 1908, **he** began to write atonal music. This term indicates that **it** does not have any key.

3) The word "**he**" refers to
   (A) Schoenberg
   (B) German Romantic tradition
   (C) Brahms
   (D) Wagner

4) The word "**it**" refers to
   (A) his career
   (B) German Romantic music
   (C) atonal music
   (D) any key

Practice #3

Read the passage. Then answer the following questions.

Researchers suggest that tribes that had been living in the British Isles for more than 10,000 years began to adopt Celtic cultural practices in about 600 BCE. **They** may have been influenced by a few Celtic immigrants from Europe. Tribes began to build Celtic-style walled forts on hill tops. **These** may have been used as permanent homes or temporary shelters.

5) The word "**They**" refers to
   (A) researchers
   (B) tribes
   (C) British Isles
   (D) cultural practices

6) The word "**These**" refers to
   (A) immigrants
   (B) tribes
   (C) walled forts
   (D) hill tops

Practice #4

Read the passage. Then answer the questions that follow.

The popularity of public aquariums has risen since the 1970s because they started exhibiting more varieties of sea creatures. Today, **they** promote special events, such as allowing people to touch the sea animals or hosting temporary exhibits displaying exotic creatures, in order to draw the public's attention. However, some animal rights groups do not favor such developments because the idea of keeping sea animals captive is disturbing to **them**.

7) The word "**they**" in the passage refers to
   (A) public aquariums
   (B) more varieties
   (C) sea creatures
   (D) special events

8) The word "**them**" in the passage refers to
   (A) people
   (B) sea animals
   (C) animal rights groups
   (D) developments

Practice #5

Read the passage. Then answer the following questions.

Successful reading requires readers to possess a few skills. It requires them to recognize and understand symbols such as letters and punctuation. Reading also demands that **they** relate to the written material by concentrating on **it** using memory, experience, and knowledge.

9) The word "**they**" refers to
   (A) a few skills
   (B) readers
   (C) symbols
   (D) letters

10) The word "**it**" refers to
   (A) a reader
   (B) reading
   (C) written material
   (D) knowledge

Practice #6

Read the passage. Then answer the questions that follow.

Some species of wild gerbils live in China, Russia, and Mongolia. They are usually found in deserts and sandy grasslands. Gerbils usually eat leaves, roots, and stems. Because there is little vegetation and little rainfall where **they** live, their survival depends on how well they dig. They form communities which live together in networks of holes. **These** are active day and night.

11) The word "**they**" refers to
(A) wild gerbils
(B) countries
(C) deserts
(D) sandy grasslands

12) The word "**These**" refers to
(A) sandy grasslands
(B) communities
(C) holes
(D) networks

Practice #7

Read the passage. Then answer the questions that follow.

As one of the biggest cities in the United States, the city of Chicago, which is located in the state of Illinois, has many nicknames. The American poet Carl Sandburg called **it** the "City of the Big Shoulders." Other popular nicknames include "City of Broad Shoulders," "The Windy City," and the "City that Works." All of **these** are still being used to this day.

13) The word "**it**" refers to
(A) the United States
(B) the city of Chicago
(C) Illinois
(D) American poet

14) The word "**these**" refers to
(A) the United States
(B) the biggest cities
(C) nicknames
(D) Broad Shoulders

Practice #8

Read the passage. Then answer the following questions.

Among the European colonial powers, the English came late to the Americas. By the time England colonized the "New World," settlers from Spain and Portugal had already arrived **there**. Additionally, **they** had already established colonies in the Americas.

15) The word "**there**" refers to
(A) the Americas
(B) England
(C) Spain
(D) Portugal

16) The word "**They**" refers to
(A) European colonial powers
(B) the English
(C) the Americas
(D) Spanish and Portuguese settlers

Practice #9

Read the passage. Then answer the questions that follow.

Human beings depend greatly on rubber. In fact, it would be impossible for modern-day people to survive without it. However, this is usually not the case with other materials. If people lack one resource, they can often substitute it with **another**. For example, plastic can replace glass if **it** is scarce.

17) The word "**another**" refers to
    (A) rubber
    (B) the case
    (C) resource
    (D) glass

18) The word "**it**" refers to
    (A) resource
    (B) another
    (C) plastic
    (D) glass

Practice #10

Read the passage. Then answer the questions that follow.

The exact time and place in which geometry originated is debatable. However, historical records show that **it** has been used at least since 2000 BCE by the Egyptians, and later by the Babylonians and the Greeks. Ancient Egyptians used geometric shapes to build their temples. The squares and triangles that make up the pyramids are examples of **these**.

19) The word "**it**" refers to
    (A) time
    (B) place
    (C) geometry
    (D) history record

20) The word "**these**" refers to
    (A) the Greeks
    (B) ancient Egyptians
    (C) geometric shapes
    (D) their temples

Select the vocabulary word or phrase that has the closest meaning.

1. **especially**
   A. particularly
   B. typically
   C. practically
   D. modestly

2. **refer to**
   A. choose to
   B. like to
   C. point to
   D. offer to

3. **normally**
   A. rarely
   B. overly
   C. hardly
   D. usually

4. **locate**
   A. find
   B. define
   C. ignore
   D. lose

5. **pretend**
   A. prefer
   B. fake
   C. assume
   D. believe

6. **threatened**
   A. in existence
   B. in safety
   C. in danger
   D. in harmony

7. **afraid**
   A. hopeful
   B. fearful
   C. angry
   D. confused

8. **fragrant**
   A. aromatic
   B. practical
   C. important
   D. bland

9. **competition**
   A. exploration
   B. research
   C. consideration
   D. contest

10. **tradition**
    A. purpose
    B. experience
    C. custom
    D. intention

11. **counterpart**
    A. piece
    B. material
    C. shape
    D. mate

12. **inhabitant**
    A. neighbor
    B. resident
    C. stranger
    D. foreigner

13. **adopt**
    A. accept
    B. favor
    C. affect
    D. practice

14. **controversial**
    A. conventional
    B. unique
    C. arguable
    D. particular

15. **immigrant**
    A. resource
    B. settler
    C. influence
    D. enemy

16. **permanent**
    A. lasting
    B. precise
    C. changing
    D. gone

17. **exhibit**
    A. prevent
    B. exercise
    C. understand
    D. display

18. **variety**
    A. product
    B. assortment
    C. necessity
    D. unity

19. **promote**
    A. describe
    B. evaluate
    C. attend
    D. advertise

20. **captive**
    A. safe
    B. competitive
    C. confined
    D. special

21. **require**
    A. recommend
    B. recognize
    C. develop
    D. need

22. **depend on**
    A. move on
    B. advise on
    C. rely on
    D. work on

23. **substitute**
    A. complete
    B. illustrate
    C. replace
    D. achieve

24. **origin**
    A. knowledge
    B. beginning
    C. effect
    D. outcome

25. **debatable**
    A. questionable
    B. definite
    C. certain
    D. extraordinary

1A 2C 3D 4A 5B 6C 7B 8A 9D 10C 11D 12B 13A 14C
15B 16A 17D 18B 19D 20C 21D 22C 23C 24B 25A

Exercises

Exercise #1 Read the passage. Then answer the questions that follow.

Some researchers have discovered that humans have been trading **goods** and services for at least 150,000 years. By doing so, prehistoric peoples most likely were able to develop special skills and divide up labor among their communities. For example, a hunter with extra animals might trade **them** for pottery from a neighbor **who** had extra pottery. **Gradually**, each person would get better at a chosen task and develop the required skill set. Then **it** would be **handed down** to the next generation.

1) The word "**goods**" is closest in meaning to
   (A) secrets
   (B) skills
   (C) items
   (D) ideas

2) The word "**them**" refers to
   (A) goods and services
   (B) people
   (C) special skills
   (D) animals

3) The word "**who**" refers to
   (A) labor
   (B) a hunter
   (C) pottery
   (D) a neighbor

4) The word "**Gradually**" means
   (A) interestingly
   (B) slowly
   (C) particularly
   (D) especially

5) The word "**it**" refers to
   (A) the neighbor
   (B) extra pottery
   (C) each
   (D) skill set

6) The expression "**handed down**" means
   (A) taught
   (B) sold
   (C) sent
   (D) led

Exercise #2 Read the passage. Then answer the questions that follow.

In pre-literate societies, there were limitations to how much knowledge people could share or pass on. **Elders** were the main sources of stored knowledge. As a result, when **they** became sick or died, oral traditions could easily be forgotten. However, knowledge became more **accessible** when people began to develop **minimal** units of written expression, such as picture symbols. **These** allowed people to share knowledge across time and distance, as long as they could **interpret** the symbols.

7) The word "**Elders**" means
   (A) close friends
   (B) younger generations
   (C) family members
   (D) older people

8) The word "**they**" refers to
   (A) societies
   (B) limitations
   (C) people
   (D) elders

9) The word "**accessible**" means
   (A) available
   (B) different
   (C) challenging
   (D) accurate

10) The word "**minimal**" means
   (A) complex
   (B) vast
   (C) basic
   (D) average

11) The word "**These**" refers to
   (A) sources of stored knowledge
   (B) oral traditions
   (C) units of written expression
   (D) time and distance

12) The word "**interpret**" means
   (A) engage
   (B) help
   (C) translate
   (D) write

Exercise #3 Read the passage. Then answer the questions that follow.

The peoples of Africa have traditionally created an **immense** variety of sculptures. The materials and meanings of **these depend upon** the peoples' ways of life. Settled **agricultural** peoples have long traditions of creating sculptures from different types of wood, metal, and stone. However, **nomadic ones** who live by hunting and gathering have created very few large sculptures.

13) The word "**immense**" means
   (A) large
   (B) new
   (C) mysterious
   (D) clear

14) The word "**these**" refers to
   (A) peoples
   (B) sculptures
   (C) materials
   (D) meanings

15) The phrase "**depend upon**" means
   (A) fight with
   (B) rely on
   (C) steal from
   (D) take in

16) The word "**agricultural**" means
   (A) hunting
   (B) educated
   (C) aggressive
   (D) farming

17) The word "**nomadic**" probably means
   (A) strong
   (B) hostile
   (C) traveling
   (D) primitive

18) The word "**ones**" refers to
   (A) peoples
   (B) traditions
   (C) sculptures
   (D) different types

Exercise #4 Read the passage. Then answer the questions that follow.

Many people who study music want to become professional performers or composers. However, **competition** is **keen** among musicians. In fact, relatively **few** earn a living **solely** by performing or composing because careers in popular music are **difficult to come by** and offer little security. A rock group that **suddenly** becomes popular may become unpopular just as quickly.

19) The word "**competition**" means
   (A) peace
   (B) rivalry
   (C) comfort
   (D) cooperation

20) The word "**keen**" is closest in meaning to
   (A) pleasant
   (B) intense
   (C) smart
   (D) possible

21) The word "**few**" refers to
   (A) people
   (B) performers
   (C) composers
   (D) musicians

22) The word "**solely**" is closest in meaning to
   (A) only
   (B) really
   (C) rarely
   (D) mostly

23) The phrase "**difficult to come by**" means
   (A) difficult to discuss
   (B) difficult to play
   (C) difficult to achieve
   (D) difficult to like

24) The word "**suddenly**" probably means
   (A) nearly
   (B) clearly
   (C) certainly
   (D) quickly

Exercise #5 Read the passage. Then answer the questions that follow.

Strategy board games have been played by countless societies for many ages. **Most** need more than one player. One strategy game called "Go" is very difficult, though it has simple rules. Go is played on a board with horizontal and vertical lines. The **object** of the game is to **capture territory** by surrounding **it** with pieces called "stones." Go **originated** in China where it is called *weiqi*. Today, professional Go players earn large salaries, as the game is very popular in many Asian countries such as Japan and South Korea.

25) The word "**Most**" refers to
   (A) strategy board games
   (B) countless societies
   (C) many ages
   (D) simple rules

26) The word "**object**" means
   (A) time
   (B) winner
   (C) goal
   (D) topic

27) The word "**capture**" means
   (A) grant
   (B) use
   (C) wish
   (D) take

28) The word "**territory**" means
   (A) detail
   (B) area
   (C) knowledge
   (D) style

29) The word "**it**" refers to
   (A) board
   (B) object
   (C) game
   (D) territory

30) The word "**originated**" means
   (A) was invented
   (B) was found
   (C) was enjoyed
   (D) was seen

I. What Is a Fact and Detail Question?

Fact and Detail

The fact and detail question asks you to identify a fact or detail from the passage.
- A **fact** is something that can be proven and that agrees with an experience or observation.
- A **detail** is a piece of information used to support the main idea of a passage.
- Facts and details are directly stated in the passage.

A. FACT AND DETAIL QUESTION MODEL

Corn, also known as *maize*, is believed to have been originally harvested by native people living in Central Mexico. Corn-growing extended to Europe as explorers and traders imported corn back to their countries of origin. Because of its ability to grow in various climates, many other nations started growing their own supplies of corn. Currently, the United States produces the largest amount of corn in the world, followed by China.

3. According to the passage, where did corn originally come from?
   (A) Central Mexico
   (B) Europe
   (C) the United States
   (D) China

B. FACT AND DETAIL QUESTION FORMATS

What _____?   Which _____?   Why _____?   Where _____?   When _____?   How _____?
Which statement BEST describes _____?   What does the author say about _____?
What is the main cause of _____?   Which of the following is an example of _____?
Which of the following is true?

C. TIPS

1. The correct answer may be a paraphrase* of the passage's information.
   Paraphrase: the restatement of information in a different form
2. Incorrect answers may:
   - restate information from the passage without correctly answering the question
   - state information from the passage incorrectly
   - be false according to the information in the passage
   - be unnecessary or not mentioned in the passage

CHAPTER 3
FACT AND DETAIL QUESTION

II. Hacking Strategy

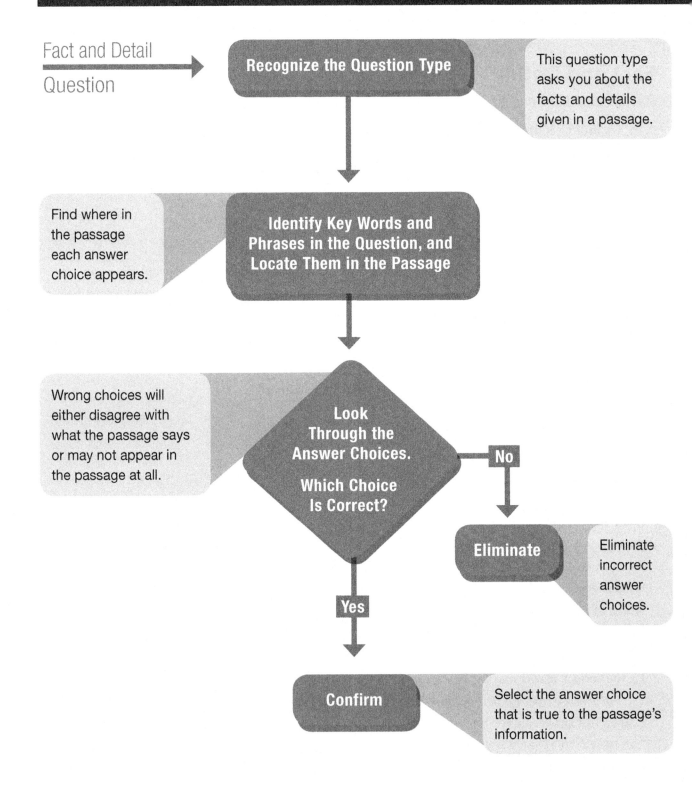

Fact and Detail Question → **Recognize the Question Type**

This question type asks you about the facts and details given in a passage.

Identify Key Words and Phrases in the Question, and Locate Them in the Passage

Find where in the passage each answer choice appears.

Wrong choices will either disagree with what the passage says or may not appear in the passage at all.

Look Through the Answer Choices.

Which Choice Is Correct?

No → **Eliminate**

Eliminate incorrect answer choices.

Yes → **Confirm**

Select the answer choice that is true to the passage's information.

Recognize the Question Type

Corn, also known as *maize*, is believed to have been originally harvested by native people living in Central Mexico. Corn-growing extended to Europe as explorers and traders imported corn back to their countries of origin. Because of its ability to grow in various climates, many other nations started growing their own supplies of corn. Currently, the United States produces the largest amount of corn in the world, followed by China.

According to the passage, where did corn originally come from?
(A) Central Mexico
(B) Europe
(C) the United States
(D) China

Identify Key Words and Phrases in the Question, and Locate Them in the Passage

According to the passage, where did **corn originally come from**?

Corn, also known as *maize*, is believed to have been originally harvested by people living in Central Mexico. Corn-growing extended to Europe as explorers and traders imported corn back to their countries of origin. Because of its ability to grow in various climates, many other nations started growing their own supplies of corn. Currently, the United States produces the largest amount of corn in the world, followed by China.

Look Through the Answer Choices.

Which Choice Is Correct?

By looking at the key words and phrases, we see that our answer is in the first sentence. Even though we believe that we have found the correct answer, it is still a good idea to look further in the passage to be sure. Check thoroughly.

• Select **Choice A** because the passage states that "Corn...is believed to have been originally harvested...in Central Mexico."

Eliminate Incorrect Choices

• Eliminate **Choice B** because Europe is mentioned in the passage, but it is not where corn was *originally harvested*. Instead, it is where corn spread to.
• Eliminate **Choices C** and **D** because these countries are mentioned in the passage, but they are countries where the most corn is produced, not where corn was *originally harvested*.

Confirm

Select the correct answer — **Choice A**.

III. Quick Look

Transitions Used to Introduce Facts and Details

Illustrating — *provides description*

For example	Next	Such	For instance	To illustrate	Such as

Explaining — *reveals more to provide better understanding*

Specifically	Furthermore	In fact	Because	How	In this case

Adding — *provides more supporting information*

Also	Finally	Moreover	Another	Furthermore	Too

Giving Reasons — *states why something is*

Because of	One reason is	Because	Due to	Since

Contrasting — *presents information that is different from what was provided before*

Although	Instead	Rather	However	Nevertheless	Like/Unlike

Comparing — *notes how things are similar to or different from/than each other*

Both	Like	Similarly	Equally important	The same	Similar to

Showing Results — *states the outcome*

Accordingly	Consequently	Therefore	Thus	Otherwise

Limiting — *puts boundaries on the information's scope or reach*

Although	Except for	However	But	Even though	Yet

Emphasizing — *highlights important information*

Clearly	In fact	Surely	Certainly	Indeed	Most importantly

IV. Warm Up

Identify whether each sentence contains a fact (F) or an opinion (O).

1. Green parrots are the prettiest type of parrots. _____

2. Seoul is the capital of South Korea. _____

3. The sweetest smelling flowers in the world are roses. _____

4. The colors of the United States of America's flag are red, white, and blue. _____

5. The Earth completes one full rotation every 24 hours. _____

6. When the Northern Hemisphere experiences winter, the Southern Hemisphere experiences summer. _____

7. Every person who has a job needs the money to survive. _____

8. Dogs make better pets than cats do because they are more friendly and loyal. _____

9. Blackberries are classified as fruits. _____

10. Red apples are the most delicious type of apples. _____

11. People consider diabetes to be the worst disease. _____

12. Teenagers have better taste in music than adults. _____

13. Avocados are actually a type of a fruit, not a vegetable. _____

14. Lunch should be your biggest meal of the day. _____

15. There are usually 365 calendar days in a year. _____

16. The month of February comes before the month of March. _____

17. Sushi is the best way to eat raw fish. _____

18. Driving a car to work is better than taking a bus. _____

19. Washington, D.C., is the capital of the United States. _____

20. There are many different time zones used throughout the world. _____

V. Quick Practice

Practice #1

Read the passage. Then answer the questions that follow.

Choosing light bulbs carefully can save energy. Some types may provide the same amount of light as others but use less electricity. For example, incandescent bulbs produce 100 lumens per 5 watts while **fluorescent tubes** produce 100 lumens per watt. Moreover, the former may last 750 hours while the latter may last 10,000 hours.

1) The author mentions "**fluorescent tubes**" as examples of
   (A) lights that look attractive
   (B) lights that save energy
   (C) lights that last indefinitely
   (D) lights that are clear

2) Which of the following is true?
   (A) Fluorescent tubes produce weaker light than incandescent bulbs.
   (B) Fluorescent tubes last longer than incandescent bulbs.
   (C) All lighting is either fluorescent or incandescent.
   (D) Incandescent bulbs are better for humans.

Practice #2

Read the passage. Then answer the questions that follow.

People sometimes choose a hobby without realizing it. They first pursue an interest in something. Then they learn more about the subject. Their interest becomes fascination. After a while, they seek information from references, such as **books and magazines**, about the subject. Some hobbyists even join organizations in which they can discuss their hobby with fellow enthusiasts.

3) What helps people choose a hobby?
   (A) Studying a topic over time
   (B) Reading a reference book
   (C) Meeting new people
   (D) Taking part in many events

4) The items "**books and magazines**" are mentioned as examples of
   (A) why people choose their hobbies
   (B) how people learn about their hobbies
   (C) where people find their hobbies
   (D) what people do as their hobbies

Practice #3

Read the passage. Then answer the questions that follow.

The Sargasso Sea has no land borders: it is surrounded by the Atlantic Ocean. Different ocean currents meet in the sea, creating a huge, clear whirlpool or spiral. Because of this characteristic, the currents carry a great deal of marine life as well as trash that ends up in the sea. The currents also bring in warm water. The warm water supports the genus of seaweeds known as *Sargassum*, which gives the sea its name.

5) What MOSTLY gives the Sargasso Sea its features?
 (A) Its depth and danger to ships
 (B) Its organisms and pollutants that form its environment
 (C) Its location as a center of several currents
 (D) Its Atlantic Ocean boundary

6) Why is this section of the ocean called the Sargasso Sea?
 (A) It is in the middle of a bigger sea.
 (B) It has several currents flowing into it.
 (C) It is home to various sea animals.
 (D) It has specific plants that grow there.

Practice #4

Read the passage. Then answer the questions that follow.

A camera works like the human eye. It receives light and focuses the light into a picture. Unlike the human eye, the camera records pictures either digitally or on film. As a result, the picture is made permanent and can be seen by many people.

7) How is a camera similar to an eye?
 (A) It changes light into an image.
 (B) It holds light in a box.
 (C) It gives light to human beings.
 (D) It stops light from moving.

8) How are pictures used?
 (A) Stopping time temporarily
 (B) Explaining ideas digitally
 (C) Sharing memories with other people
 (D) Helping people focus better

Practice #5

Read the passage. Then answer the questions that follow.

Over a period of time, scientists have discovered more than 1.7 million animal species. Of these, 1 million are insects. Nowadays, scientists discover thousands of new insect species every year. They believe that there may be 5 to 30 million insect species still unknown.

9) How many insect species do scientists know about now?
 (A) 1 million
 (B) 1.7 million
 (C) 5 million
 (D) 30 million

10) According to the passage, what happens every year?
 (A) 1.7 million animal species are discovered.
 (B) Insects are eaten by animals.
 (C) Insects become extinct.
 (D) Scientists find more insect types.

Practice #6

Read the passage. Then answer the questions that follow.

San Francisco is built on 40 different hills. Some of the steepest streets in the world are in San Francisco, such as those on Nob Hill and Russian Hill. These hills can rise up to 115 meters in just a few blocks. As a result, cable cars amaze onlookers, resembling elevators as they climb or descend the hills.

11) How are the streets in San Francisco described?
   (A) Highly praised
   (B) Beautifully decorated
   (C) Outstandingly inclined
   (D) Annoyingly bumpy

12) What does the author say about cable cars on San Francisco's hills?
   (A) They have no trouble climbing hills.
   (B) They look terrifying.
   (C) They only operate on two hills.
   (D) They disturb people.

Practice #7

Read the passage. Then answer the questions that follow.

Categorized as tropical storms, hurricanes are also called *cyclones* or *typhoons*. They are one of the most dangerous natural disasters in the world. Forming first in the open seas, hurricanes can damage buildings, trees, and cars with their strong winds and heavy rain. They are most likely to occur when the weather is warm. Thus, hurricanes frequently develop from June to November in the Northern Hemisphere and between January and March in the Southern Hemisphere.

13) What is one condition that contributes to the development of hurricanes?
   (A) Heavy rain
   (B) Strong wind
   (C) Warm weather
   (D) Northern Hemisphere

14) What is one characteristic of a typical hurricane?
   (A) It is typically created in open land.
   (B) It occurs when the weather is cold.
   (C) It is often seen between January and March in the Northern Hemisphere.
   (D) It can cause property damage.

Practice #8

Read the passage. Then answer the questions that follow.

Cleopatra was a queen of ancient Egypt. Little is known about her exact appearance, but some things about her are well known. She was said to have intelligence, charisma, and ambition. These traits may have led Rome's leaders—**Julius Caesar and Mark Antony**—to court her.

15) For what was Cleopatra BEST known?
   (A) Her appearance
   (B) Her character
   (C) Her words
   (D) Her activity

16) "**Julius Caesar and Mark Antony**" are mentioned as examples of
   (A) fathers of Cleopatra
   (B) leaders who fought against Cleopatra
   (C) subjects of Cleopatra
   (D) romantic interests of Cleopatra

Practice #9

Read the passage. Then answer the questions that follow.

Clara Barton was a school teacher who became one of the first women to work for the United States government, beginning her career as a clerk in 1855. After the U.S. Civil War broke out in 1861, she risked her life working as a nurse close to the battles. She later helped organize military hospitals in Europe during the Franco-Prussian War. She returned home and founded the American Red Cross in 1881, which helps soldiers in wartime and meets human needs during emergencies to this day.

17) Which world events shaped Clara Barton's experiences?
(A) Public schools growing in number
(B) Two wars, at home and abroad
(C) The invention of the hospital in Europe
(D) The development of ways to heal war injuries

18) Clara Barton's clearest influence on the world today is
(A) working as a U.S. clerk
(B) nursing soldiers during the Civil War
(C) founding the American Red Cross
(D) serving in the Franco-Prussian War

Practice #10

Read the passage. Then answer the questions that follow.

Novels are a form of fiction that attempts to bring many types of relationships and feelings into focus. There are several kinds of novels. *Realistic fiction* represents situations that could actually have happened and aims to provide wisdom or insight into some aspect of life as the characters develop. In contrast, *genre fiction*—such as romance, science fiction, and mystery novels—may simply aim to entertain. The characters in genre fiction are often idealized types of people; instead of focusing on how characters change, the attention may be on the plot or action.

19) What might readers expect from realistic fiction?
(A) Escaping from real life for awhile
(B) Gaining knowledge about history
(C) Following characters exactly like themselves
(D) Learning something about life

20) What tends to be true about genre fiction?
(A) It may have many different types of characters in it.
(B) What happens in the plot may be more important than the characters' development.
(C) It is often more optimistic than realistic fiction.
(D) The characters usually mature by the end.

Select the vocabulary word or phrase that has the closest meaning.

1. **harvest**
   A. gather
   B. observe
   C. spend
   D. trade

2. **describe**
   A. excuse
   B. explain
   C. reason
   D. defend

3. **confirm**
   A. cancel
   B. contest
   C. question
   D. verify

4. **spread**
   A. yield
   B. return
   C. extend
   D. store

5. **nevertheless**
   A. moreover
   B. however
   C. consequently
   D. lastly

6. **certainly**
   A. doubtfully
   B. possibly
   C. impossibly
   D. definitely

7. **classify**
   A. categorize
   B. manage
   C. rearrange
   D. expand

8. **attractive**
   A. common
   B. unusual
   C. attentive
   D. appealing

9. **indefinite**
   A. intelligent
   B. incredible
   C. undefined
   D. undone

10. **spiral**
    A. heavy load
    B. curled shape
    C. straight line
    D. thick layer

11. **characteristic**
    A. difference
    B. experience
    C. tradition
    D. feature

12. **period**
    A. era
    B. clock
    C. series
    D. schedule

13. **discover**
    A. discard
    B. conceal
    C. uncover
    D. screen

14. **outstandingly**
    A. unnecessarily
    B. exceptionally
    C. typically
    D. similarly

15. **inclined**
    A. reduced
    B. raised
    C. lowered
    D. expanded

16. **operate**
    A. work
    B. occur
    C. develop
    D. organize

17. **disturb**
    A. comfort
    B. support
    C. bother
    D. force

18. **exact**
    A. precise
    B. general
    C. beautiful
    D. extra

19. **ambition**
    A. attitude
    B. skill
    C. perception
    D. aspiration

20. **court**
    A. avoid
    B. ignore
    C. entice
    D. sue

21. **risk**
    A. endanger
    B. restrain
    C. ruin
    D. approach

22. **organize**
    A. break
    B. return
    C. originate
    D. arrange

23. **represent**
    A. confuse
    B. regret
    C. symbolize
    D. describe

24. **idealized**
    A. comfortable
    B. perfect
    C. questionable
    D. imaginative

25. **optimistic**
    A. pessimistic
    B. opportunistic
    C. hopeful
    D. obsessive

I. What Is a Negative Fact Question?

Negative Fact

The negative fact question asks you to identify the answer choice that is not described in the passage or is not true according to the passage.

A. NEGATIVE FACT QUESTION MODEL

Dogs have been called "man's best friend" for many reasons. Dogs evolved from wolves that were particularly social, so dogs almost always want to be with their human companions. Furthermore, they are often fun to spend time with because of their enthusiasm over the simple joys in life. Most of all, they show their owners great affection, which many people find comforting.

4. All of the following describe the reasons why dogs are "man's best friend" EXCEPT:
   (A) Dogs are tamed from dangerous wild animals.
   (B) Dogs desire to be in social situations.
   (C) Dogs take pleasure in ordinary life.
   (D) Dogs demonstrate their love and devotion.

B. NEGATIVE FACT QUESTION FORMATS

Which of the following is NOT mentioned in the passage?

What is NOT mentioned as _____?

What is NOT given as a reason for _____?

All are examples of _____ EXCEPT _____.

All describe _____ EXCEPT _____.

All statements are true EXCEPT _____.

All are mentioned EXCEPT _____.

_____ involves all EXCEPT _____.

C. TIPS

1. When you see questions with words EXCEPT or NOT, three of the answer choices will be true.
2. Remember, you are looking for an answer that is untrue or is not included in the passage.

II. Hacking Strategy

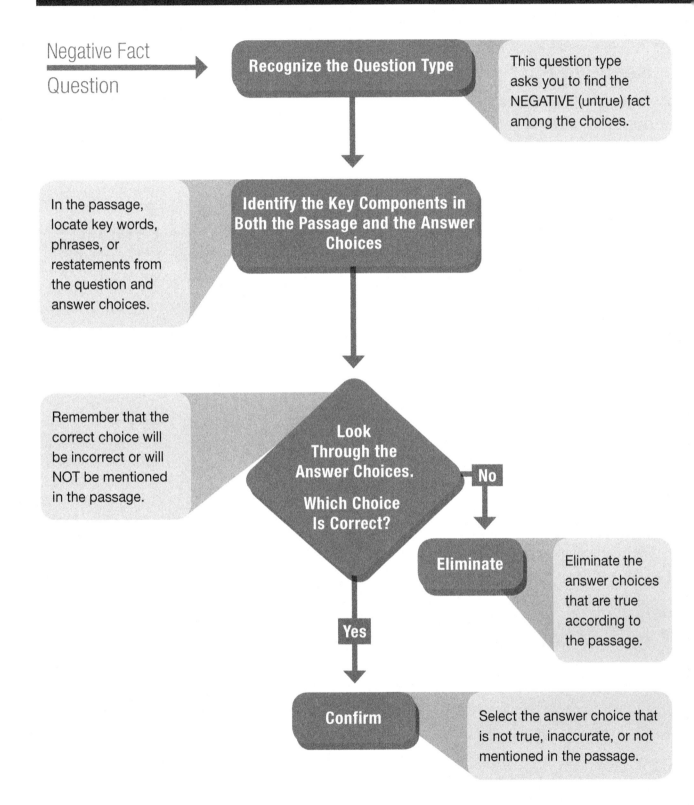

Negative Fact Question →

Recognize the Question Type

This question type asks you to find the NEGATIVE (untrue) fact among the choices.

Identify the Key Components in Both the Passage and the Answer Choices

In the passage, locate key words, phrases, or restatements from the question and answer choices.

Look Through the Answer Choices.

Which Choice Is Correct?

Remember that the correct choice will be incorrect or will NOT be mentioned in the passage.

No →

Eliminate

Eliminate the answer choices that are true according to the passage.

Yes ↓

Confirm

Select the answer choice that is not true, inaccurate, or not mentioned in the passage.

EXAMPLE

Recognize the Question Type

Dogs have been called "man's best friend" for many reasons. Dogs evolved from wolves that were particularly social, so dogs almost always want to be with their human companions. Furthermore, they are often fun to spend time with because of their enthusiasm over the simple joys in life. Most of all, they show their owners great affection, which many people find comforting.

All of the following describe the reasons why dogs are "man's best friend" EXCEPT:

(A) Dogs are tamed from dangerous wild animals.
(B) Dogs desire to be in social situations.
(C) Dogs take pleasure in ordinary life.
(D) Dogs demonstrate their love and devotion.

Identify the Key Components in Both the Passage and the Answer Choices

All of the following describe the reasons why dogs are "**man's best friend**" EXCEPT:

Dogs have been called "man's best friend" for many reasons. Dogs evolved from wolves that were particularly social, so dogs almost always want to be with their human companions. Furthermore, they are often fun to spend time with because of their enthusiasm over the simple joys in life. Most of all, they show their owners great affection, which many people find comforting.

(A) Dogs are tamed from dangerous wild animals.
(B) Dogs desire to be in social situations.
(C) Dogs take pleasure in ordinary life.
(D) Dogs demonstrate their love and devotion.

Look Through the Answer Choices.

Which Choice Is Correct?

Which choice is NOT something the passage says?

• Select **Choice A** because dogs "evolved from wolves that were particularly social," which are not described as *dangerous wild animals*.

Eliminate Incorrect Choices

• Eliminate **Choices B, C**, and **D** because they paraphrase correct reasons that dogs are "man's best friend."

Confirm

Select the correct answer — **Choice A**.

III. Quick Look

Negative Fact Questions

Look at the images below. Then select which answer is a negative fact.

A. This is an animal.

B. This can be tamed.

C. This is a cat.

D. This has fur.

Choice C is the negative fact because the image shows a dog, not a cat (untrue to the image).

A. This is a pen.

B. This is used to write.

C. This has ink.

D. This is used to speak.

Choice D is the negative fact because a pen is used to write, not to speak (false information).

IV. Warm Up

Choose the answer that does NOT belong in each group.

1. (A) car
   (B) motorcycle
   (C) truck
   (D) bicycle
   (E) bus

2. (A) apple
   (B) orange
   (C) lettuce
   (D) strawberry
   (E) mango

3. (A) eyes
   (B) nose
   (C) mouth
   (D) ears
   (E) legs

4. (A) cat
   (B) dog
   (C) bird
   (D) elephant
   (E) giraffe

5. (A) happy
   (B) sad
   (C) excited
   (D) scared
   (E) frozen

6. (A) stove
   (B) chair
   (C) couch
   (D) table
   (E) desk

7. (A) pencil
   (B) doll
   (C) pen
   (D) paper
   (E) eraser

8. (A) computer
   (B) television
   (C) dictionary
   (D) refrigerator
   (E) microwave

9. (A) ocean
   (B) river
   (C) lake
   (D) forest
   (E) stream

10. (A) Japan
    (B) Italy
    (C) Hawaii
    (D) India
    (E) Austria

11. (A) Asia
    (B) Africa
    (C) Antarctica
    (D) Russia
    (E) Europe

12. (A) ruby
    (B) sapphire
    (C) emerald
    (D) diamond
    (E) fossil

13. (A) tea
    (B) juice
    (C) cake
    (D) coffee
    (E) lemonade

14. (A) lion
    (B) cheetah
    (C) tiger
    (D) zebra
    (E) leopard

15. (A) ring
    (B) earrings
    (C) necklace
    (D) wristwatch
    (E) shoes

16. (A) bean sprouts
    (B) carrots
    (C) onions
    (D) blueberries
    (E) green beans

17. (A) wild fire
    (B) tornado
    (C) lake
    (D) earthquake
    (E) hurricane

18. (A) volleyball
    (B) baseball
    (C) basketball
    (D) gymnastics
    (E) football

19. (A) squirrel
    (B) pigeon
    (C) owl
    (D) parrot
    (E) lovebird

20. (A) flamenco
    (B) waltz
    (C) tango
    (D) opera
    (E) ballet

V. Quick Practice

Practice #1

Read the passage. Then answer the question that follows.

Some natural resources cannot be exhausted. Salt and some minerals are so abundant that they will never be used up. Wind and solar energy are also natural resources that will always supply energy. Earth will always have an abundance of water, yet some places lack clean, fresh water.

1) All of the resources are inexhaustible EXCEPT
(A) certain minerals
(B) sunlight
(C) wind energy
(D) uncontaminated water

Practice #2

Read the passage. Then answer the question that follows.

Since the 1800s, farming has become more productive. For example, the use of fertilizers has led to bigger harvests. Furthermore, selective breeding has improved livestock production. Technological improvements, such as the development of machines, also have reduced the need for labor, making farming much easier for people.

2) What is NOT a cause of increased farm productivity?
(A) Controlling animal reproduction
(B) Better chemicals
(C) Increased number of laborers
(D) Motorized devices

Practice #3

Read the passage. Then answer the question that follows.

Suppose that you are looking at a rainbow. When you do, you are at its center. Likewise, a person next to you is at the center of a different rainbow. Thus, no two people will ever see the exact same rainbow.

3) What is NOT true of a rainbow?
   (A) A viewer is always at its center.
   (B) Nearby viewers see a different one.
   (C) No one sees the same one.
   (D) It is always moving.

Practice #4

Read the passage. Then answer the question that follows.

Although the name suggests otherwise, the funny bone is not actually a bone. It is a nerve that runs from the pinky finger through the back of the elbow to the spinal cord. Although this nerve is like any other nerve, it is located in a less protected area. Thus, when the nerve gets hit or hits a hard surface, a person feels a slight shock or numbness in the area.

4) What is NOT true about the funny bone?
   (A) It is found in the brain.
   (B) It is in a vulnerable spot.
   (C) It is connected to the backbone.
   (D) A strange sensation is felt when it is hit.

Practice #5

Read the passage. Then answer the question that follows.

Airplanes come in many sizes. Some airplanes have only two seats. Others are jumbo jets that can carry hundreds of passengers. Ninety percent of airplanes have only one engine and carry just a few passengers.

5) What is NOT true about airplanes?
   (A) Some are for two people.
   (B) Large ones are called "jumbo."
   (C) Ninety percent of people use them.
   (D) They are often small in size.

Practice #6

Read the passage. Then answer the question that follows.

There are more than 250 species of turtles worldwide. Eight of these are sea turtles. Except for the Arctic and Antarctic regions, turtles live everywhere on Earth. Some species like to be completely underwater most of the time, while others like to get out and lay in the Sun.

6) What is NOT true about turtles?
(A) There are hundreds of kinds of turtles.
(B) Different species live in the polar regions of Earth.
(C) Some turtles enjoy being underwater for a long time.
(D) There are more types of freshwater turtles than saltwater turtles.

Practice #7

Read the passage. Then answer the question that follows.

The Blue Mountains in Australia are not mountains at all. They are a high plain divided by extremely deep, narrow, damp, fern-covered canyons. Some drop more than 600 meters and feature long waterfalls. The global positioning system, or GPS for short, does not work inside the canyons. Thus, explorers must bring maps.

7) What is NOT true about the Blue Mountains?
(A) They contain canyons that are usually wet and support plants.
(B) They are broken up by steep canyons.
(C) They have canyons so deep that GPS does not work in them.
(D) They are plains that are blue at certain times of the day.

Practice #8

Read the passage. Then answer the question that follows.

The French captain Jacques Cartier thought that he had found a Pacific passage to Asia when he sailed into the Gulf of Saint Lawrence. To his surprise, he discovered a land full of natural resources and tribes of Huron-Iroquois living in two different communities. In the name of the King of France, Jacques Cartier claimed the land. Today, these communities—which the Huron-Iroquois called *Stadacona* and *Hochelaga*—are the French-speaking cities Québec and Montréal.

8) What is NOT true about this passage?
(A) People in Québec and Montréal speak French to this day.
(B) Cartier found what are now Québec and Montréal by mistake.
(C) Cartier was looking for natural resources and new tribes.
(D) Huron-Iroquois tribes lived in what is now Québec and Montréal.

Practice #9

Read the passage. Then answer the question that follows.

People's perceptions of cats have varied greatly over the centuries. For example, in ancient Egypt it was illegal to kill cats because they were considered sacred animals. In medieval Europe, some people believed that black cats should be avoided because they were frightening and unlucky. In parts of Asia, cats were, and still are, thought to bring luck and prosperity. Today, they are often beloved household pets.

9) What is NOT mentioned about cats?
   (A) Opinions about cats have changed with time and place.
   (B) Egyptians have viewed cats as holy creatures.
   (C) It was often illegal for ordinary people to raise them.
   (D) Medieval Europeans did not favor black cats.

Practice #10

Read the passage. Then answer the question that follows.

In 1666, Sir Isaac Newton invented the color wheel. He identified three primary colors: yellow, red, and blue. These cannot be created from any combination of colors. The secondary colors are orange, green, and purple. They can be produced by combining different primary colors. Finally, there are tertiary colors, which are created by blending primary and secondary colors.

10) Which of the following is NOT true about the color wheel?
   (A) Orange, green, and purple are mixtures of colors.
   (B) There are more than six colors in the color wheel.
   (C) A color wheel has three categories of colors.
   (D) Sir Isaac Newton invented colors.

POP QUIZ

Select the vocabulary word or phrase that has the closest meaning.

5. **tamed**
   A. reduced
   B. domesticated
   C. honored
   D. comforted

6. **look for**
   A. finish
   B. attend
   C. seek
   D. count

7. **false**
   A. wrong
   B. unseen
   C. valid
   D. far

1. **evolve from**
   A. live with
   B. develop from
   C. chase after
   D. grow with

8. **exhaust**
   A. refresh
   B. build
   C. increase
   D. drain

2. **companion**
   A. partner
   B. neighbor
   C. instructor
   D. parent

9. **abundant**
   A. rare
   B. abnormal
   C. plentiful
   D. brief

3. **enthusiasm**
   A. excitement
   B. ambition
   C. anger
   D. confusion

10. **inexhaustible**
   A. endless
   B. limited
   C. necessary
   D. large

4. **affection**
   A. disrespect
   B. honesty
   C. expectation
   D. fondness

11. **uncontaminated**
   A. abundant
   B. stable
   C. unknown
   D. clean

12. **productive**
   A. proper
   B. efficient
   C. restrictive
   D. respected

13. **breeding**
   A. feeding
   B. breathing
   C. reproducing
   D. learning

14. **improve**
   A. introduce
   B. weaken
   C. better
   D. discover

15. **reduce**
   A. expand
   B. decrease
   C. include
   D. retain

16. **device**
   A. detection
   B. detail
   C. term
   D. tool

17. **vulnerable**
   A. reliable
   B. unprotected
   C. closed
   D. ordinary

18. **kind**
   A. type
   B. system
   C. method
   D. part

19. **feature**
   A. raise
   B. display
   C. change
   D. divide

20. **by mistake**
   A. knowingly
   B. accidentally
   C. carefully
   D. surprisingly

21. **perception**
   A. introduction
   B. exhibition
   C. perspective
   D. production

22. **avoid**
   A. evade
   B. accept
   C. endure
   D. affect

23. **frightening**
   A. significant
   B. scary
   C. comforting
   D. well-known

24. **primary**
   A. fair
   B. final
   C. basic
   D. ideal

25. **mixture**
   A. simplicity
   B. category
   C. application
   D. combination

Exercises

Exercise #1 Read the passage. Then answer the questions that follow.

Cupido, more commonly known as Cupid, is the god of love in Roman mythology. He is also called Amor. Cupido may be the counterpart of the Greek god Eros; they share many similar traits. The Romans believed that Cupid was the son of the goddess Venus.

The first Greek images of Cupid's forerunner, Eros, show him as a handsome young man. By the 300s BCE, he was portrayed as a naked baby with wings, holding a bow and arrows. In myth, a person shot with one of Eros' gold-tipped arrows fell in love. His lead-tipped arrows had the opposite effect.

1) Based on Paragraph 1, what is NOT a name that describes the god of love?
(A) Cupido
(B) Amor
(C) Eros
(D) Venus

2) Based on Paragraph 2, which of the following is NOT a description of Eros' looks, according to the first images of him?
(A) Young
(B) Handsome
(C) Chubby
(D) Man

3) According to Paragraph 2, what had happened to Eros by the 300s BCE?
(A) His appearance changed.
(B) His meaning became unclear.
(C) His Roman roots were lost.
(D) His bow and arrow became bigger.

4) According to Paragraph 2, what happened to characters in myths who were shot with the god of love's lead-tipped arrows?
(A) They became angry.
(B) They fell out of love.
(C) They went crazy.
(D) They got special powers.

Exercise #2 Read the passage. Then answer the questions that follow.

People have tried to understand the mind for centuries. Scientists of all kinds, including philosophers, psychologists, and computer scientists, have added to people's knowledge of the mind. However, experts still debate what the mind is.

Most animals with a nervous system have something like a mind. A mind allows animals to react to, and make sense of, their surroundings. In human beings, the mind also allows for and processes abstract thoughts and feelings.

5) According to Paragraph 1, what is TRUE about the mind?
    (A) It is used only by scientists.
    (B) It is not well understood.
    (C) It is only three centuries old.
    (D) It is not fun to study.

6) According to Paragraph 2, what is indicated about most animals with a nervous system?
    (A) They think like human beings.
    (B) They are known for their development of feelings.
    (C) They cannot easily process their surroundings.
    (D) They can respond to changes in their environment.

7) According to Paragraph 2, how does the human mind differ from the animal mind?
    (A) It is studied by scientists.
    (B) It makes sense of surroundings.
    (C) It has complex ideas and emotions.
    (D) It reacts to the environment.

8) According to Paragraphs 1 and 2, what is NOT true of the mind?
    (A) It has been studied for many years.
    (B) It allows people to react to their surroundings.
    (C) It makes people nervous.
    (D) It has feelings and thoughts.

Exercise #3 Read the passage. Then answer the questions that follow.

The 1890s have been characterized as a happy time in the United States history and thus called the "Gay Nineties." Some Americans did well during this time. But the decade also witnessed an economic depression, labor unrest, and the Spanish-American War. As a result of these events, few Americans living in the 1890s ever regarded the period as particularly happy.

The term "Gay Nineties" started being used during the Great Depression of the 1930s. During that time, people looked for a comfortable past. They chose to remember only the good years and events of the 1890s.

9) Based on Paragraph 1, what negative occurrence is NOT true of the 1890s?

(A) Problems with crops

(B) A bad economy

(C) Workers protesting

(D) An international conflict

10) According to Paragraph 1, how did MOST Americans living in the 1890s feel?

(A) Hopeful

(B) Troubled

(C) Bored

(D) Comfortable

11) According to Paragraph 2, why was the term "Gay Nineties" created?

(A) It created more choices.

(B) It stopped a bad economy.

(C) It made people feel good.

(D) It sounded promising.

12) According to Paragraphs 1 and 2, what is NOT true of the 1890s?

(A) It was referred to as the "Gay Nineties" in the 1930s.

(B) Some Americans enjoyed financial stability.

(C) It featured great economic success.

(D) The Spanish-American War occurred during this period.

Exercise #4 Read the passage. Then answer the questions that follow.

The coriander plant first grew wild in the Mediterranean region. The stems grow about 50 centimeters high and bear feathery leaves and small white flowers. The plant, also known as *cilantro*, is a member of the carrot family. Coriander is now grown and eaten in many cultures. The leaves, stems, and roots are added to sauces and salads, and the seeds are especially useful.

   Coriander seeds can be dried or roasted, and then ground up and used as a sweet spice in curries, stews, cakes, and other dishes. There is evidence that the seeds were used in Israel more than 8,000 years ago. Ancient Egyptians and Greeks used coriander to flavor drinks; they also added its oil to perfume. Some cultures have traditionally boiled the seeds to make medicine.

13) According to Paragraph 1, what is NOT a characteristic of coriander?

(A) It may grow about half a meter.

(B) Its blossoms are small and white.

(C) Its leaves are thick and tough.

(D) It is related to carrots.

14) According to Paragraph 1, what has changed about the coriander plant?

(A) It no longer grows wild in the Mediterranean climate.

(B) It is now taller, and its name has changed.

(C) It is now used mostly in sauces and salads.

(D) Its use spread from one area to many areas.

15) Based on Paragraph 2, the taste of coriander seed is

(A) sweet

(B) carrot-like

(C) dry

(D) roasted

16) According to Paragraph 2, coriander seeds have been used in all of the following ways EXCEPT

(A) as a spice

(B) in perfume

(C) in medicine

(D) as a grain

Exercise #5 Read the passage. Then answer the questions that follow.

The earliest paintings are known to be at least 30,000 years old. They were made during the Paleolithic Period, also known as the Old Stone Age. Most of the paintings discovered are images of animals. These paintings are found on the walls of caves in Australia, France, Italy, Portugal, and Spain.

No one really knows why early artists painted. It is likely that these drawings were not for decoration because many of them are found in dark and isolated parts of caves. It has been suggested that the paintings might have been used for religious purposes because people then may have believed that the animals depicted were gods. Some scholars suggest that the paintings were used as form of communication between groups of people. Others suggest that some of the images might have been used as a way to measure time like a calendar.

17) According to Paragraph 1, what is TRUE about early paintings?
(A) They were created by animals.
(B) They were found mostly in Europe.
(C) They were put on building walls.
(D) They were made within two centuries.

18) According to Paragraph 1, which country is NOT associated with early paintings?
(A) Austria
(B) France
(C) Italy
(D) Portugal

19) According to Paragraph 2, why were early paintings probably NOT decorative?
(A) They were drawn on cave walls.
(B) They were completed in a short time.
(C) They were hard to find and see.
(D) They were very ugly and strange.

20) According to Paragraph 2, which of the following is probably NOT a purpose of early paintings?
(A) Ceremonies to honor animals
(B) Way to interact with others
(C) Method to track time
(D) Predictions of the future

I. What Is a Coherence Question?

Coherence

The coherence question asks you to create a more logical or coherent passage by adding a new sentence that will improve the overall information.

A. COHERENCE QUESTION MODEL

Visiting the beach is a popular pastime for many people. **A** They can surf in it or just swim in the water. **B** However, there can be dangers in the ocean, such as very strong waves. **C**

5. Look at the squares [■] that indicate where the following sentence could be added.

   Some of them enjoy going in the ocean.

   Where would the sentence best fit?

   Circle the square [■] to add the sentence.

All other coherence questions have four squares that indicate where the bold-faced sentence can be added. Above is a simplified example.

B. COHERENCE QUESTION FORMATS

Look at the squares [■] that indicate where the following sentence could be added.

(A bold-faced sentence)

Where would the sentence best fit?

Circle the square [■] to add the sentence.

C. TIPS

1. When taking the official Internet-based TOEFL test, you will be asked to *click on* the correct answer choice rather than *circle* it.
2. Understanding the purpose of the passage will help you identify the correct placement of the new sentence.
3. Look for transitions to indicate what kind of information should come next if the given information seems unrelated.
4. Check that all of the pronouns have referents. If a referent is missing, that omission can give you a clue as to where the new sentence should be placed.
5. An incorrect answer may:
   - stop the logical continuation of ideas between sentences
   - conflict with the function of the transitions
   - disrupt the relationship between a pronoun and its referent

II. Hacking Strategy

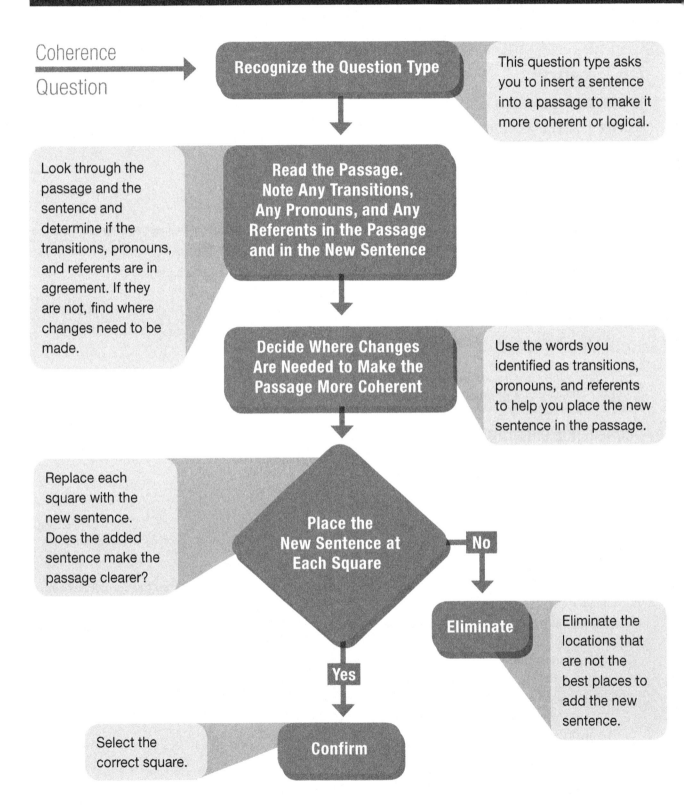

Coherence
Question

Recognize the Question Type

This question type asks you to insert a sentence into a passage to make it more coherent or logical.

Look through the passage and the sentence and determine if the transitions, pronouns, and referents are in agreement. If they are not, find where changes need to be made.

Read the Passage. Note Any Transitions, Any Pronouns, and Any Referents in the Passage and in the New Sentence

Decide Where Changes Are Needed to Make the Passage More Coherent

Use the words you identified as transitions, pronouns, and referents to help you place the new sentence in the passage.

Replace each square with the new sentence. Does the added sentence make the passage clearer?

Place the New Sentence at Each Square

No

Eliminate

Eliminate the locations that are not the best places to add the new sentence.

Yes

Select the correct square.

Confirm

Recognize the Question Type

Visiting the beach is a popular pastime for many people. **A** They can surf in it or just swim in the water. **B** However, there can be dangers in the ocean, such as very strong waves. **C**

Look at the squares [■] that indicate where the following sentence could be added.

Some of them enjoy going in the ocean.

Where would the sentence best fit?

Circle the square [■] to add the sentence.

Note Any Transitions, Any Pronouns, and Any Referents in the Passage and in the New Sentence

Sentence 1: Visiting **the beach** (**the beach** is a possible referent for a pronoun) is a popular pastime for many people (**people** is a referent for the pronoun **they**).

Sentence 2: **They** (**They** is a pronoun referring back to **people**) can surf in **it** (**it** is a pronoun referring back to a possible referent) or just swim in the water.

Sentence 3: **However**, (**However** is a transition word) there can be dangers in the ocean, such as very strong waves.

Decide Where Changes Are Needed to Make the Passage More Coherent

Notice the pronoun "it" in the second sentence. "It" refers to what people can surf in. The only possible referent in the first sentence is *the beach*.

However, this does not make sense because the beach is the area of land that touches the ocean, not the body of water where people can surf. So, we have identified a problem here with the pronoun-referent agreement.

Place the New Sentence at Each Square

• **Choice A**: Visiting the beach is a popular pastime for many people. **Some of them enjoy going in the ocean.** They can surf in it or just swim in the water.
• **Choice B**: They can surf in it or just swim in the water. **Some of them enjoy going in the ocean.** However, there can be dangers in the ocean, such as very strong waves.
• **Choice C**: However, there can be dangers in the ocean, such as very strong waves. **Some of them enjoy going in the ocean.**

Check the Answer Choice

As seen, there is a logical problem with the pronoun-referent agreement between **beach** and **it** in sentences 1 and 2. However, when we add the new sentence between the two, the passage becomes more coherent because the pronoun *it* (sentence 2) now refers back to the ocean (new sentence), a body of water.

Confirm

Select the correct square — **A** — by circling it.

III. Quick Look

Transitions Used in Coherence Questions

1. Addition signals that more information similar to the previous sentence is going to be introduced

Also   Another   Other   First, Second, etc.   And so on

Topic: Cheeseburger   Choices

2. Contrast signals that information different from the previous sentence is going to follow

Although   However   In contrast   While   But

Topic: Contrast   Choices

3. Cause / Result signals that results from information in the previous sentence will follow

Because / Since   Consequently   Therefore   Thus   To conclude

Topic: Actions   Choices

4. Example signals that a supporting example is going to follow

For example   For instance   Including   Such as   First, Second, etc.

Topic: Animals   Choices

IV. Warm Up

Read each sentence below. Then put the sentences in the correct order by labeling each choice as 1, 2, or 3.

1. ____ Thus, in 1863 President Abraham Lincoln declared Thanksgiving a national holiday to be held each November.
   ____ Until the 1860s, it had been celebrated for more than two centuries in individual states, but not as a nation.
   ____ Thanksgiving is a holiday celebrated in the United States every year in November.

2. ____ By visiting other countries, people learn about different cultures and peoples.
   ____ Many people like to travel to have new experiences.
   ____ Travelers may come to appreciate other cultures' food and traditions more.

3. ____ It is very important for people to sleep enough hours every night.
   ____ One consequence may be trouble concentrating the next day.
   ____ Otherwise, the body and brain will not function at their best.

4. ____ The most populated country in the world is China.
   ____ India is the second most populated country.
   ____ China has more than 1 billion people.

5. ____ Many Native Americans still do rain dances today.
   ____ Long ago, Native Americans did rain dances, which they believed would bring rain.
   ____ The dances were usually done during dry summers.

6. ____ Each color of fruit and vegetable has a different positive effect on a person's health.
   ____ For example, yellow fruit such as pineapple has a chemical that may help protect against cancer.
   ____ Eating a variety of differently colored fruits and vegetables is important.

7. ____ Exercising regularly is important for your health.
   ____ This activity can be broken up into 30 minutes of exercise, five days a week.
   ____ One recommended weekly exercise is walking.

8. ____ This makes them the fastest land animals in the world.
   ____ Cheetahs can run extremely fast.
   ____ They can go from 0 to 100 kilometers per hour in less than 3 seconds.

9. ____ The invention of the Internet has made life easier for us.
   ____ But now, a quick search on the Internet will tell you most things that you want to know.
   ____ Before the Internet, people had to look up information in books.

10. ____ In fact, four major walls were built during different Chinese dynasties.
    ____ However, it is actually not just one wall, but several.
    ____ The Great Wall of China is a big part of Chinese history.

V. Quick Practice

Practice #1

Read the passage. Then answer the question that follows.

A People in every country celebrate this day as a holiday. **B** The celebrations are most often joyful but are sometimes serious as well. **C** Many people make New Year's resolutions to stop bad habits or start good ones. **D**

1) Look at the squares [■] that indicate where the following sentence could be added.

   New Year's Day is the first day of the year.

   Where would the sentence best fit?
   Circle the square [■] to add the sentence.

Practice #2

Read the passage. Then answer the question that follows.

A European colonists and Native Americans had different ways of life. **B** Although the lifestyles were different, some colonists tried to treat Native Americans fairly. **C** When Native Americans fought back, horrible battles occurred. **D**

2) Look at the squares [■] that indicate where the following sentence could be added.

   Others cheated them and took their land.

   Where would the sentence best fit?
   Circle the square [■] to add the sentence.

Practice #3

Read the passage. Then answer the question that follows.

A The moon does not really have an atmosphere. **B** However, some gases are present above its surface. **C** People sometimes call these gases an "atmosphere." **D**

3) Look at the squares [■] that indicate where the following sentence could be added.

   In fact, some asteroids have similar "atmospheres."

   Where would the sentence best fit?
   Circle the square [■] to add the sentence.

Practice #4

Read the passage. Then answer the question that follows.

A Walt Disney was born in Chicago on December 5, 1901. **B** After high school, he joined the Kansas City Film Ad Company. **C** There, he made cartoon advertisements that were shown in movie theaters. **D**

4) Look at the squares [■] that indicate where the following sentence could be added.

However, he spent his childhood on a farm in Missouri.

Where would the sentence best fit?
Circle the square [■] to add the sentence.

Practice #5

Read the passage. Then answer the question that follows.

A Teeth are important in speech. **B** They are used along with the tongue to make sounds and words. **C** For example, to produce the "th-" sound, the tongue is positioned against the upper front teeth. **D**

5) Look at the squares [■] that indicate where the following sentence could be added.

Consequently, a person without these teeth cannot make this sound.

Where would the sentence best fit?
Circle the square [■] to add the sentence.

Practice #6

Read the passage. Then answer the question that follows.

A The horse is no longer an important means of transportation. **B** Trains and cars have replaced it in most countries. **C** However, people still use horses for sport and work. **D**

6) Look at the squares [■] that indicate where the following sentence could be added.

Some popular activities include horse racing, cattle herding, and weekend riding.

Where would the sentence best fit?
Circle the square [■] to add the sentence.

Practice #7

Read the passage. Then answer the question that follows.

A For thousands of years, people have worn clothing. **B** They made their first clothes from the animals that they killed. **C** They used these fibers to make fabric. **D**

7) Look at the squares [■] that indicate where the following sentence could be added.

Gradually, they learned to use other materials such as plant fibers.

Where would the sentence best fit?
Circle the square [■] to add the sentence.

Practice #8

Read the passage. Then answer the question that follows.

A Quick-freezing saves food better than slow-freezing. **B** Quick-freezing simply freezes the water inside the food without making any changes to the food's structure. **C** Unlike quick-freezing, slow-freezing changes the structure of the food. **D**

8) Look at the squares [■] that indicate where the following sentence could be added.

For example, vegetables become soft and meats become tough.

Where would the sentence best fit?
Circle the square [■] to add the sentence.

Practice #9

Read the passage. Then answer the question that follows.

Since 1945, scientists have developed peaceful uses for nuclear energy. **A** Electric power production is one way of using nuclear energy peacefully. **B** For example, during the electric power production process, the energy from nuclei creates heat. **C** Then the steam can be used to move machines that create electric power. **D**

9) Look at the squares [■] that indicate where the following sentence could be added.

In turn, this can be used to make steam.

Where would the sentence best fit?
Circle the square [■] to add the sentence.

Practice #10

Read the passage. Then answer the question that follows.

A For example, many ancient civilizations observed the movement of the stars to determine the planting and harvesting seasons. **B** Ancient Egyptian and Chinese civilizations developed sundials that displayed time in regards to the movement of the Sun throughout the day. **C** It was not until 1275 when the first mechanical clock was developed. **D**

10) Look at the squares [■] that indicate where the following sentence could be added.

Before the invention of the modern time-keeping methods, people relied on different techniques to measure time.

Where would the sentence best fit?
Circle the square [■] to add the sentence.

**P O P
Q U I Z**

Select the vocabulary word or phrase that has the closest meaning.

1. coherent
A. vague
B. common
C. logical
D. confusing

2. pastime
A. chore
B. task
C. hobby
D. work

3. indicate
A. conceal
B. avoid
C. pretend
D. specify

4. purpose
A. result
B. benefit
C. knowledge
D. intention

5. identify
A. recognize
B. access
C. maintain
D. divide

6. clue
A. conflict
B. truth
C. hint
D. secret

7. transition
A. shift
B. trouble
C. point
D. region

8. disrupt
A. locate
B. disprove
C. remind
D. obstruct

9. insert
A. develop
B. make
C. force
D. place

10. select
A. delete
B. choose
C. observe
D. save

11. signal
A. indicate
B. find
C. promise
D. know

12. conclusion
A. similarity
B. contrast
C. result
D. condition

13. previous
A. useful
B. preceding
C. following
D. current

14. declare
A. prepare
B. explain
C. state
D. measure

15. celebrate
A. forget
B. exhibit
C. honor
D. ignore

16. function
A. communicate
B. operate
C. flow
D. protect

17. joyful
A. bright
B. merry
C. gloomy
D. amazing

18. resolution
A. translation
B. representation
C. innovation
D. determination

19. horrible
A. awful
B. honorable
C. thoughtful
D. unsatisfactory

20. produce
A. plan
B. stop
C. join
D. make

21. position
A. insure
B. argue
C. warn
D. place

22. replace
A. review
B. locate
C. substitute
D. compare

23. determine
A. decide
B. present
C. emphasize
D. question

24. display
A. show
B. associate
C. complain
D. dislike

25. rely on
A. depend on
B. bring on
C. focus on
D. try on

15C 16B 17B 18D 19A 20D 21D 22C 23A 24A 25A
1C 2C 3D 4D 5A 6C 7A 8D 9D 10B 11A 12C 13B 14C

I. What Is an Inference Question?

Inference

The inference question asks you to assume, or *infer*, an idea about a passage based on the information presented. In an inference question, you must be aware that the author does not directly state an idea, but implies it. The author will state specific facts and details that will lead you to the unstated idea.

A. INFERENCE QUESTION MODEL

A *rumor* is a story passed on from person to person over a period of time. The rumor is often about a famous person or a controversial issue. Typically, there is no real proof that the rumor is true. Often, details of the rumor change slightly over time.

6. What can be inferred about rumors from the passage?
   (A) They are interesting stories about history.
   (B) They are a way of praising important people.
   (C) There is enough evidence to prove that they are true.
   (D) They gradually change as many people retell them.

B. INFERENCE QUESTION FORMATS

What can be inferred about _____?   It can be inferred from _____ that _____.

Which statement is MOST LIKELY true about _____?   What can be inferred from Paragraph _____?

What PROBABLY occurred after/before/during _____?   What is a probable belief of the author?

Which of the following MOST ACCURATELY reflects the author's opinion?

C. TIPS

1. An inference can be made from just one sentence or from the entire passage.
2. Often the answer choices paraphrase the ideas of the passage, so it is important to understand the passage well.
3. An incorrect answer may:
   • be too broad or unclear
   • be off-topic or unrelated to the passage
   • be false or not supported by stated information
   • restate information already given in the passage

II. Hacking Strategy

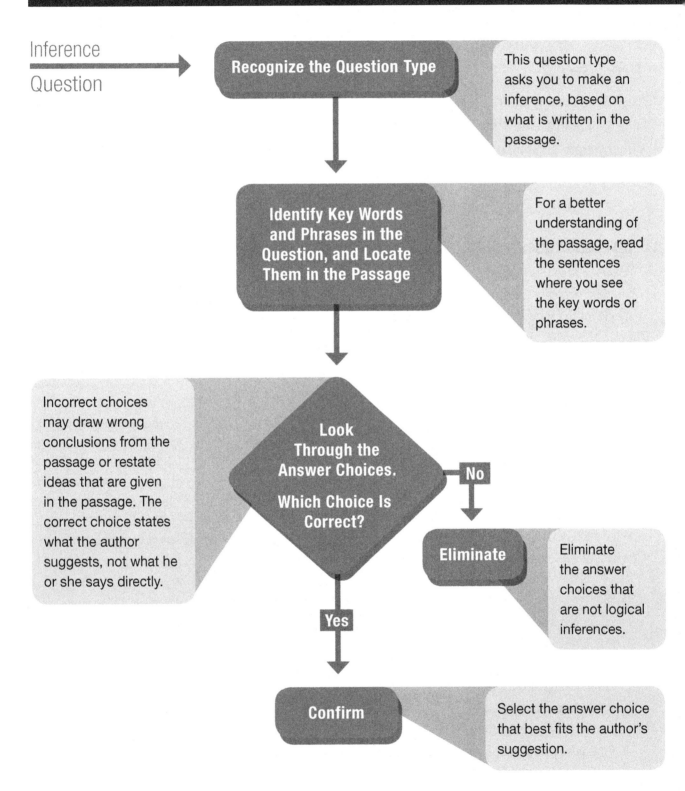

Inference
Question

Recognize the Question Type

This question type asks you to make an inference, based on what is written in the passage.

Identify Key Words and Phrases in the Question, and Locate Them in the Passage

For a better understanding of the passage, read the sentences where you see the key words or phrases.

Incorrect choices may draw wrong conclusions from the passage or restate ideas that are given in the passage. The correct choice states what the author suggests, not what he or she says directly.

Look Through the Answer Choices. Which Choice Is Correct?

No

Eliminate

Eliminate the answer choices that are not logical inferences.

Yes

Confirm

Select the answer choice that best fits the author's suggestion.

Recognize the Question Type	A *rumor* is a story passed on from person to person over a period of time. The rumor is often about a famous person or a controversial issue. Typically, there is no real proof that the rumor is true. Often, details of the rumor change slightly over time. **What can be inferred about rumors from the passage?** (A) They are interesting stories about history. (B) They are a way of praising important people. (C) There is enough evidence to prove that they are true. (D) They gradually change as many people retell them.
Identify Key Words and Phrases in the Question, and Locate Them in the Passage	A *rumor is a story* passed on from person to person over a period of time. The rumor is often about a famous person or a controversial issue. Typically, there is no real proof that the rumor is true. Often, details of the rumor change slightly over time. **What can be inferred about rumors from the passage?** (A) They are interesting stories about history. (B) They are a way of praising important people. (C) There is enough evidence to prove that they are true. (D) They gradually change as many people retell them.
Look Through the Answer Choices. **Which Choice Is Correct?**	Which choice is **NOT STATED** in the passage but is **SUGGESTED?** • Select **Choice D** because the last sentence of the passage states that "details of the rumor change slightly over time." This leads us to conclude that people telling rumors may change the information.
Eliminate Incorrect Choices	• Eliminate **Choice A** because it mentions *stories about history*, which is unrelated to rumors, the main idea of the passage. • Eliminate **Choice B** because it says that rumors are *a way of praising* people. The passage does not mention anything about the purpose of rumors. • Eliminate **Choice C** because it gives information that directly opposes the information from the passage.
Confirm	Select the correct answer — **Choice D**.

III. Quick Look

Making Inferences

Inference: An *inference* is an idea that you create on your own BASED ON the information that is directly stated in the passage.

1.

Choices

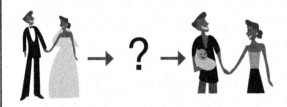

2.

Choices

3.

Choices

IV. Warm Up

Choose the MORE LIKELY inference from each of the following sentences.

1. The ancient Egyptian goddess Bastet had the head of a cat and the body of a woman.
   - Ⓐ Ancient Egyptians considered cats to be divine creatures.
   - Ⓑ Ancient Egyptians believed that cats were insignificant.

2. Timothy picked six apples to bring home, but by the time he returned home, he had only five apples left.
   - Ⓐ Timothy does not like apples.
   - Ⓑ Timothy ate one apple.

3. Keiko put many potatoes in the vegetable soup that she was making for her family, but only a few carrots.
   - Ⓐ Keiko's family likes potatoes a lot.
   - Ⓑ Keiko's favorite dish is vegetable soup.

4. Every time Herbert eats a banana, his throat swells up.
   - Ⓐ Herbert has caught a cold.
   - Ⓑ Herbert is allergic to bananas.

5. Long ago, some people believed that the Earth was flat.
   - Ⓐ People at that time were less intelligent.
   - Ⓑ People at that time did not have the technology to know the truth.

6. When Lily asked Marshall what color her purple dress was, Marshall replied that it was blue.
   - Ⓐ Marshall cannot tell purple from blue.
   - Ⓑ Marshall likes the color blue.

7. Although it was raining outside, Kelly still went for a long walk.
   - Ⓐ Kelly does not mind the rain.
   - Ⓑ Kelly was looking for something that she left outside.

8. Whenever the boy saw pandas on television, he would smile and laugh.
   - Ⓐ The boy liked watching television.
   - Ⓑ The boy liked pandas.

9. Although she liked the white car, Allison was more eager to buy the black one.
   - Ⓐ Allison liked the color black better than white.
   - Ⓑ Allison was shopping for black cars only.

10. Some animals sleep through cold winter months to save their energy while others travel to warmer climates.
   - Ⓐ Animals that sleep during winter are lazy.
   - Ⓑ Animals have different ways of surviving in the cold.

V. Quick Practice

Practice #1

Read the passage. Then answer the question that follows.

Trucking is a big industry in developed countries. In the United States, trucks carry 75 percent of industrial products. They also carry most goods that need to be moved short distances.

1) What can be inferred from this information?
   (A) Truck drivers make big salaries.
   (B) Most American products are industrial.
   (C) Americans rely greatly on trucks.
   (D) Few goods move short distances.

Practice #2

Read the passage. Then answer the question that follows.

A whale is a large sea animal that looks like a fish. It has fins and lives in the ocean. However, whales are not fish. They belong to the group of animals called mammals.

2) What can be inferred about whales?
   (A) They have been mistaken for fish.
   (B) They fight with large fish.
   (C) They used to be much smaller.
   (D) They often scare people.

Practice #3

Read the passage. Then answer the question that follows.

Wolves were once extinct in Yellowstone Park, but park rangers reintroduced wolves to keep the balance in the environment. Wolves help control the population of plant-eaters, which otherwise would eat young trees. With more trees growing, beavers are able to build more dams across streams. The dams help create ponds, which in turn leads to an increase in fish, frog, and bird populations.

3) What can be inferred about wolves?
   (A) They move around between parks and ranches.
   (B) They create conditions that support more types of animals.
   (C) They scare all the animals in the park by hunting them.
   (D) They balance out the beaver population and in turn save more trees.

Practice #4

Read the passage. Then answer the question that follows.

Although Puerto Ricans are citizens of the United States, Puerto Rico is not a U.S. state. The U.S. Census Bureau does not count the island's residents as part of the U.S. population; thus, the nearly 3.7 million Puerto Rican U.S. citizens are not included in the U.S. population.

4) What can be inferred from this information?
   (A) Few people live on Puerto Rico.
   (B) Counting an island population is difficult.
   (C) U.S. Census figures are not entirely accurate.
   (D) Puerto Ricans are angry at the United States.

Practice #5

Read the passage. Then answer the question that follows.

It is impossible to know how old dancing is because it has been around since before people started recording history. Regardless of when it developed, dancing may have helped early people bond, communicate, and, therefore, survive.

5) What can be inferred about dancing?
   (A) It is not important to modern humans.
   (B) Researchers expect to discover its beginning.
   (C) If people dance more, they may become more modern.
   (D) Dancing was important to prehistoric people.

Practice #6

Read the passage. Then answer the question that follows.

Georgia was the last American colony to be founded by England. The first group of English settlers arrived there in 1733. The colony was named for King George II of England.

6) What can be inferred from this information?
   (A) More English settlers arrived after 1733.
   (B) King George II lived in the colony until 1733.
   (C) The English settlers did not care for Georgia.
   (D) Every colony was named for a king.

Practice #7

Read the passage. Then answer the question that follows.

Taxes are as old as government. The tax rate depends on the role of government. In modern times, the need for taxes has become great.

7) What can be inferred from this information?
   (A) Change depends on taxes.
   (B) People like modern governments.
   (C) Taxes were created before government.
   (D) The role of government is increasing.

Practice #8

Read the passage. Then answer the question that follows.

Skyscrapers are buildings that are so tall that they seem to *scrape*, or touch, the sky. People started using the term to express awe when buildings of 10 or more stories began appearing in New York and Chicago in the late 1800s. One special thing about these skyscrapers was that they had elevators. Before skyscrapers, a few medieval cities in Europe and the Arab world had tall buildings, but they were made of stone and brick and only had stairs.

8) What can be inferred from this passage?
(A) Building designers came up with new technology by the late 19th century.
(B) Tall buildings in New York and Chicago look like ones in Europe and the Arab world.
(C) People were not amazed by European and Arab buildings since they had to climb stairs.
(D) People have always perceived tall buildings as positive and inspiring.

Practice #9

Read the passage. Then answer the question that follows.

The *Renaissance* refers to a "rebirth" of thinking and expression that took hold in Europe at the end of the Medieval period. The Renaissance began in Italy around 1300. The ideas associated with it spread through Europe as a middle class developed. As a result, people began traveling and trading more, and a gradual increase in literacy made books more desirable.

9) What can be inferred about the Renaissance?
(A) In other countries, it was considered a noble Italian way of thinking.
(B) Learning about the world was important to many people during this time.
(C) The middle class feared the changes brought about by the Renaissance.
(D) European life in 1300 was gloomy, and people were mostly poor.

Practice #10

Read the passage. Then answer the question that follows.

Gaia is the idea that on Earth, living things and nonliving things affect each other in a balanced system. According to the theory, this balanced system regulates itself so that the organisms on Earth can continue to survive. The theory states that this balanced system controls atmospheric factors such as global temperature and water-salt ratios in oceans. For example, trees make air breathable for animals, and in turn, animals make air usable for trees.

10) What can be inferred about *Gaia*?
(A) It is focused on the potentially harmful effects of organisms on environment.
(B) It is considered more of a story than a theory by scientists.
(C) It is a theory about matters that cannot be proven true or false.
(D) It illustrates that both living and nonliving things are important.

Select the vocabulary word or phrase that has the closest meaning.

5. proof
A. theory
B. notion
C. evidence
D. provision

6. slightly
A. greatly
B. notably
C. commonly
D. inconsiderably

7. probable
A. preventable
B. questionable
C. possible
D. interesting

8. reflect
A. complete
B. express
C. prohibit
D. prepare

9. logical
A. perfect
B. reasonable
C. direct
D. intentional

10. consider
A. regard
B. teach
C. enable
D. prefer

11. bring
A. follow
B. maintain
C. transport
D. borrow

12. industry
A. subject
B. building
C. problem
D. business

13. build
A. destroy
B. carry
C. receive
D. construct

14. figure
A. letter
B. piece
C. symbol
D. term

15. accurate
A. precise
B. normal
C. important
D. misleading

16. angry at
A. joyful of
B. sad at
C. fearful of
D. upset at

17. start
A. leave
B. begin
C. finish
D. ignore

18. awe
A. rage
B. fear
C. amazement
D. happiness

19. perceive
A. present
B. misinterpret
C. view
D. disregard

20. affect
A. contain
B. influence
C. examine
D. mimic

21. regulate
A. control
B. confront
C. leave
D. adopt

22. state
A. remember
B. question
C. declare
D. deny

23. in turn
A. independently
B. initially
C. considerably
D. subsequently

24. focus on
A. build on
B. concentrate on
C. move on
D. rely on

25. illustrate
A. imagine
B. attract
C. show
D. support

1. assume
A. doubt
B. explain
C. refuse
D. suppose

2. imply
A. suggest
B. define
C. state
D. express

3. specific
A. particular
B. insignificant
C. vague
D. general

4. typically
A. clearly
B. usually
C. rarely
D. definitely

15A 16D 17B 18C 19C 20B 21A 22C 23D 24B 25C
1D 2A 3A 4B 5C 6D 7C 8B 9B 10A 11C 12D 13D 14C

Exercises

Exercise #1 Read the passage. Then answer the questions that follow.

A Not all birds can fly. **B** For example, ostriches and penguins are flightless. **C** For this type of movement, they need their wings mostly for balance. **D**

   E For instance, ostriches have developed strong legs so that they can run fast. **F** They are capable of running as fast as 70 kilometers per hour. **G** Penguins, on the other hand, have developed outstanding diving skills so that they can feed on sea animals such as fish and squid. **H**

---

1) Look at the squares [■] that indicate where the sentence below could be added to Paragraph 1.

   Instead of flying, these two birds walk or run.

   Where would the sentence best fit?
   Circle the square [■] to add the sentence.

2) Look at the squares [■] that indicate where the sentence below could be added to Paragraph 2.

   Because they cannot fly, these birds have developed other special characteristics.

   Where would the sentence best fit?
   Circle the square [■] to add the sentence.

Exercise #2 Read the passage. Then answer the questions that follow.

Hemlock is a toxic herb. As a result, people who mistake hemlock for parsley can become poisoned. Children are also sometimes harmed by hemlock when they make whistles from its stems.

   The ancient Greeks made a poisonous drink from hemlock. They gave it to criminals condemned to death. For example, the philosopher Socrates died from drinking this beverage.

---

3) What can be inferred about hemlock from Paragraph 1?
   (A) It smells good to children.
   (B) It has short stems.
   (C) It looks like parsley.
   (D) It looks like a whistle.

4) What can be inferred from Paragraph 2?
   (A) Hemlock was expensive.
   (B) Socrates was considered a criminal.
   (C) The Greeks made a big mistake.
   (D) No Greeks liked Socrates.

Exercise #3 Read the passage. Then answer the questions that follow.

A Bamboo is a giant grass famous for its hollow stem. **B** It is related to wheat, oats, and barley. **C** Some types grow up to 37 meters in height and 30 centimeters in diameter. **D**

     E Bamboo is essential in many tropical countries. **F** They wear bamboo clothing and eat bamboo food. **G** Without bamboo, their lifestyles would be impossible. **H**

5) Look at the squares [■] that indicate where the sentence below could be added to Paragraph 1.

    But unlike these grasses, bamboo is usually humongous.

    Where would the sentence best fit?

    Circle the square [■] to add the sentence.

6) Look at the squares [■] that indicate where the sentence below could be added to Paragraph 2.

    In these places, many people live in bamboo houses and sleep on bamboo beds.

    Where would the sentence best fit?

    Circle the square [■] to add the sentence.

Exercise #4 Read the passage. Then answer the questions that follow.

Vampire bats received their name because blood is their main food source. The name refers to an imaginary, frightening creature called a *vampire* who sucks blood from unwilling victims.

    Vampire bats can spread diseases through their bites, but their bites are small and heal quickly. Although these bats usually feed on animal blood, there are incidents when they have attacked people who are sleeping.

7) What can be inferred about vampire bats from Paragraph 1?
   (A) They are hard to find.
   (B) They scare people.
   (C) They are supernatural animals.
   (D) They were discovered recently.

8) What can be inferred about vampire bats from Paragraph 2?
   (A) They can be dangerous.
   (B) They can attack and bite animals quickly.
   (C) They can easily be killed by diseases.
   (D) They only feed on the blood of people who are sleeping.

Exercise #5 Read the passage. Then answer the questions that follow.

A Until the 1800s, fires often destroyed whole cities. **B** When a fire occurred, everyone ran toward the flames. **C** People formed a row and passed buckets of water. **D**

      E In 27 BCE, Emperor Augustus started a group called the *vigiles*. **F** This group walked the streets to look for fires. **G** They also served as the police force in Rome. **H**

9) Look at the squares [■] that indicate where the sentence below could be added to Paragraph 1.

As cities grew, this system became inefficient and fire departments were organized.

Where would the sentence best fit?
Circle the square [■] to add the sentence.

10) Look at the squares [■] that indicate where the sentence below could be added to Paragraph 2.

The first firefighting organization was created in ancient Rome.

Where would the sentence best fit?
Circle the square [■] to add the sentence.

Exercise #6 Read the passage. Then answer the questions that follow.

Because the brain is an extremely complex organ, *neuroscientists*, or researchers who investigate the brain, still have much to discover. One aspect of neuroscience is learning how the brain grows.

      A baby's brain weighs about 0.5 kilograms at birth, and most of the brain nerve cells are already developed at this stage. By the time a child is 6 years old, the weight of the brain increases to about 1.4 kilograms, which is its full weight. This increase in brain weight is due to nerve-cell growth.

11) What can be inferred about the brain from Paragraph 1?
(A) It is quickly increasing in size.
(B) It is the only source of knowledge.
(C) It is still not fully understood.
(D) It controls human growth.

12) What can be inferred from Paragraph 2?
(A) Brain nerve cells are completely developed at birth.
(B) Scientists have difficulty weighing the brain.
(C) Nerve cells continue to grow in the brain until death.
(D) The brain is not completely formed at birth.

Exercise #7 Read the passage. Then answer the questions that follow.

A International newspapers have fewer pages than American ones. **B** For example, many European papers have about 10 pages. **C** Also, they have much less advertising. **D**

   E By 1830, the United States had about 1,000 papers. **F** Most of these papers concentrated on business or political news. **G** They sold for about 6 cents a copy. **H**

13) Look at the squares [■] that indicate where the sentence below could be added to Paragraph 1.

   Most of their stories focus on political or governmental subjects.

   Where would the sentence best fit?
   Circle the square [■] to add the sentence.

14) Look at the squares [■] that indicate where the sentence below could be added to Paragraph 2.

   This was far more than working people could afford.

   Where would the sentence best fit?
   Circle the square [■] to add the sentence.

Exercise #8 Read the passage. Then answer the questions that follow.

American writer John Steinbeck published *The Grapes of Wrath* in 1939. The fictional novel follows a poor family that travels to California with the hope of finding stable farm jobs. Arriving in California, the family finds little work because landowners control workers with the help of brutal police officers. Hence, the family is forced to join masses of starving people in the search for work.

   Many California farmers said that the novel was deceptive, and it was even burned and banned in some places. Despite these criticisms, it won major prizes and awards and even became a bestseller in the United States in 1939.

15) What can be inferred about John Steinbeck from Paragraph 1?
   (A) He was a farm worker in California during the 1930s.
   (B) He wanted people to stop traveling to California for jobs.
   (C) He thought that the California farm economy was unjust.
   (D) He was mostly interested in writing about California landowners.

16) Based on Paragraph 2, most Americans in 1939 PROBABLY
   (A) had never heard of the book
   (B) had strong opinions about the book
   (C) did not understand the book's story
   (D) believed that the book was nonfiction

Exercise #9 Read the passage. Then answer the questions that follow.

A Plastics are long molecular chains. **B** These chains are made of repeating patterns of relatively large molecules. **C** Each of these molecules forms a connection in the longer chain. **D**

 E Plastics are very useful. **F** However, they do have some disadvantages. **G** As a result, disposing of plastics is a big environmental concern. **H**

17) Look at the squares [■] that indicate where the sentence below could be added to Paragraph 1.

This overall structure gives plastics the ability to be shaped.

Where would the sentence best fit?
Circle the square [■] to add the sentence.

18) Look at the squares [■] that indicate where the sentence below could be added to Paragraph 2.

The biggest one is that they take a very long time to decay.

Where would the sentence best fit?
Circle the square [■] to add the sentence.

Exercise #10 Read the passage. Then answer the questions that follow.

For about one out of every three people on Earth, clean water is *scarce,* or not plentiful enough. This lack of clean water causes millions of people, mostly children, to die each year from infections and illnesses caused by waterborne bacteria. Unfortunately, global water shortages will likely get much worse, partly because of melting glaciers.

 Inventors are constantly coming up with many products to help produce and filter clean water. One example is a greenhouse that can use salt water from the ocean. The greenhouse pumps and filters the water using solar power, creating fresh water for the greenhouse crops.

19) What can be inferred from Paragraph 1?
 (A) Water shortages force people to rely on dirtier water.
 (B) It is always difficult to keep children away from polluted water.
 (C) One-third of the global population depends on glacier water.
 (D) Melting glaciers will provide more clean water.

20) What can be inferred from Paragraph 2?
 (A) Salt water is the only solution to the global water shortage.
 (B) People are trying to adapt to environmental changes.
 (C) Inventors only rely on solar power to create fresh water.
 (D) Someday all farming will take place in greenhouses.

I. What Is a Purpose Question?

Purpose

The purpose question asks you to identify the ways in which certain pieces of information help you understand either a detail or the main idea of the passage. A *purpose* is the reason why the author included particular information in a passage. For example, the purpose of a passage can be to inform you about a topic or to persuade the reader.

A. PURPOSE QUESTION MODEL

The parrot is considered one of the most intelligent birds. All parrots can imitate sounds, such as words spoken by humans. They can also imitate sounds made by other animals. Some species of parrots have shown that they can use tools and solve puzzles.

7. Why does the author mention that parrots can imitate sounds?
   (A) To introduce the example of human words as sounds
   (B) To give an example of how parrots are intelligent birds
   (C) To show that parrots are more fun than other birds
   (D) To tell the reader about parrots

B. PURPOSE QUESTION FORMATS

The author discusses _____ in order to _____.
The author mentions _____ in order to _____.
Why does the author discuss _____?
Why does the author compare _____ to _____?
Why does the author mention _____?
Why does the author order the information by _____?
Why does the author use the word/the punctuation mark when discussing _____?

C. TIPS

1. Generally, purpose questions ask you to create logical connections between sentences or paragraphs.
2. The overall purpose sometimes can be found in the topic sentence, which is normally the first sentence.
3. Incorrect answers are too vague, false according to the passage, or unrelated to the passage.

II. Hacking Strategy

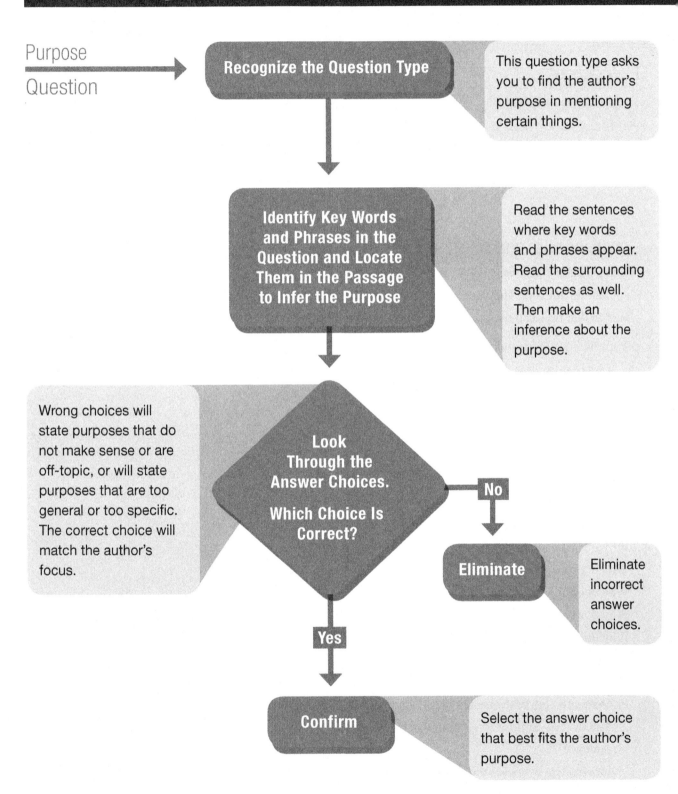

Purpose
Question

Recognize the Question Type

This question type asks you to find the author's purpose in mentioning certain things.

Identify Key Words and Phrases in the Question and Locate Them in the Passage to Infer the Purpose

Read the sentences where key words and phrases appear. Read the surrounding sentences as well. Then make an inference about the purpose.

Wrong choices will state purposes that do not make sense or are off-topic, or will state purposes that are too general or too specific. The correct choice will match the author's focus.

Look Through the Answer Choices.

Which Choice Is Correct?

No

Yes

Eliminate

Eliminate incorrect answer choices.

Confirm

Select the answer choice that best fits the author's purpose.

Recognize the Question Type

The parrot is considered one of the most intelligent birds. All parrots can imitate sounds, such as words spoken by humans. They can also imitate sounds made by other animals. Some species of parrots have shown that they can use tools and solve puzzles.

Why does the author mention that parrots can imitate sounds?
(A) To introduce the example of human words as sounds
(B) To give an example of how parrots are intelligent birds
(C) To show that parrots are more fun than other birds
(D) To tell the reader about parrots

Identify Key Words and Phrases in the Question, and Locate Them in the Passage to Infer the Purpose

Why does the author mention that parrots can imitate sounds?

Make an inference about the purpose. Let's examine the sentences in which the key words appear. Before the author tells us that "*all parrots can imitate sounds*," the author says that "*the parrot is considered one of the most intelligent birds*." Given this introduction, we can infer that the author tells us that parrots imitate sounds as an example of how parrots are intelligent.

Look Through the Answer Choices.

Which Choice Is Correct?

(A) To introduce the example of human words as sounds
(B) To give an example of how parrots are intelligent birds
(C) To show that parrots are more fun than other birds
(D) To tell the reader about parrots

Look for the choice that stays focused on what the passage is mainly saying.

• Select **Choice B** because this matches our inference about the relationship between imitation and intelligence.

Eliminate Incorrect Choices

• Eliminate **Choice A** because the passage is about parrots, so an answer about human words is off topic.
• Eliminate **Choice C** because the author does not mention anything about birds being fun.
• Eliminate **Choice D** because the passage focuses specifically on parrot intelligence, so this choice is too broad.

Confirm

Select the correct answer — **Choice B**.

CHAPTER 7 Purpose Question | 81

III. Quick Look

Words Used in Purpose Answer Choices

Word	Definition
Argue	to try to prove a point
Caution	to warn against
Classify	to put in a category
Compare	to examine two or more things in relation to each other
Contrast	to show that one thing is different from the other
Criticize	to show something's faults
Define	to tell what something is
Describe	to provide details about what something is like
Emphasize	to highlight important information
Explain	to tell why something is
Give Examples	to provide instances in order to further explain something
Identify	to tell what something is (similar to **Define**)
Illustrate	to give further information (similar to **Describe**)
Introduce	to bring forward a new idea or information
Persuade	to try to convince the reader to agree
Point Out	to bring something to attention
Praise	to admire or compliment something
Predict	to foretell something
Prove	to show that something is true
Show	to state something
Summarize	to state something in a shorter way, giving only the main ideas
Support	to show that something is true; to provide evidence for it
Trace	to follow the course of something's development
Warn	to give caution about something

IV. Warm Up

Read each topic and each detail below. Then choose whether the purpose of each detail is to:

*Persuade = PER   *Describe = DES   *Criticize = CR

1. **Topic:** Eating a balanced diet _____
   Detail: It is wise to eat many whole, fresh foods such as fruits, vegetables, nuts, and beans.

2. **Topic:** Eating a balanced diet
   Detail: A *balanced* diet refers to the _____ principle of eating food from each food group.

3. **Topic:** Swimming
   Detail: One disadvantage of swimming _____ for fitness is that it does not greatly strengthen bones.

4. **Topic:** Swimming
   Detail: Because it is a low-impact _____ activity, swimming is the ideal exercise for anyone with painful knees.

5. **Topic:** Paying attention
   Detail: The length of time a person can _____ concentrate on an activity is called his or her *attention span*, and it varies with age.

6. **Topic:** Paying attention _____
   Detail: Unfortunately, some Roman emperors succeeded in turning the public's attention away from social problems by using "bread and circuses," or free food and violent stadium games.

7. **Topic:** Egyptian pyramids _____
   Detail: More than 100 ancient pyramids have been discovered in Egypt.

8. **Topic:** Egyptian pyramids _____
   Detail: One of the Egyptian pyramids is the Great Pyramid of Giza, which was built in 2560 BCE as a tomb for a ruler named Khufu.

9. **Topic:** Giving flowers _____
   Detail: The cut-flower industry causes massive ecological damage just so customers can give a gift that will die within days.

10. **Topic:** Giving flowers _____
    Detail: There is no gift that is equal to flowers to convey love, cheer someone up, or just say, "You matter to me."

V. Quick Practice

Practice #1

Read the passage. Then answer the question that follows.

A mask is a covering worn over the face. In some theaters, actors wear masks to show emotions. In **ancient Greece**, actors wore masks to express anger, joy, sorrow, and love.

1) Why does the author mention "**ancient Greece**" in the passage?
   (A) To introduce a different main idea
   (B) To trace the history of masks
   (C) To contrast one type of mask with another
   (D) To give an example of uses for theater masks

Practice #2

Read the passage. Then answer the question that follows.

City planners try to foresee future needs. They try to predict the effects of factors such as large **changes in population**. These predictions help a government plan for the future.

2) Why does the author mention "**changes in population**" in the passage?
   (A) To praise city planners for their work
   (B) To give an example of what city planners predict
   (C) To explain why people become city planners
   (D) To show how city planners have changed

Practice #3

Read the passage. Then answer the question that follows.

Although it is still being explored, the Moon seems to lack evidence of any life forms. Compared with **Earth**, its surface has shown little change over billions of years while many things have changed on Earth.

3) Why does the author mention "**Earth**" in the passage?
   (A) To criticize the Moon
   (B) To show why the Moon exists
   (C) To define what a planet is
   (D) To contrast with the Moon

Practice #4

Read the passage. Then answer the question that follows.

Doctor Tim Fitzgerald believes that exercise is the **"cure"** for many chronic conditions. Such conditions include high blood pressure, diabetes, and heart disease.

4) Why does the author put quotation marks around "**cure**" in the passage?
   (A) To show that it is the doctor's opinion, not the author's
   (B) To indicate that the use of the word is ironic
   (C) To define the word for readers
   (D) To explain that the word is foreign

Practice #5

Read the passage. Then answer the question that follows.

Sigmund Freud, one of the most famous thinkers of the 20th century, remains both the most influential and the most debated psychologist. Although many find his theories controversial, most psychologists accept his belief that the unconscious mind plays a big role in behavior.

5) Why does the author mention "**Sigmund Freud**" in the passage?
   (A) To illustrate problems regarding psychology
   (B) To contrast an old with a new psychologist
   (C) To show his influence on modern psychology
   (D) To criticize him as an inexperienced psychologist

Practice #6

Read the passage. Then answer the question that follows.

People have always tried to understand why things happen. Today, people use **science** to answer these questions. But in the past, people relied on myths. In other words, natural events were explained in terms of the actions of gods and goddesses.

6) Why does the author mention "**science**" in the passage?
   (A) To introduce a new topic
   (B) To contrast with myths
   (C) To criticize ancient people
   (D) To answer a question

Practice #7

Read the passage. Then answer the question that follows.

No one knows when cats were first domesticated. However, some historians believe that it happened around 4000 BCE in **Egypt**. There, cats were encouraged to kill mice and rats on farms and in homes.

7) Why does the author mention "**Egypt**" in the passage?
   (A) To trace the first use of the word "cat"
   (B) To describe a myth about cats
   (C) To explain a possible origin of domesticated cats
   (D) To contrast domestic cats with wild cats

Practice #8

Read the passage. Then answer the question that follows.

Many Arab Americans have combined traditions from their homelands with American practices and fashions. For example, a Muslim girl may wear a headscarf, but she may also wear Western-influenced clothing, such as **jeans and sneakers**.

8) Why does the author mention "**jeans and sneakers**" in the passage?
   (A) To give an example of typical Muslim clothing
   (B) To show that Arab Americans are like other Americans
   (C) To contrast American and Muslim clothing
   (D) To persuade readers to like Arab Americans

Practice #9

Read the passage. Then answer the question that follows.

The Colossus of Rhodes was a statue that stood on Rhodes, a Greek island in the Aegean Sea. Although he never saw it finished, **Chares of Lindos**, a Greek sculptor, started construction on this massive statue around 292 BCE. The statue, completed 12 years later, was built to honor and praise the sun god Helios.

9) Why does the author mention "**Chares of Lindos**" in the passage?
   (A) To introduce the creator of the statue
   (B) To give the subject of the statue
   (C) To give the title of the statue
   (D) To show where the statue is located

Practice #10

Read the passage. Then answer the question that follows.

The word *democracy* comes from a Greek term that translates to "rule of the people." During the 19th century, United States President **Abraham Lincoln** added to the definition, stating that "Democracy is the government of the people, by the people, for the people."

10) Why does the author mention "**Abraham Lincoln**" in the passage?
   (A) To describe democracy in greater detail
   (B) To give an example of a democratic leader
   (C) To contrast two different democracies
   (D) To persuade readers that democracy is good

Select the vocabulary word or phrase that has the closest meaning.

5. **species**
   A. brand
   B. breed
   C. source
   D. level

6. **solve**
   A. learn about
   B. serve as
   C. talk about
   D. figure out

7. **mention**
   A. state
   B. blame
   C. judge
   D. notice

1. **inform**
   A. ask
   B. question
   C. convince
   D. tell

2. **criticize**
   A. create
   B. praise
   C. discredit
   D. reduce

3. **intelligent**
   A. smart
   B. interesting
   C. insane
   D. normal

4. **imitate**
   A. trace
   B. irritate
   C. mimic
   D. write

8. **introduce**
   A. examine
   B. imagine
   C. use
   D. present

9. **emphasize**
   A. highlight
   B. forget
   C. ignore
   D. exclude

10. **persuade**
    A. prepare
    B. prevent
    C. convince
    D. converse

11. **predict**
    A. foretell
    B. trust
    C. think
    D. focus

12. **warn**
    A. caution
    B. watch
    C. relate
    D. forward

13. **balanced**
    A. fortunate
    B. popular
    C. kind
    D. stable

14. **principle**
    A. property
    B. standard
    C. maintenance
    D. attention

15. **painful**
    A. skillful
    B. tiresome
    C. agonizing
    D. violent

16. **ecological**
    A. environmental
    B. improper
    C. possible
    D. acceptable

17. **sorrow**
    A. grief
    B. happiness
    C. trust
    D. rage

18. **foresee**
    A. remember
    B. anticipate
    C. collect
    D. restrict

19. **condition**
    A. state
    B. variety
    C. manner
    D. outline

20. **influential**
    A. factual
    B. intentional
    C. extreme
    D. effectual

21. **unconscious**
    A. significant
    B. unaware
    C. dazed
    D. alert

22. **domesticated**
    A. tamed
    B. excited
    C. defined
    D. released

23. **probably**
    A. certainly
    B. possibly
    C. randomly
    D. definitely

24. **encouraged**
    A. expected
    B. determined
    C. supported
    D. forced

25. **massive**
    A. ancient
    B. graceful
    C. enormous
    D. decorative

CHAPTER **8**
PARAPHRASE QUESTION

I. What Is a Paraphrase Question?

Paraphrase

The paraphrase question asks you to identify the answer choice that best restates the meaning of the sentence(s) in a given passage. The restatement may summarize the main ideas in a simpler way and omit less important details. The paraphrase may use *synonyms*, or different words that have similar meanings, to convey the same ideas. Furthermore, sentences may change when paraphrased: the sentence length and/or the sentence structure—the order of the words and the clauses within the sentence—may vary from the original.

A. PARAPHRASE QUESTION MODEL

Thomas Edison is regarded as one of the greatest inventors in the world. Through many experiments, he developed devices such as the electric light bulb and motion picture camera that are still used to this day.

8. Which of the following best paraphrases the passage?
   (A) Thomas Edison loved the electric light bulb and motion picture camera, so he became an inventor.
   (B) Through many experiments, Thomas Edison's inventions became some of the greatest inventions in the world.
   (C) Thomas Edison, one of the greatest inventors in the world, developed many devices that influence the world to this day.
   (D) Because of his many creative inventions, Thomas Edison is still the world's most famous inventor.

B. PARAPHRASE QUESTION FORMATS

Which of the following best expresses the highlighted section?
Which of the following best expresses the highlighted section of Paragraph _____?
Which of the following best paraphrases _____?

C. TIPS

1. Look for paraphrases that contain the necessary information.
2. Incorrect answers may:
   • include unnecessary information
   • omit essential information
   • add information not in the passage
   • be inaccurate according to the passage
   • have a different meaning than the original passage

II. Hacking Strategy

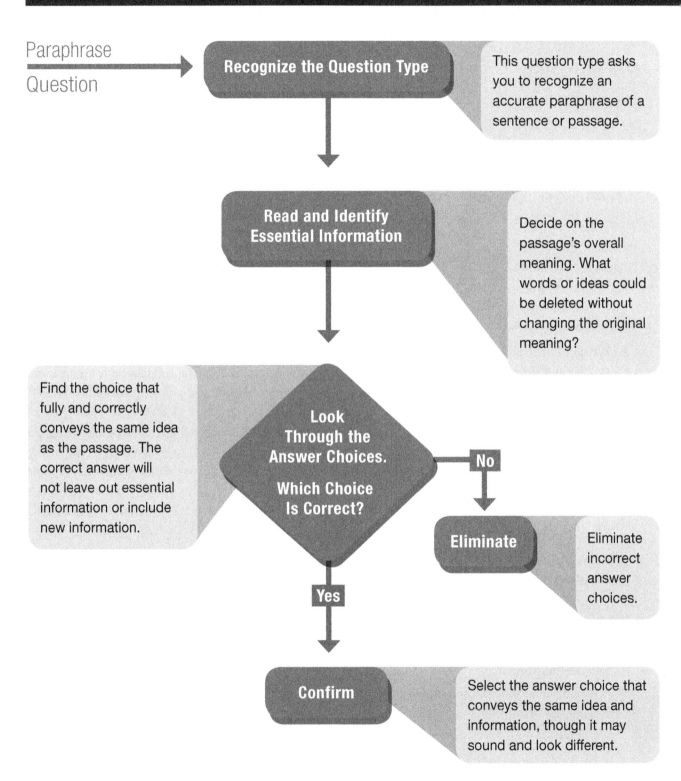

Paraphrase Question

Recognize the Question Type

This question type asks you to recognize an accurate paraphrase of a sentence or passage.

Read and Identify Essential Information

Decide on the passage's overall meaning. What words or ideas could be deleted without changing the original meaning?

Find the choice that fully and correctly conveys the same idea as the passage. The correct answer will not leave out essential information or include new information.

Look Through the Answer Choices.

Which Choice Is Correct?

No

Yes

Eliminate

Eliminate incorrect answer choices.

Confirm

Select the answer choice that conveys the same idea and information, though it may sound and look different.

Recognize the Question Type	Thomas Edison is regarded as one of the greatest inventors in the world. Through many experiments, he developed devices such as the electric light bulb and motion picture camera that are still used to this day. **Which of the following best paraphrases the passage?** (A) Thomas Edison loved the electric light bulb and motion picture camera, so he became an inventor. (B) Through many experiments, Thomas Edison's inventions became some of the greatest inventions in the world. (C) Thomas Edison, one of the greatest inventors in the world, developed many devices that influence the world to this day. (D) Because of his many creative inventions, Thomas Edison is still the world's most famous inventor.
Read and Identify Essential Information	*Thomas Edison* is regarded as *one of the greatest inventors in the world*. Through many experiments, he *developed devices* such as the *electric light bulb and motion picture camera* that are still *used to this day*. The passage calls Thomas Edison one of the greatest inventors, and we can convey this idea without listing details, such as Edison's creations of the electric light bulb and motion picture camera.
Look Through the Answer Choices. **Which Choice Is Correct?**	Which choice conveys the main idea in a different way, without introducing new conclusions or details? • Select **Choice C** because it conveys the main ideas, such as Edison being one of the greatest inventors ever and his inventions still being used today.
Eliminate Incorrect Choices	• Eliminate **Choice A** because the passage does not describe what Edison felt or why he became an inventor. • Eliminate **Choice B** because the passage does not conclude that Edison's inventions became great through *many experiments*. • Eliminate **Choice D** because the passage does not state anything about Edison's inventions being *creative* or that he is *the world's most famous inventor*.
Confirm	Select the correct answer — **Choice C**.

III. Quick Look

Paraphrase Structure Types

Type 1	Type 2	Type 3
Type 1 changes the wording and uses different sentence structure or different ordered clauses.	Type 2 uses synonyms and other expressions to convey the same idea.	Type 3 uses the referent instead of the pronoun to convey the same idea.
Original Sentence	**Original Sentence**	**Original Sentence**
People exercise, 1 for their health and looks. 2 Clause 2 Clause 1 destination (resulting sentence)	People **love** having fun. love enjoy	**Eating** is a way to survive. Also, **it** gives people pleasure. Eating / It referent pronoun
Paraphrase	**Paraphrase**	**Paraphrase**
For their health and looks, 2 people exercise. 1 Clause 1 Clause 2 destination (resulting sentence)	People **enjoy** having fun. enjoy love	**Eating**, a way to survive, gives people pleasure. Eating referent

IV. Warm Up

Read each sentence below. Then choose the answer that provides the more accurate paraphrase.

1. Native Americans did not just hunt buffalos for food, but for clothes and tools as well.
   A) Native Americans killed buffalos for food, tools, and clothes.
   B) Buffalos were killed mainly for food, not for tools or clothes.

2. Many people use spices to add a wider variety of flavors to their food.
   A) Most people add spices to give their food a new taste.
   B) People are always eager to try different foods and spices.

3. Because handmade gifts require time and effort, they are often more appreciated than store-bought gifts.
   A) People often treasure presents made by hand more than gifts bought from stores.
   B) People prefer giving handmade gifts to be appreciated by others.

4. Even though Susan spent the whole day resting, she still felt too sick to go to the party.
   A) Susan did not go to the party because she was too sick.
   B) Resting did not help Susan recover from her illness in time for the party.

5. Khan and Cindy both enjoy watching movies, and that is why they became good friends.
   A) Khan and Cindy are friends because they both like movies.
   B) Khan and Cindy watched movies in order to become friends.

6. Rebecca hates being cold, so she stays indoors when it is snowing outside.
   A) Rebecca hates the cold but likes watching the snow while indoors.
   B) Rebecca stays indoors when it snows because she hates feeling cold.

7. Cats will run away from loud noises because they are scared of them and prefer quiet.
   A) Cats like quiet, but they are often unconcerned about loud noises.
   B) Cats do not like loud sounds and tend to quickly hide from them.

8. Pho, a well-known Vietnamese noodle soup, is popular in the United States.
   A) Vietnamese people introduced pho to the United States.
   B) The Vietnamese food called *pho* is well liked in the United States.

9. Vegetarians choose not to eat meat for different reasons, such as religious beliefs.
   A) Religious beliefs are one reason some vegetarians follow their diet.
   B) Vegetarians do not like to eat meat because their religion disapproves it.

10. Tina was always shy in class until she started talking to other students.
    A) Tina felt uncomfortable while talking to other students in class.
    B) Talking to other students in class made Tina become less shy.

CHAPTER 8
PARAPHRASE QUESTION

V. Quick Practice

Practice #1

Read the passage. Then answer the question that follows.

Although many schools have good libraries, some schools are unable to provide adequate learning facilities.

1) Which of the following best paraphrases the sentence?
   (A) Teachers like school libraries more than students.
   (B) Most schools have excellent libraries.
   (C) Some schools have better libraries than others.
   (D) All schools have poor libraries nowadays.

Practice #2

Read the passage. Then answer the question that follows.

Certain jobs require only a high school education, but many jobs require additional schooling.

2) Which of the following best paraphrases the sentence?
   (A) Many jobs require additional education after high school.
   (B) Job training is hard for high school graduates without proper experience.
   (C) Few high school graduates train for jobs while in high school.
   (D) Most students prefer college to high school for education.

Practice #3

Read the passage. Then answer the question that follows.

Although Mount Kilimanjaro lies near the equator, it is covered with snow for much of the year.

3) Which of the following best paraphrases the sentence?
   (A) Half of Mount Kilimanjaro has snow, but half does not.
   (B) If people are on top of Mount Kilimanjaro in winter, they can see the equator.
   (C) People cannot see the top of Mount Kilimanjaro most of the time.
   (D) Despite its location, Mount Kilimanjaro has snow almost the entire year.

Practice #4

Read the passage. Then answer the question that follows.

A good biography describes what its subject did and why the person acted in certain ways.

4) Which of the following best paraphrases what the sentence says about a biography?
(A) It is short but contains a lot of information.
(B) It discusses the actions of many different people.
(C) It is supposed to provide the facts of a person's life.
(D) It mainly talks about two different things at the same time.

Practice #5

Read the passage. Then answer the question that follows.

Benjamin Franklin was known for his ability and excellence in many different fields.

5) Which of the following best paraphrases what is said about Benjamin Franklin?
(A) He was so famous that he had to do everything perfectly.
(B) He was always changing his job due to his many abilities.
(C) He was trained by different people who excelled in various fields.
(D) He was highly talented in multiple areas.

Practice #6

Read the passage. Then answer the question that follows.

Albert Einstein once said: "The only source of knowledge is experience."

6) Which of the following best paraphrases Albert Einstein's quote?
(A) Experience is the only way to learn.
(B) People gain experience from knowledge.
(C) The only way to experience is through knowledge.
(D) Practice makes perfect.

Practice #7

Read the passage. Then answer the question that follows.

While punctuation marks were used more frequently in the past, today the trend is to use fewer and fewer marks.

7) Which of the following best paraphrases the sentence?
(A) It is best to learn punctuation from an old teacher.
(B) No one clearly understands punctuation anymore.
(C) Punctuation is not used as much as it used to be.
(D) The look of punctuation has recently changed.

Practice #8

Read the passage. Then answer the question that follows.

Despite a growing interest in ballet, ballet companies worldwide struggle to survive even during good economic times.

8) Which of the following best paraphrases the sentence?
(A) When more people attend ballets, ballet companies survive.
(B) Changes in the economy create interest in ballet.
(C) People only attend ballet when they have money.
(D) No matter what, ballet companies have financial difficulties.

Practice #9

Read the passage. Then answer the question that follows.

Arizona, once thought to be a worthless desert, has become one of the most prosperous American states.

9) Which of the following best paraphrases the sentence?
(A) When people moved to Arizona, the deserts became big cities.
(B) Arizona ended up being more valuable than people predicted.
(C) Only very rich people live in the state of Arizona.
(D) People who are traveling in Arizona have more than enough money.

Practice #10

Read the passage. Then answer the question that follows.

Because a horse has eyes on the sides of its head, it has almost a full range of vision except for blind spots directly in front of and behind it.

10) Which of the following best paraphrases the sentence?
(A) A horse may lose its vision in blind spots because of the placement of the eyes on the sides of the horse's head.
(B) The location of a horse's eyes provides a wide vision field, but a horse also has limited vision in some areas.
(C) The location of a horse's eyes causes the horse not to have a large field of vision except for certain ranges.
(D) A horse's blind spots are to the left and the right of the horse, preventing it from seeing these areas.

POP QUIZ

Select the vocabulary word or phrase that has the closest meaning.

1. **paraphrase**
   A. persuade
   B. complete
   C. restate
   D. introduce

2. **regard as**
   A. consider as
   B. reveal as
   C. arrange as
   D. prove as

3. **influence**
   A. affect
   B. generate
   C. burden
   D. create

4. **include**
   A. excuse
   B. contain
   C. reject
   D. want

5. **omit**
   A. deliver
   B. exclude
   C. apply
   D. obtain

6. **essential**
   A. minor
   B. trivial
   C. optional
   D. vital

7. **overall**
   A. collective
   B. elaborate
   C. unimportant
   D. implied

8. **convey**
   A. understand
   B. express
   C. insist
   D. accept

9. **leave out**
   A. consider
   B. involve
   C. exclude
   D. supply

10. **mainly**
    A. commonly
    B. mostly
    C. generally
    D. normally

11. **spice**
    A. fragrance
    B. perfume
    C. flavor
    D. seasoning

12. **appreciated**
    A. absorbed
    B. carried
    C. cherished
    D. amazed

13. **prefer**
    A. praise
    B. dislike
    C. favor
    D. prohibit

14. **recover**
    A. rest
    B. heal
    C. grow
    D. change

15. **tend**
    A. be free
    B. be used
    C. be made
    D. be likely

16. **disapprove**
    A. favor
    B. respect
    C. oppose
    D. display

17. **adequate**
    A. abandoned
    B. suitable
    C. expensive
    D. passionate

18. **additional**
    A. excessive
    B. official
    C. proper
    D. extra

19. **excellence**
    A. superiority
    B. necessity
    C. support
    D. exercise

20. **frequently**
    A. particularly
    B. often
    C. rarely
    D. faintly

21. **struggle**
    A. surrender
    B. continue
    C. remain
    D. battle

22. **worthless**
    A. useless
    B. enormous
    C. unknown
    D. faithless

23. **prosperous**
    A. economic
    B. definitive
    C. problematic
    D. successful

24. **valuable**
    A. vacant
    B. current
    C. useful
    D. private

25. **placement**
    A. arrangement
    B. opening
    C. amount
    D. enjoyment

1C 2A 3A 4B 5B 6D 7A 8B 9C 10B 11D 12C 13C 14B 15D 16C 17B 18D 19A 20B 21D 22A 23D 24C 25A

Exercises

Exercise #1 Read the passage. Then answer the questions that follow.

The Native American people known as the Sioux live in the northern plains of North America. The Sioux are well known for their **bravery and political skills**.

The **Dakota Sioux** live in what is now Minnesota. On the other hand, the **Lakota Sioux** are spread out over the central and midwest regions of the United States. Some members of these groups still hunt and farm.

1) Why does the author mention "**bravery and political skills**" in Paragraph 1?
   (A) To question the Sioux
   (B) To criticize the Sioux
   (C) To describe the Sioux
   (D) To warn about the Sioux

2) Why does the author mention the "**Dakota Sioux**" and "**Lakota Sioux**" in Paragraph 2?
   (A) To introduce two Sioux tribes
   (B) To argue which Sioux tribe is better
   (C) To name two Sioux leaders
   (D) To support Sioux culture

Exercise #2 Read the passage. Then answer the questions that follow.

Fish live in mountain streams and in underground rivers. They even live in the cold Arctic Sea, as well as in the warm fresh water of tropical jungles.

Another interesting fact about fish is their variety. The kinds of fish differ so greatly in shape, color, and size, that it is hard to believe that they all belong to the same class.

3) Which of the following best paraphrases Paragraph 1?
   (A) Fish still have a great deal to teach people.
   (B) Fish travel among various bodies of water annually.
   (C) Fish live almost anywhere there is water on Earth.
   (D) Fish can only survive where the conditions are just right.

4) Which of the following best paraphrases Paragraph 2?
   (A) Physically, fish are so varied that they sometimes appear to belong in different groups of animals.
   (B) Scientists cannot believe how much fish have taught them about other animals.
   (C) Because fish have become so diverse, scientists have a hard time grouping them all.
   (D) No one in their lifetime will ever see all the different fish that exist on the planet.

Exercise #3 Read the passage. Then answer the questions that follow.

A quilt is a cloth bedcover. The top part of a quilt may be decorated with **geometric designs and patterns of certain animals, plants, or people**. The center part is filled with cotton or wool.

Quilting originated in prehistoric times. Quilting in the United States began during colonial days. During that time, immigrants from **Europe** began practicing the quilting skills that they had learned in their countries.

5) Why is the highlighted phrase used in Paragraph 1?
   (A) To describe the appearance of some quilts
   (B) To contrast different quilt subjects
   (C) To show how quilts are changing
   (D) To make readers interested in quilts

6) Why is "**Europe**" mentioned in Paragraph 2?
   (A) To introduce where colonists first learned quilting
   (B) To explain why colonists quilted
   (C) To compare two types of quilting
   (D) To criticize American quilts

Exercise #4 Read the passage. Then answer the questions that follow.

Accidental injuries and deaths in the workplace have gone down in the United States within the last century. In 1997, there were four work-related deaths for every 100,000 workers, a 90 percent decline from 1933.

Many changes have been made to help improve job safety. For example, industries such as mining have improved their safety techniques. Companies in the U.S. also offer more desk jobs now to meet ever-changing commercial needs. In fact, these days there are more deaths from accidents in the home than on the job these days.

7) Which of the following best paraphrases Paragraph 1?
   (A) In 1997, there were 100,000 workers in the U.S., 90 percent more than in 1933.
   (B) Unintended injuries and deaths have gone down in the last 100 years.
   (C) During the 20th century, work environments became less risky for laborers.
   (D) Proper job training led to a decline in work-related injuries and deaths.

8) Which of the following best paraphrases Paragraph 2?
   (A) Mining used to be much more dangerous, but now there are improved standards.
   (B) Due to industrial and economic changes, job safety has improved more than home safety.
   (C) More people die from accidents in their homes annually than have ever died at the workplace.
   (D) Working at a desk at the workplace has become 90 percent safer than working at home.

Exercise #5 Read the passage. Then answer the questions that follow.

Locoweed is a poisonous plant in North America. The name *locoweed* comes from the Spanish word for "crazy." Locoweed has harmful effects on animals; when they eat it, they act strangely.

Locoweed's effects come from two factors. Swainsonine is the main toxin in locoweed that causes illness in livestock. Scientists also believe that the plant's effects result from its absorption of large amounts of the element **selenium**.

9) Why does the author italicize "*locoweed*" in Paragraph 1?
(A) To criticize the name of the plant
(B) To introduce the word in the passage
(C) To show that locoweed came from Spain
(D) To indicate that the name is of foreign origin

10) Why does the author mention "**selenium**" in Paragraph 2?
(A) To explain why locoweed is poisonous
(B) To contrast locoweed with another plant
(C) To describe what locoweed needs to survive
(D) To persuade readers not to eat locoweed

Exercise #6 Read the passage. Then answer the questions that follow.

Since ancient times, toys have played a big role in children's lives. They enable children to have fun while learning about the world around them.

Before the development of toy factories, parents or crafters made toys. In fact, up to the early 1900s, most children in the United States played with homemade toys.

11) Which of the following best paraphrases Paragraph 1?
(A) Toys have been important in human development because they help people learn.
(B) Toys expose children to ancient knowledge from an early age.
(C) Children used to prefer bigger toys but now prefer smaller versions.
(D) Toys have always been beneficial learning tools for children.

12) Which of the following best paraphrases Paragraph 2?
(A) Children started working in toy factories in the 1900s.
(B) American parents used to copy crafters to make toys.
(C) Only American children played with handmade toys before 1900.
(D) Until the 20th century, children's toys were made by hand.

Exercise #7 Read the passage. Then answer the questions that follow.

Henry Ford is the **father** of the American automobile industry. He started the Ford Motor Company in the early 1900s. From 1908 to 1927, half the cars sold in the United States were Fords.

Henry Ford was always interested in politics. Today, some of his views would be considered inappropriate. He made many discriminatory remarks about race. He also opposed labor unions.

13) Why does the author mention "**father**" in Paragraph 1?
  (A) To persuade readers to like Henry Ford
  (B) To illustrate that Henry Ford was an inventor
  (C) To imply that Henry Ford launched the American car industry
  (D) To indicate that Henry Ford had many children

14) What is the MAIN purpose of Paragraph 2?
  (A) To explain why he liked politics
  (B) To describe Henry Ford's early life
  (C) To appeal to older readers
  (D) To criticize Henry Ford

Exercise #8 Read the passage. Then answer the questions that follow.

African Americans were enslaved in the United States before 1865. As they worked, they developed songs about Biblical stories called spirituals. Many of these songs were also about freedom.

Slaves used stories to voice their true feelings. For example, one spiritual, "Go Down, Moses," includes the repeated phrase, "Let my people go."

15) Which of the following best paraphrases Paragraph 1?
  (A) African Americans have recently written a number of songs about freedom.
  (B) Religious songs about freedom were created by enslaved African Americans.
  (C) Songs that people made up during historical times are now free because no one owns them.
  (D) Before slavery was abolished, African Americans sang many religious songs.

16) Which of the following best paraphrases Paragraph 2?
  (A) Slaves used metaphor as their way of expression.
  (B) One song included lines about freedom and spirituality.
  (C) African Americans sang a song telling Moses to go "down," or out.
  (D) Spirituals repeated certain phrases to make the meaning of the song clearer.

Exercise #9 Read the passage. Then answer the questions that follow.

Time is one of the world's biggest mysteries. No one can say exactly what it is. Yet, the ability to measure time makes **modern lifestyles** possible.

However, clocks around the world do not show the same time because the world is divided into different time zones. **Suppose that they all did show the same time**—3 p.m., for example. At that time, people in some countries would see the sun rise while people in other countries would see it set.

17) Why does the author mention "**modern lifestyles**" in Paragraph 1?
   (A) To criticize people's focus on time
   (B) To show how important time is
   (C) To argue for a new kind of time
   (D) To make readers better understand time

18) Why is the phrase "**Suppose that they all did show the same time**" mentioned in Paragraph 2?
   (A) To illustrate why society needs time zones
   (B) To describe how time was measured in the past
   (C) To criticize people who think that time should be measured differently
   (D) To give an example of one of the world's biggest mysteries

Exercise #10 Read the passage. Then answer the questions that follow.

Many scientists believe that Antarctica was once a part of a supercontinent called Gondwana. It consisted of lands such as Antarctica, Australia, New Zealand, India, Africa, and South America. However, over many years, Gondwana slowly divided and broke up into the smaller continents and islands that exist today.

Some pieces of the evidence for the supercontinent theory are the fossils found in Antarctica. For example, fossils of one type of reptile have been found not only in Antarctica, but also in India, South America, Africa, and Australia.

19) Which of the following best paraphrases Paragraph 1?
   (A) Lands such as Antarctica and Australia are divided into smaller continents.
   (B) Gondwana and Antarctica are two of the supercontinents in the world.
   (C) Many scientists are discovering new small continents and islands.
   (D) Many continents and islands may have been one large continent in the past.

20) Which of the following best paraphrases Paragraph 2?
   (A) India, South America, Africa, and Australia have fossils of only one type of reptile.
   (B) Certain fossils found in different regions of the world support the existence of Gondwana.
   (C) The presence of Antarctica is the evidence of the existence of Gondwana.
   (D) One type of reptile is the only evidence that supports the existence of Gondwana.

I. What Is a Summary Question?

Summary

The summary question asks you to select the sentences that best support the main idea of a given passage. A summary states the major ideas in shorter form.

A. SUMMARY QUESTION MODEL

Moving to a new place can be both stressful and exciting. There are many things to consider. Location is one of them. People must decide how far they would travel to their jobs or schools from home. People also must consider the safety of the area. They should pick an area without high crime rates.

9. **Directions**: *An introductory sentence for a summary of the passage is provided. Complete the summary by selecting the TWO answer choices that are the most important. Some sentences do not belong.*

There are many things to consider when choosing a new home.

-
-

Answer Choices
1. People must decide how far they are willing to travel each day.
2. People can be stressed and excited about moving at the same time.
3. People have to find out how to bring their pets with them.
4. People should try to move to a safe place without much crime.

*Typical summary questions will have three correct choices out of six possible choices. Above is a simplified example.

B. TIPS

1. Make sure that you choose an answer that includes the most important ideas in the passage.
2. You can choose a paraphrase that omits minor ideas or details as long as the passage's meaning remains the same.
3. Incorrect answers are inaccurate or irrelevant, or contain minor ideas or details.
4. Because these questions ask you to select multiple correct answers, they are worth up to 2 points rather than 1 point.
5. You must select two correct answers to receive 1 point and three correct answers for 2 points.

II. Hacking Strategy

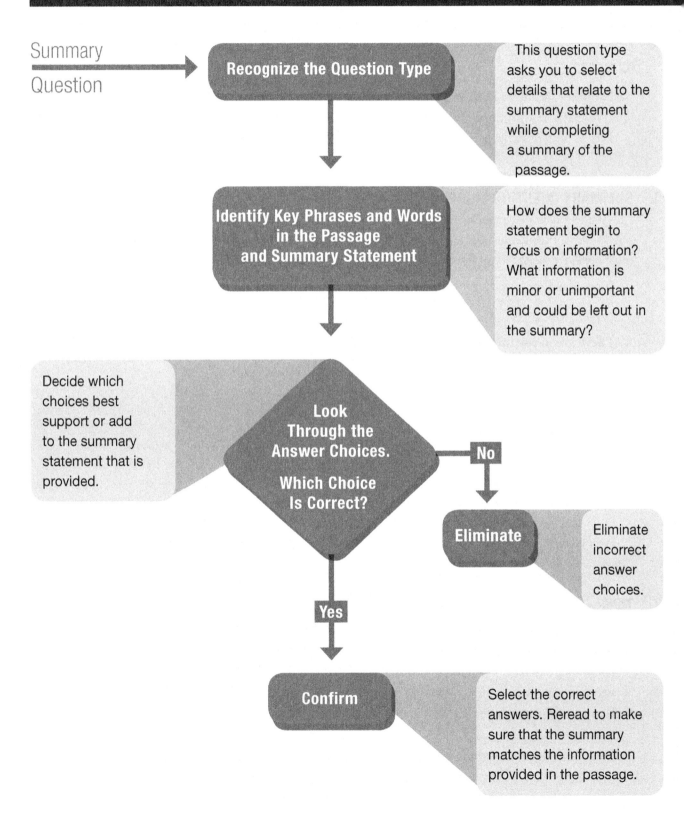

Summary Question → **Recognize the Question Type**

This question type asks you to select details that relate to the summary statement while completing a summary of the passage.

Identify Key Phrases and Words in the Passage and Summary Statement

How does the summary statement begin to focus on information? What information is minor or unimportant and could be left out in the summary?

Decide which choices best support or add to the summary statement that is provided.

Look Through the Answer Choices. Which Choice Is Correct?

No

Eliminate

Eliminate incorrect answer choices.

Yes

Confirm

Select the correct answers. Reread to make sure that the summary matches the information provided in the passage.

Recognize the Question Type	Moving to a new place can be both stressful and exciting. There are many things to consider. Location is one of them. People must decide how far they would travel to their jobs or schools from home. People also must consider the safety of the area. They should pick an area without high crime rates.

Directions: An introductory sentence for a summary of the passage is provided. Complete the summary by selecting the TWO answer choices that are the most important. Some sentences do not belong.

There are many things to consider when choosing a new home.
-
-

Answer Choices
1. People must decide how far they are willing to travel each day.
2. People can be stressed and excited about moving at the same time.
3. People have to find out how to bring their pets with them.
4. People should try to move to a safe place without much crime.

Identify Key Phrases and Words in the Passage and Summary Statement

There are many things to consider when choosing a new place to move to.

Moving to a new place can be both <u>stressful and exciting</u>. There are many things to consider. <u>Location</u> is one of them. People must decide <u>how far they would travel to their jobs or schools from home</u>. People also must consider the <u>safety</u> of the area. They should pick an area <u>without high crime rates</u>.

Look Through the Answer Choices.

Which Choice Is Correct?

Find choices that are discussed in the passage AND logically connect to the introductory sentence: *"There are many things to consider when choosing a new home."*
- Select **Choice 1** because the passage states that *people must decide how far they would travel*, which matches the choice.
- Select **Choice 4** because the passage states that people *should pick an area without high crime rates*, which matches the choice.

Eliminate Incorrect Choices

- Eliminate **Choice 2** because the idea is true according to the passage, but it does not match the introductory sentence given and does not support the main idea.
- Eliminate **Choice 3** because it is not mentioned anywhere in the passage.

Confirm

Select the correct answers — **Choices 1** and **4**.

III. Quick Look

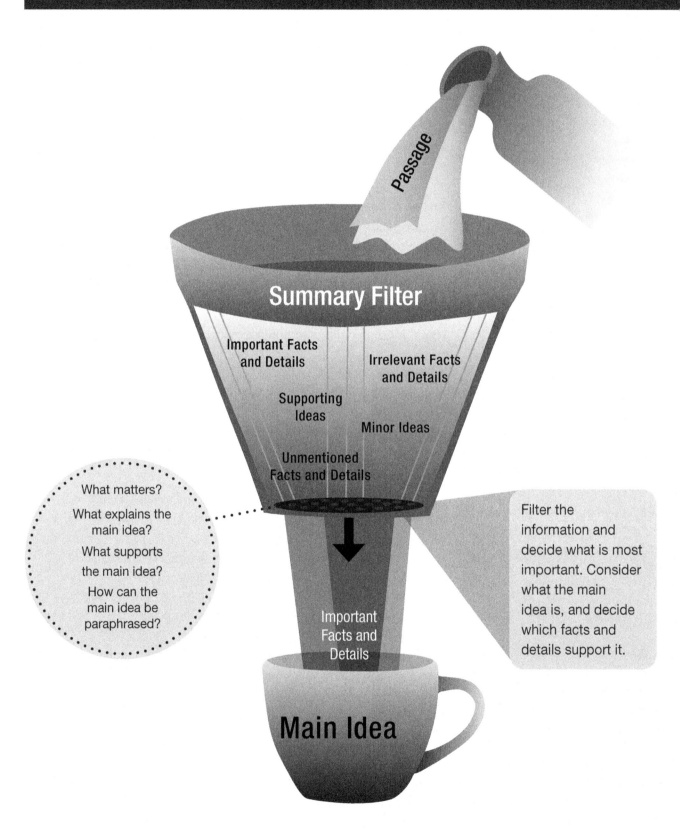

Passage

Summary Filter

Important Facts and Details

Irrelevant Facts and Details

Supporting Ideas

Minor Ideas

Unmentioned Facts and Details

What matters?

What explains the main idea?

What supports the main idea?

How can the main idea be paraphrased?

Filter the information and decide what is most important. Consider what the main idea is, and decide which facts and details support it.

Important Facts and Details

Main Idea

IV. Warm Up

Below is a topic sentence and three supporting details. Put a check mark next to the one detail that does NOT support the main idea.

1. Topic sentence: **There are many benefits to having a dog as a pet.**

    _____ Support #1: People can train dogs to do tricks or to help them.

    _____ Support #2: Dogs require a lot of time and effort and can be unsanitary.

    _____ Support #3: Dogs love people and can be great friends to them.

2. Topic sentence: **There are many different types of movies that you can watch.**

    _____ Support #1: Due to a lack of technology, the first movies had no color or audio.

    _____ Support #2: Comedy movies are funny and make people laugh.

    _____ Support #3: Some people enjoy horror movies, which are scary.

3. Topic sentence: **Our solar system has eight major planets.**

    _____ Support #1: Our planet Earth is one of them and is the third planet away from the Sun.

    _____ Support #2: The largest major planet is Jupiter.

    _____ Support #3: NASA is searching for another life form in the universe.

4. Topic sentence: **Mother's Day is celebrated in countries around the world to honor mothers.**

    _____ Support #1: Father's Day is a day when fathers are celebrated.

    _____ Support #2: Mother's Day around the world is most commonly celebrated in the spring.

    _____ Support #3: Many people give their mothers a card or gift on that day.

5. Topic sentence: **There are many good luck symbols.**

    _____ Support #1: In China, the color red is considered good luck.

    _____ Support #2: Pigs are considered good luck in several countries, such as Germany.

    _____ Support #3: In the United States, the number 13 is thought to bring bad luck.

6. Topic sentence: **People all over the world enjoy many different kinds of hobbies.**

_____ Support #1: Many people in the world work overtime, so they have no time for hobbies.

_____ Support #2: One of the most popular hobbies in the world is listening to music.

_____ Support #3: Many people in the world enjoy collecting interesting objects, such as shoes and stamps.

7. Topic sentence: **Smoking cigarettes is bad for a person's health.**

_____ Support #1: People still choose to smoke cigarettes, even though they know that it is unhealthy.

_____ Support #2: Ninety percent of people with lung cancer contracted the disease from smoking cigarettes.

_____ Support #3: Smoking increases the risk of developing heart disease.

8. Topic sentence: **Blue whales are the largest known animals in the world.**

_____ Support #1: The longest blue whale ever recorded was 33.6 meters long.

_____ Support #2: Blue whales usually live alone or with only one other whale.

_____ Support #3: The heaviest blue whale ever recorded weighed 190 metric tons.

9. Topic sentence: **People around the world have different colored eyes.**

_____ Support #1: The most common eye color in the world is brown, and blue is the second most common.

_____ Support #2: Green is the rarest eye color in the world.

_____ Support #3: People can change their eye color by using colored contact lenses.

10. Topic sentence: **The development of new technology has made life much easier for people today.**

_____ Support #1: The invention of elevators helped people go up and down many stories with ease.

_____ Support #2: Air pollution became a big problem after motorized vehicles were introduced.

_____ Support #3: Cellphones made communicating with others much more convenient.

V. Quick Practice

Practice
#1

Read the passage. Then answer the question that follows.

Many colonists in North America came from Europe. Many of them came because they wanted to escape from problems that they were experiencing in their homelands. Some had no land of their own to farm and lived in poverty; some were tired of constant wars; and some held religious beliefs that were outlawed.

1) **Directions**: *An introductory sentence for a summary of the passage is provided. Complete the summary by selecting the THREE answer choices that are the most important. Some sentences do not belong.* **This question is worth 2 points.**

> **Colonists came to North America for many reasons.**

-
-
-

Answer Choices

1. They had few economic opportunities at home.
2. They could not find food.
3. They wanted to escape conflict.
4. They had escaped from jail.
5. They desired non-farming jobs.
6. They wanted religious freedom.

Practice #2

Read the passage. Then answer the question that follows.

Small businesses are on the rise worldwide. Often, they allow individuals to make more money than does employment with corporations. Small businesses also give people a sense of control over their lives. They may create fewer environmental problems as well.

2) **Directions**: *An introductory sentence for a summary of the passage is provided. Complete the summary by selecting the THREE answer choices that are the most important. Some sentences do not belong.* **This question is worth 2 points.**

Answer Choices

1. They create new corporations.
2. They make the world smaller.
3. They tend to pay a higher salary.
4. They result in less pollution.
5. They empower people personally.
6. They earn more money than large businesses.

Small businesses have several benefits.

-
-
-

Practice #3

Read the passage. Then answer the question that follows.

There are many reasons to learn a new language. Studying new languages increases one's opportunities for interesting and diverse communication. Foreign-language learners also acquire more knowledge of their own language and about the world in general. Additionally, speaking more than one language may delay memory loss in old age.

3) **Directions**: *An introductory sentence for a summary of the passage is provided. Complete the summary by selecting the THREE answer choices that are the most important. Some sentences do not belong.* **This question is worth 2 points.**

Answer Choices

1. It improves memory among elderly people.
2. It increases understanding of a person's native language.
3. It makes the world more peaceful.
4. It gives a person more job opportunities.
5. It improves a person's communication abilities with other people.
6. It encourages people to travel.

There are many reasons for learning a new language.

-
-
-

Practice #4

Read the passage. Then answer the question that follows.

Adolescence is the time between childhood and adulthood. There are many challenges during this stage of life. Adolescents tend to take more risks than adults. Many adolescents experiment with alcohol or tobacco. Violating the law is more common in this period than at other stages of life. Adolescents are also learning about themselves as sexual beings.

4) **Directions**: *An introductory sentence for a summary of the passage is provided. Complete the summary by selecting the THREE answer choices that are the most important. Some sentences do not belong.* **This question is worth 2 points.**

Answer Choices

1. Some young people start to drink or smoke.
2. Most young people must find a job.
3. Some young people commit crimes.
4. Most young people figure out their sexuality.
5. Some young people run away from home.
6. Most young people do not enjoy learning.

There are many challenges during adolescence.

-
-
-

Practice #5

Read the passage. Then answer the question that follows.

Although he was loved by most people, President Franklin Roosevelt had his critics. They claimed that Roosevelt gave the federal government too much power. Some critics accused him of taking over rights belonging to the states, and they feared that his public welfare programs would lead to socialism.

5) **Directions**: *An introductory sentence for a summary of the passage is provided. Complete the summary by selecting the THREE answer choices that are the most important. Some sentences do not belong.* **This question is worth 2 points.**

Answer Choices

1. They did not feel that he was powerful enough.
2. They believed that he relied too much on federal government.
3. They felt that he disrespected state governments.
4. They thought that he was destroying capitalism.
5. They believed that his public welfare programs were well designed.
6. They disagreed with his policies on socialism.

Franklin Roosevelt was feared and hated by some Americans.

-
-
-

Practice #6

Read the passage. Then answer the question that follows.

The effects of colonialism outlast it. For example, many former colonies still speak the language of their colonizers. Former colonies frequently struggle because they were less economically developed while colonized. They may also be left with borders that are not of their choosing; the borders of former colonies may enclose or divide groups unnaturally.

6) **Directions**: *An introductory sentence for a summary of the passage is provided. Complete the summary by selecting the THREE answer choices that are the most important. Some sentences do not belong.* **This question is worth 2 points.**

Answer Choices

1. It discourages the use of local languages.
2. It prevents economic self-sufficiency.
3. It leads to conflicts among people.
4. It builds up security at national borders.
5. It establishes unnatural boundaries of countries.
6. It eases tensions over a longer period of time.

Colonialism has long-lasting effects.

-
-
-

Practice #7

Read the passage. Then answer the question that follows.

Animal experimentation is the use of animals in laboratory research. Members of animal rights groups call for an end to animal experimentation because they say that it causes animals to suffer. They also say that the benefits gained from it are trivial, as animals are physically different from humans. They believe that there are more useful research methods that do not involve using animals and thus support developing laboratory tests that do not use animals.

7) **Directions**: *An introductory sentence for a summary of the passage is provided. Complete the summary by selecting the THREE answer choices that are the most important. Some sentences do not belong.* **This question is worth 2 points.**

Answer Choices

1. They want researchers to only use insects.
2. They feel that there are better ways to perform laboratory experiments.
3. They think that little can be learned from it.
4. They believe that it costs too much money.
5. They feel that animals are too much like humans.
6. They do not like the way it affects animals.

Some people object to the idea of animal experimentation.

-
-
-

Practice #8

Read the passage. Then answer the question that follows.

When humans feel heat from a stove, they are sensing infrared radiation. Waves of infrared energy have a longer wavelength and a lower frequency than waves of visible light. However, some goggles, cameras, and telescopes can convert infrared radiation into viewable images. The images will be in the shape and form of anything that is warmer than its surroundings. The technology is useful for search-and-rescue missions, even in the dark or in thick fog or smoke.

8) **Directions**: *An introductory sentence for a summary of the passage is provided. Complete the summary by selecting the THREE answer choices that are the most important. Some sentences do not belong.* **This question is worth 2 points.**

Answer Choices

1. It consists of waves of energy that differ from visible light.
2. It travels further than visible light.
3. It can be presented visually using technology.
4. It is used to make goggles, cameras, and telescopes.
5. It radiates from warm objects and people.
6. It produces fog and smoke.

Infrared radiation is a form of energy with various qualities.

-
-
-

Practice #9

Read the passage. Then answer the question that follows.

Crocodile and alligator species tend to lay their eggs in nests, but they do not sit on the nests to keep their eggs warm. Instead, the nest materials emit heat as they *decompose*, or break down. The temperature of the nest determines whether the babies will be male or female. In some alligator species, for example, a nest of decomposing leaves will provide more heat and produce males while a nest of marsh grasses will be cooler and produce females.

9) **Directions**: *An introductory sentence for a summary of the passage is provided. Complete the summary by selecting the THREE answer choices that are the most important. Some sentences do not belong.* **This question is worth 2 points.**

Answer Choices

1. The nests break down the eggs.
2. The nests prevent the parents from sitting on the eggs.
3. The nests warm the eggs by decomposing.
4. The nests' temperature determines the offspring's gender.
5. The nests are made from nearby materials.
6. The nests' materials decay at varying temperatures.

Crocodilian nests play an important role in the species' reproduction.

-
-
-

Practice #10

Read the passage. Then answer the question that follows.

Some athletic competitors use drugs to succeed. Many of the abused drugs have legitimate medical purposes, but they are illegal when used to enhance athletic performance. For example, doctors may prescribe anabolic steroids in order to treat weakness caused by cancer. However, some athletes take anabolic steroids illegally in order to build extra muscle. Excessive use of steroids can lead to the development of physical characteristics of the opposite sex, as well as life-threatening heart and liver problems, aggressive behavior, and hair loss.

10) **Directions**: *An introductory sentence for a summary of the passage is provided. Complete the summary by selecting the THREE answer choices that are the most important. Some sentences do not belong.* **This question is worth 2 points.**

> **There are several objections to using drugs in sports.**

-
-
-

Answer Choices

1. They are unlawful when used in competitive sports.
2. They can create too much muscle mass.
3. They always cause unacceptable behavior.
4. They sometimes cause weakness and cancer.
5. They can cause male athletes to develop feminine traits.
6. They can lead to severe health problems.

**P O P
Q U I Z**

Select the vocabulary word or phrase that has the closest meaning.

5. search for
A. seek
B. start
C. ignore
D. follow

6. invention
A. condition
B. alteration
C. collection
D. creation

7. vehicle
A. effect
B. building
C. automobile
D. robot

8. escape from
A. endure
B. flee
C. honor
D. retain

9. opportunity
A. approval
B. design
C. truth
D. opening

10. empower
A. protest
B. authorize
C. impress
D. attract

11. acquire
A. accuse
B. lose
C. obtain
D. remind

12. adolescence
A. preadulthood
B. informality
C. adulthood
D. childhood

13. violation
A. importance
B. wrongdoing
C. anger
D. control

14. critic
A. praiser
B. teacher
C. writer
D. reviewer

15. destroy
A. build
B. destruct
C. create
D. restore

16. former
A. remaining
B. next
C. previous
D. formal

17. economically
A. financially
B. selfishly
C. considerably
D. socially

18. call for
A. answer
B. determine
C. question
D. demand

19. benefit
A. amazement
B. opposition
C. miracle
D. profit

20. trivial
A. insignificant
B. useful
C. valuable
D. effective

21. convert
A. combine
B. answer
C. change
D. explore

22. marsh
A. ocean
B. lake
C. swamp
D. river

23. prevent
A. stop
B. cause
C. encourage
D. limit

24. performance
A. existence
B. elimination
C. experience
D. efficiency

25. aggressive
A. satisfied
B. passive
C. successful
D. offensive

1. willing
A. unlikely
B. ready
C. forced
D. reluctant

2. irrelevant
A. apparent
B. necessary
C. important
D. unrelated

3. minor
A. specific
B. unimportant
C. common
D. massive

4. effort
A. efficiency
B. acceptance
C. endeavor
D. respect

1B 2D 3B 4C 5A 6D 7C 8B 9D 10B 11C 12A 13B 14D
15B 16C 17A 18D 19D 20A 21C 22C 23A 24D 25D

I. What Is an Organization Question?

Organization

The organization question asks you to identify the facts and details that best fit the two to three subtopics of the passage. A passage has one main topic. To support the main topic, a passage can have multiple subtopics. Subtopics are supported by their own facts and details.

A. ORGANIZATION QUESTION MODEL

The largest bodies of water on planet Earth are oceans. Oceans contain salt water and cover about 70 percent of the Earth's surface. Lakes are another type of body of water. They are much smaller than oceans and are usually fresh water, though there are some saltwater lakes. Like oceans, lakes have many kinds of plants and aquatic animals. Water birds such as ducks live on them.

10. **Directions**: *Select the sentences that most appropriately match the descriptions of each body of water. TWO of the answers will NOT be used.*

Answer Choices	Bodies of Water
1. These are made up of salt water.	**Oceans**
2. These are very small in size.	•
3. These cover more than half of Earth's surface.	•
4. These cover about 30 percent of Earth's surface.	**Lakes**
5. These provide homes for ducks.	•
6. These are most often made up of fresh water.	•

All other organization questions have either five or seven correct answer choices. Above is a simplified example.

B. TIPS
1. Note any facts in the paragraph that refer to a subtopic.
2. Correct answers should be easily found in the passage.
3. An incorrect answer will be inaccurate, unrelated, or illogical according to the passage.
4. Because these questions ask you to select multiple correct answers, they are worth either 3 or 4 points.
5. If you are asked to select five correct choices, you must answer three out of five correctly for 1 point, four out of five for 2 points, and five out of five for 3 points. If you are asked to select seven correct choices, you must answer four out of seven correctly for 1 point, five out of seven for 2 points, six out of seven for 3 points, and seven out of seven for 4 points.

II. Hacking Strategy

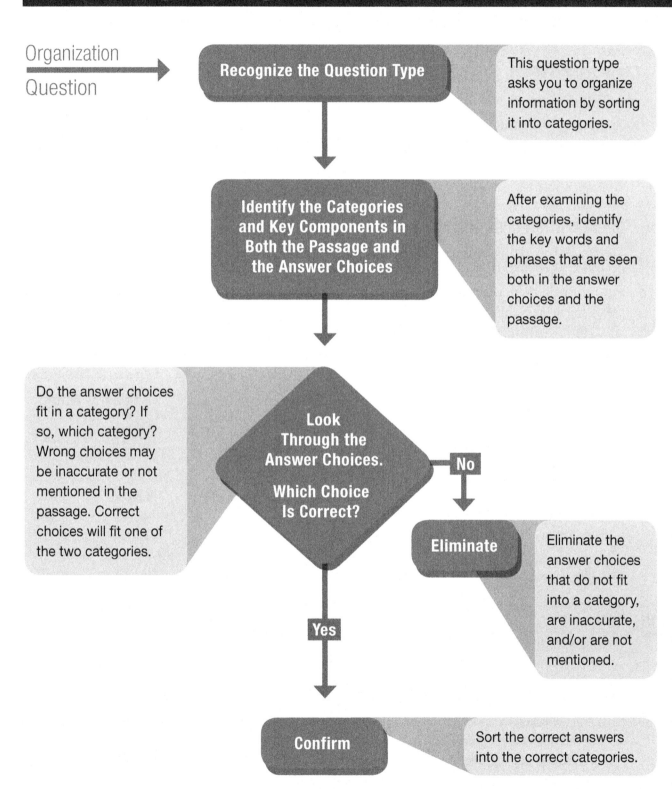

Organization
Question

Recognize the Question Type

This question type asks you to organize information by sorting it into categories.

Identify the Categories and Key Components in Both the Passage and the Answer Choices

After examining the categories, identify the key words and phrases that are seen both in the answer choices and the passage.

Do the answer choices fit in a category? If so, which category? Wrong choices may be inaccurate or not mentioned in the passage. Correct choices will fit one of the two categories.

Look Through the Answer Choices.

Which Choice Is Correct?

No

Eliminate

Eliminate the answer choices that do not fit into a category, are inaccurate, and/or are not mentioned.

Yes

Confirm

Sort the correct answers into the correct categories.

EXAMPLE

The largest bodies of water on planet Earth are oceans. Oceans contain salt water and cover about 70 percent of the Earth's surface. Lakes are another type of body of water. They are much smaller than oceans and are usually fresh water, though there are some saltwater lakes. Like oceans, lakes have many kinds of plants and aquatic animals. Water birds such as ducks live on them.

Recognize the Question Type

Answer Choices
1. These are made up of salt water.
2. These are very small in size.
3. These cover more than half of Earth's surface.
4. These cover about 30 percent of Earth's surface.
5. These provide homes for ducks
6. These are most often made up of fresh water.

Bodies of Water
Oceans
•
•

Lakes
•
•

Identify the Categories and Key Components in Both the Passage and the Answer Choices

The category types are "oceans" and "lakes."
The largest bodies of water on planet Earth are oceans. Oceans contain salt water and cover about 70 percent of the Earth's surface. Lakes are another type of body of water. They are much smaller than oceans and are usually fresh water, though there are some saltwater lakes. Like oceans, lakes have many kinds of plants and aquatic animals. Water birds such as ducks live on them.

Look Through the Answer Choices.

Which Choice Is Correct?

Compare key words in the choices to key words in the passage. Do they have the same information? Does the choice fit into one of the categories?

Oceans
• Select **Choice 1** because this information appears in the second sentence and describes oceans.
• Select **Choice 3** because this information appears in the second sentence and describes oceans.

Lakes
• Select **Choice 5** because this information appears in the last sentence and describes lakes.
• Select **Choice 6** because the fourth sentence states that lakes are usually fresh water.

Eliminate Incorrect Choices

• Eliminate **Choice 2** because the passage states that lakes are smaller than oceans, but it does not indicate that they *are very small*.
• Eliminate **Choice 4** because it is not mentioned anywhere in the passage.

Confirm

Select the correct answers and put them into the correct category.
Oceans — Choices 1 and **3** / **Lakes — Choices 5** and **6**

III. Quick Look

Organization Diagram

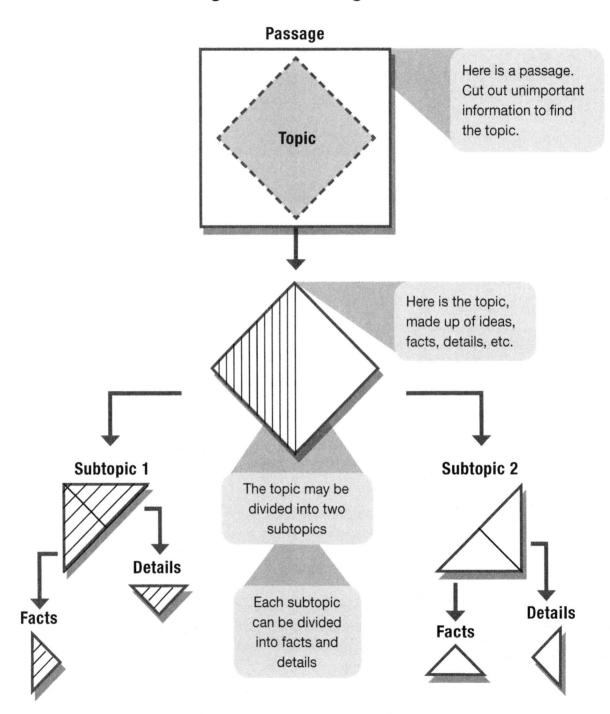

Passage

Topic

Here is a passage. Cut out unimportant information to find the topic.

Here is the topic, made up of ideas, facts, details, etc.

Subtopic 1

Details

Facts

The topic may be divided into two subtopics

Each subtopic can be divided into facts and details

Subtopic 2

Facts

Details

IV. Warm Up

Below are two categories and six answer choices. Four of the answers belong in the categories. Put the four appropriate answer choices into their corresponding categories.

1. **Desktop**   **Laptop**

    ____   ____

    ____   ____

    Choices

    1. It is hard to carry around.
    2. It only comes in black.
    3. It can be folded.
    4. It needs to be charged to use.
    5. It is usually very unreliable.
    6. It must be plugged in to operate.

3. **Nose**   **Eye**

    ____   ____

    ____   ____

    Choices

    1. It helps people see objects.
    2. It helps people smell.
    3. It is used to breathe.
    4. Nobody is born with it.
    5. It is the strongest part of the body.
    6. It produces tears.

2. **Angry**   **Happy**

    ____   ____

    ____   ____

    Choices

    1. This is an action that we take.
    2. This is a positive emotion.
    3. This is a negative emotion.
    4. This takes a long time to form.
    5. When we feel this, we smile.
    6. When we feel this, we are stressed.

4. **Car**   **Motorcycle**

    ____   ____

    ____   ____

    Choices

    1. It mostly rides on two wheels.
    2. Wearing a seatbelt is required to ride it.
    3. It does not have an engine.
    4. It is used in the water.
    5. Wearing a helmet is often required to ride it.
    6. It mostly rides on four wheels.

5. **Trees**   **Flowers**

     _____   _____

     _____   _____

Choices

1. These can grow very tall.
2. These often smell pleasing.
3. These usually grow in the ocean.
4. These are often given as gifts to women.
5. Children and cats like to climb these.
6. These do not like sunlight.

6. **Halloween**   **Christmas**

     _____   _____

     _____   _____

Choices

1. This holiday is in October.
2. People celebrate the new year on this holiday.
3. People wear costumes on this holiday.
4. This holiday is in December.
5. People give gifts on this holiday.
6. This holiday is in January.

7. **Spring**   **Winter**

     _____   _____

     _____   _____

Choices

1. It is when flowers generally start to bloom.
2. It is the best season of all.
3. It is the coldest season of the year.
4. It is associated with birth or new life.
5. It is associated with snow.
6. It is the hottest season of the year.

8. **Skateboard**   **Snowboard**

     _____   _____

     _____   _____

Choices

1. It rides on wheels.
2. It can only be used on snow.
3. It is world's most popular sport.
4. It can be used on the streets.
5. It is used in the water.
6. It requires a special set of boots.

9. **Desert**   **Forest**

     _____   _____

     _____   _____

Choices

1. It is a place with little rainfall.
2. It is where sharks live.
3. It is associated with trees.
4. It is known for its cacti.
5. It is usually green.
6. It is heavily populated by humans.

10. **Rural**   **Urban**

     _____   _____

     _____   _____

Choices

1. Streets are very busy here.
2. Not many people are often seen here.
3. Farms are easy to find here.
4. It is always sunny here.
5. Tall buildings are seen here.
6. No one lives here.

V. Quick Practice

Practice #1

Read the passage. Then answer the question that follows.

Angiosperms and gymnosperms are two groups of plants. Angiosperms are flowering plants that make up the majority of all plants. They produce seeds in a protective case. Gymnosperms include conifers, palms, and ginkgos. They produce unprotected seeds, which are contained in cones. These seeds are usually spread by the wind, allowing gymnosperms to reproduce.

1) **Directions**: *Select the sentences that most appropriately match the descriptions of each group of plant. TWO of the answers will NOT be used.* **This question is worth 3 points.**

Answer Choices	Groups of Plants
1. They have flowers and shielded seeds.	**Angiosperms**
2. They produce cones that have seeds inside.	•
3. They rely on wind to distribute their seeds.	•
4. They include most plants.	**Gymnosperms**
5. They include moss and ferns.	•
6. They have bare seeds.	•
7. They have seeds of different colors.	•

Practice #2

Read the passage. Then answer the question that follows.

Butterflies and moths are similar, but they are different, too. Both feed on flowers, have wings covered in dust, and have three-part bodies. However, while butterflies feed during the day, moths feed during the night. Additionally, while butterflies have thin bodies and rest with their wings upright, moths have thick bodies and rest with their wings outspread.

2) **Directions**: *Select the sentences that most appropriately match the descriptions of each species of insect. TWO of the answers will NOT be used.* **This question is worth 3 points.**

Answer Choices	Species of Insects
1. They have bulky bodies.	**Butterflies**
2. They are slim and eat during the daytime.	•
3. They crawl on the ground.	•
4. Their wings are standing when resting.	**Moths**
5. They have bodies with six parts.	•
6. Their wings are extended when resting.	•
7. They look for food in the darkness.	•

Practice #3

Read the passage. Then answer the question that follows.

Two popular forms of ancient drama from Western civilization are tragedy and comedy. *Tragedy* has an overall somber mood, with some moments of comedy. It has a hero who is great but flawed in some way. The hero's death raises questions about life's meaning. On the other hand, *comedy* tries to provoke laughter, but also can have serious moments. Unlike tragedy, it usually ends with a happy resolution.

3) **Directions**: *Select the sentences that most appropriately match the descriptions of each form of drama. TWO of the answers will NOT be used.* **This question is worth 3 points.**

Answer Choices	Forms of Drama
1. It is mostly funny but sometimes serious.	**Tragedy**
2. It is mostly serious but sometimes funny.	•
3. It has an imperfect hero who often dies.	•
4. It has a happy ending, not a sad one.	**Comedy**
5. It is mostly strange but sometimes normal.	•
6. It has the goal of making people laugh.	•
7. It has a perfect hero who questions life's meaning.	•

Practice #4

Read the passage. Then answer the question that follows.

Malware is computer software created with a harmful purpose. The most common type is the Trojan horse, which may present itself as a free gift or useful software. Once it gains access to a computer, it may steal, spy, or install other software. Trojan horses can spread through computer worms. Worms use networks to actively send copies of themselves to other computers. They do not need users to open anything in order to gain access. After gaining access, worms duplicate needless information and can clog a network.

4) **Directions**: *Select the sentences that most appropriately match the descriptions of each type of malware. TWO of the answers will NOT be used.* **This question is worth 3 points.**

Answer Choices	Types of Malware
1. It can reproduce itself.	**Trojan horse**
2. It pretends to be helpful.	•
3. It blocks a network with useless material.	•
4. It can damage or take personal information.	•
5. It is sometimes useful.	**Computer worm**
6. It can create new networks.	•
7. It can set up unwanted programs.	•

Practice #5

Read the passage. Then answer the question that follows.

The Stone Age lasted for at least 3.5 million years. People pounded stone against stone to make tools with sharp edges or points. They also used wood, bone, shells, plants, deer antlers, and animal skins in daily life. When people learned to make bronze metal, life changed forever. During the Bronze Age, people were capable of creating tough tools and materials in any shape imaginable, such as better axes, weapons, armor, buildings, and boat fixtures. Since people were able to make more useful objects, they were able to trade more easily and increase economic activity.

5) **Directions**: *Select the sentences that most appropriately match the descriptions of each age of prehistory. TWO of the answers will NOT be used.* ***This question is worth 3 points.***

Answer Choices	Ages of Prehistory
1. People were able to make a variety of metal tools.	**Stone Age**
2. People used bones and other animal parts in daily life.	•
3. People often played wood or bone instruments during ceremonies.	•
4. People were only interested in making new tools.	**Bronze Age**
5. People produced a wide variety of products, encouraging trade.	•
6. People relied on hitting rocks to craft things.	•
7. People constructed stronger buildings.	•

Practice #6

Read the passage. Then answer the question that follows.

Two common kinds of algae are brown and green algae. Brown algae, often called seaweed, grow in oceans where there are mild climates. Some seaweed can grow 60 meters up from the seafloor. Manufacturers use seaweed to help make ice cream, cosmetics, and other products. Green algae grow in fresh and salt water. Most live in lakes or streams. Sometimes, they cover an entire lake.

6) **Directions**: *Select the sentences that most appropriately match the descriptions of each kind of algae. TWO of the answers will NOT be used.* ***This question is worth 3 points.***

Answer Choices	Kinds of Algae
1. They grow only in fast moving water.	**Brown algae**
2. They grow in relatively warm salt water.	•
3. They can cover a whole lake.	•
4. They grow mostly in fresh water.	•
5. They are used to create food and makeup.	**Green algae**
6. They can be very tall.	•
7. They are found in all types of food.	•

Practice #7

Read the passage. Then answer the question that follows.

Two kinds of maps for travelers are road maps and street maps. Road maps show interstate highways, local highways, and scenic routes. They also show cities and local attractions connected by these roads. Street maps show a smaller area in great detail. People use street maps to locate an address. Both types of maps can be found on the Internet.

7) **Directions**: *Select the sentences that most appropriately match the descriptions of each kind of map. TWO of the answers will NOT be used.* ***This question is worth 3 points.***

Answer Choices	Kinds of Map
1. They are of little use to travelers.	**Road maps**
2. They show areas, such as neighborhoods, in detail.	●
3. They are only found on the Internet.	●
4. They show a larger area in less detail.	●
5. They show highways and freeways.	**Street maps**
6. They are used to find specific addresses.	●
7. They show how to get to a town or city.	●

Practice #8

Read the passage. Then answer the question that follows.

Two fields of philosophy are ethics and aesthetics. *Ethics* concerns human conduct. Studies in this branch of philosophy cover ideas of right and wrong and questions such as, "What is good and what is bad?" *Aesthetics* deals with art and beauty. Studies in this field look at people's thoughts and feelings when they see or hear artistic expression. Questions posed may include, "What makes something beautiful?"

8) **Directions**: *Select the sentences that most appropriately match the descriptions of each field of philosophy. TWO of the answers will NOT be used.* ***This question is worth 3 points.***

Answer Choices	Fields of Philosophy
1. It deals with the behavior of people.	**Ethics**
2. It makes distinctions between good and bad.	●
3. It includes the study of painting and music.	●
4. It tries to understand why an object is attractive.	●
5. It asks questions about the origin of life.	**Aesthetics**
6. It explores the moral aspect of what people should do.	●
7. It attempts to stop conflicts in philosophy.	●

Practice #9

Read the passage. Then answer the question that follows.

There are two main types of knives – fixed-blade and folding. A fixed-blade knife has a blade that is attached to a handle with glue. These are usually carried in a *sheath*, or a case that holds the blade. The Bowie knife, used for hunting, is an example of a fixed-blade knife. Folding knives have blades that close inside a handle. A pin holds the blades to the handle. A Swiss Army knife with 20 blades is an example of a folding knife.

9) **Directions**: *Select the sentences that most appropriately match the descriptions of each group of knife. TWO of the answers will NOT be used.* **This question is worth 3 points.**

Answer Choices	Groups of Knives
1. They have blades that do not move.	**Fixed-blade knives**
2. They are always used for hunting.	•
3. They may have more than one blade.	•
4. They have blades that fold into a handle.	**Folding knives**
5. They originated in Switzerland.	•
6. They are usually held in a knife cover.	•
7. They are secured with a tiny metal stick.	•

Practice #10

Read the passage. Then answer the question that follows.

Two styles of games are tile games and target games. In tile games, players have tiles marked by numbers or patterns. They try to use up all of their tiles, or they try to earn points by combining tiles. Dominos and mahjong are some examples of popular tile games. In target games, players try to get their object closest to a target. Some examples of target games include darts, marbles, and bowling.

10) **Directions**: *Select the sentences that most appropriately match the descriptions of each style of game. TWO of the answers will NOT be used.* **This question is worth 3 points.**

Answer Choices	Styles of Game
1. They may require players to aim carefully.	**Tile games**
2. They use objects with some kind of markings.	•
3. They may require players to link game pieces together.	•
4. They are usually played only by children.	•
5. They may involve winning by having nothing.	**Target games**
6. They may require a player to roll a ball at objects.	•
7. They started in China with carved wooden markers.	•

Select the vocabulary word or phrase that has the closest meaning.

5. unreliable
A. mindful
B. untrustworthy
C. responsible
D. accurate

6. associated with
A. reduced by
B. divided by
C. related to
D. detached from

7. shielded
A. organized
B. protected
C. ineffective
D. complex

1. cover
A. surround
B. exclude
C. obtain
D. allow

2. type
A. setting
B. grade
C. mark
D. kind

3. usually
A. rarely
B. clearly
C. generally
D. specifically

4. make up
A. remind
B. support
C. comprise
D. perform

8. extended
A. expired
B. closed
C. stretched
D. excused

9. somber
A. gentle
B. comical
C. exciting
D. depressing

10. provoke
A. resist
B. promote
C. incite
D. prohibit

11. imperfect
A. obedient
B. intelligent
C. flawed
D. brave

12. strange
A. familiar
B. unusual
C. normal
D. common

13. duplicate
A. inform
B. destroy
C. reproduce
D. improve

14. clog
A. secure
B. damage
C. control
D. block

15. pound
A. touch
B. carry
C. lift
D. strike

16. imaginable
A. wasteful
B. possible
C. economical
D. useful

17. mild
A. moderate
B. noisy
C. absent
D. mean

18. relatively
A. particularly
B. comparatively
C. unevenly
D. exceptionally

19. distinction
A. reaction
B. component
C. strength
D. characteristic

20. attempt
A. design
B. include
C. try
D. compete

21. conflict
A. disagreement
B. stability
C. confusion
D. approval

22. fixed
A. unsteady
B. secured
C. broken
D. loose

23. attached
A. connected
B. dropped
C. brought
D. moved

24. originate
A. be needed
B. be kept
C. be created
D. be required

25. marked
A. various
B. labeled
C. mixed
D. creative

15D 16B 17A 18B 19D 20C 21A 22B 23A 24C 25B
1A 2D 3C 4C 5B 6C 7B 8C 9D 10C 11C 12B 13C 14D

SUMMARY - ORGANIZATION QUESTIONS

Exercises

Exercise #1 Read the passage. Then answer the question that follows.

In many habitats, plants depend partly on mammals for survival. For example, certain mammals eat plant-eating insects, thus controlling their populations. Another way that mammals may help plants is by distributing their seeds. A bear might eat fruit, for example, and scatter the seeds in its droppings; or a squirrel might bury a seed to eat later, but forget about it, allowing it to grow into a plant. Finally, when mammals die, their bodies and bones fertilize the soil.

Directions: *An introductory sentence for a summary of the passage is provided. Complete the summary by selecting the THREE answer choices that are the most important. Some sentences do not belong.* **This question is worth 2 points.**

| Mammals are important for plants' survival. |

-
-
-

Answer Choices

1. Mammals consume plant-eaters.
2. Mammals provide water for plants.
3. Mammals improve the quality of soil.
4. Mammals shelter plants in several ways.
5. Mammals remember where seeds are stored.
6. Mammals move seeds around.

CHAPTERS 9-10 Exercises | 129

Exercise #2 Read the passage. Then answer the question that follows.

There are two main types of fairs – agricultural and trade. Agricultural fairs are the most common type in North America. They have contests for crops, livestock, and home-cooked food, as well as a carnival section with rides and games. Trade fairs focus on a specific product or industry. They provide exposure for new products and are held in large halls in major cities. Trade fairs limit attendance to people within the industry.

Directions: *Select the sentences that most appropriately match the descriptions of each type of fair. TWO of the answers will NOT be used.* **This question is worth 3 points.**

Answer Choices

1. They provide entertainment to attendees.
2. They emphasize a particular product or business.
3. They are usually not open to the public.
4. They are only held in very small towns.
5. They are the most popular type in Canada and the United States.
6. They focus on cooking and the farming industry.
7. They are not as popular as they used to be.

Types of Fairs

Agricultural fairs
-
-
-

Trade fairs
-
-

Exercise #3 Read the passage. Then answer the questions that follow.

Book collecting is a popular hobby. People collect books for various reasons. Many people collect books simply because they love them. For example, the American writer Ernest Hemingway once said, "There is no friend as loyal as a book." Other collectors are interested in a specific type of book. For instance, Australian Brett Chilman has filled at least two houses with comic books, the largest private collection in the world. Sometimes, people collect books because they hope that their books will increase in value.

Directions: *An introductory sentence for a summary of the passage is provided. Complete the summary by selecting the THREE answer choices that are the most important. Some sentences do not belong.* **This question is worth 2 points.**

Answer Choices

1. They have no social life.
2. They want to prove that they are smart.
3. They love and enjoy books.
4. They have great interest in a particular writer or field.
5. They believe that books are good investments.
6. They do not want to be disturbed when they are reading.

People collect books for different reasons.

-
-
-

Exercise #4 Read the passage. Then answer the question that follows.

Two modern styles of furniture are De Stijl and Art Deco. De Stijl began in the Netherlands in 1917. This style emphasized rectangular shapes and is characterized by the use of three primary colors – blue, red, and yellow. The geometric shapes of De Stijl furniture influenced most other fashions of the 1900s. Art Deco was the most popular international style of the 1920s and 1930s. Objects created in this style utilized shapes related to people's interest in technology. Steel was blended with ivory, bronze, and wood. Machine design and ancient Egyptian and African designs also were combined.

Directions: *Select the sentences that most appropriately match the descriptions of each style of furniture. TWO of the answers will NOT be used.* **This question is worth 3 points.**

Answer Choices

1. It required complex math to build.
2. It started in Egypt and Africa.
3. It mixed styles from different cultures.
4. It was made out of many materials.
5. It was limited in shape and color.
6. It sometimes looked like machinery.
7. It affected many other 20th-century styles.

Styles of Furniture

De Stijl
-
-

Art Deco
-
-
-

Exercise #5 Read the passage. Then answer the question that follows

The North Atlantic Treaty Organization (NATO), which consists of 28 nations, was established in 1949 during the start of the Cold War. Originally, the main purpose of NATO was to discourage an attack by the Soviet Union on NATO members. Since the Cold War ended, the main focus of NATO has shifted toward peacekeeping. Today, the organization's central aims include resolving international conflicts, developing international security policies, and fighting terrorism.

Directions: *An introductory sentence for a summary of the passage is provided. Complete the summary by selecting the THREE answer choices that are the most important. Some sentences do not belong.* **This question is worth 2 points.**

Answer Choices

1. It was first created to promote capitalism.
2. It was originally formed to prevent a Soviet attack.
3. It now focuses on keeping the peace.
4. It tries to create plans for global defense.
5. It operates a court dealing with terrorism.
6. It was established to end world starvation.

NATO has had various purposes over the past 50 years.

-
-
-

Exercise #6 Read the passage. Then answer the question that follows.

There are two main categories of bees – social and solitary. Social bees live in colonies with strict hierarchies among members. There may be as few as 10 or as many as 80,000 members in a colony. Honeybees have the most complex social organization, while stingless bees and bumblebees are also highly social. On the other hand, solitary bees mostly live alone, gathering with other bees sometimes to build nests together. Among solitary bees, there are no special "workers." Each female is a queen that does her own work. The best known solitary bees include carpenter bees, leaf-cutting bees, and miner bees.

Directions: *Select the sentences that most appropriately match the descriptions of each category of bee. TWO of the answers will NOT be used.* **This question is worth 3 points.**

Answer Choices

1. They are organized into hierarchies.
2. They do not like to live with other bees.
3. They have no male bees in the species.
4. They do not have any worker bees.
5. They may have thousands in one colony.
6. They always produce honey.
7. They include stingless bees and bumblebees.

Categories of Bees

Social bees
-
-
-

Solitary bees
-
-

Exercise #7 Read the passage. Then answer the question that follows.

Environmental conditions in the deep ocean are extreme. For example, the water is so cold that temperatures are just above freezing. The pressure in the deep sea can be up to 1,000 times as great as the pressure on the surface. In fact, in the ocean depths, the pressure is strong enough to crush the bodies of most life forms. Furthermore, no sunlight penetrates to the deep sea, so its creatures live in total darkness.

Directions: *An introductory sentence for a summary of the passage is provided. Complete the summary by selecting the THREE answer choices that are the most important. Some sentences do not belong.* **This question is worth 2 points.**

Answer Choices

1. It is always at very low temperatures.
2. It is 1,000 times colder than the surface.
3. It possesses great crushing pressures.
4. It has various dangerous life forms.
5. It is extremely dark all the time.
6. It provides an environment that is not difficult to explore.

The deep sea has unique environmental conditions.
-
-
-

Exercise #8 Read the passage. Then answer the question that follows.

The ancient people of the Andes Mountains in South America domesticated two similar animals that produce soft, warm wool used in clothing: the alpaca and the llama. Alpacas are about half the size of llamas, weighing no more than about 84 kilograms. Alpacas have been selectively bred to grow long coats of silky, fine hair. Llamas, besides producing wool, were bred to carry heavy weight for long distances. Llamas are very intelligent as well as tough, and they can be trained as effective guard animals for herds of sheep. Both alpacas and llamas make a "humming" sound, perhaps to provide ongoing reassurance to other members of their herd.

Directions: *Select the sentences that most appropriately match the descriptions of each type of domestic animal. TWO of the answers will NOT be used.* ***This question is worth 3 points.***

Answer Choices

1. They are strong, hardy animals.
2. They are raised mainly for their coat of hair.
3. They can be trusted to protect some other animals.
4. They weigh under 100 kilograms.
5. They are considered to be especially smart.
6. They communicate quietly to avoid predators.
7. They produce wool that is softer than sheep wool.

Types of Domestic Animal

Alpaca
-
-

Llama
-
-
-

Exercise #9 Read the passage. Then answer the questions that follow.

Scholars trace the beginnings of labor unions to different origins. Some say that the idea for labor unions came from European medieval craft guilds. The guilds were made up of skilled workers who grouped together to keep quality and prices high. Other scholars think that the rise of factories caused workers to form unions because factory owners had too much power over individual employees. Still other scholars feel that labor unions came about when market competition caused companies to cut worker pay.

Directions: *An introductory sentence for a summary of the passage is provided. Complete the summary by selecting the THREE answer choices that are the most important. Some sentences do not belong.* ***This question is worth 2 points.***

Answer Choices

1. They may have originated from groups of people who handcrafted quality goods.
2. They may have begun to join factories together.
3. They may have started because of reduced income.
4. They may have originated from employees who wanted to work less.
5. They may have been a way to reduce prices.
6. They may have begun to counter unethical employers.

Scholars believe that there are several possible origins of labor unions.
-
-
-

Exercise #10 Read the passage. Then answer the question that follows.

Of the many types of locks in use, two include warded locks and card access locks. Warded locks have obstacles called *wards* that block wrong keys from opening the lock. The correct key has marks that match the wards in the lock. However, warded locks are easy to open with wire. Therefore, people should use them only for doors such as closet doors. Card access locks are the most common electronic locks. They are found in many hotels and offices. The "key" is a flat plastic card that usually looks like a credit card that has physical patterns or computerized information that the door mechanism reads and must accept to open the lock. The data in keycards may be stored in a magnetic stripe, an electronic microchip, or a bar code.

Directions: *Select the sentences that most appropriately match the descriptions of each sort of lock. TWO of the answers will NOT be used.* **This question is worth 3 points.**

Answer Choices

1. They are opened using wards.
2. They have barriers inside the locks.
3. They need plastic cards with marks.
4. They require digital information to operate.
5. They are not very secure.
6. They can only be opened by professionals.
7. They require keys with patterns.

Sorts of Locks

Warded locks
-
-
-

Card access locks
-
-

Actual Practice

Our **Actual Practice** section provides 12 academic passages with a variety of associated questions to give students an opportunity to apply skills acquired throughout the first ten chapters before proceeding onto a simulation of a full-length TOEFL iBT Reading Test.

The Pawnee Indians

Time
00:20:00

The Pawnee people are a Native American tribe **centered** in Oklahoma that consists of about 3,240 members. Before European contact, the tribe of around 12,000 people lived on rich farmland in the Great Plains.

A Pawnee houses, often built on riverbanks, were made of soil packed over logs and branches. **B** Several families lived in each one. **C** During summer and winter months, the Pawnee left their farms and villages to hunt buffalo on the plains. While on the hunt, families lived in *teepees*, or large tents made of buffalo skins and wooden posts. **D**

Religion was important in Pawnee lives. The Pawnee believed that corn was a **sacred** gift, so they developed rituals for planting and harvesting **it**. Before 1838, the tribe even practiced **human sacrifice** once a year to ensure good crops. Other ceremonies prepared for successful buffalo hunts. These ceremonies included days of nonstop dancing.

In 1857, the United States government **forced** the tribe onto a reservation in Nebraska. However, in 1875 pressure from white settlers and attacks by other tribes forced the Pawnee to move again to what is now Oklahoma.

1) Which of the following best paraphrases Paragraph 1?
   (A) The Pawnee tribe once was bigger and lived on excellent farmland.
   (B) Oklahoma is the center of rich farmland in the Great Plains.
   (C) There used to be a Pawnee tribe, but not anymore.
   (D) The Pawnee tribe lives in a region with a population of 3,240.

2) The word "**centered**" in Paragraph 1 is closest in meaning to
   (A) extended
   (B) remembered
   (C) united
   (D) concentrated

3) Look at the squares [■] that indicate where the sentence below could be added to Paragraph 2.

   The oval-shaped homes were dug a few meters into the ground and had long entry tunnels.

   Where would the sentence best fit?
   Circle the square [■] to add the sentence.

4) What can be inferred about the Pawnee from Paragraph 2?
   (A) They farmed during spring and fall.
   (B) They preferred to live in teepees.
   (C) They raised buffalo herds.
   (D) They enjoyed hunting.

5) According to Paragraph 2, what is NOT something in which the Pawnee lived?
   (A) Earth-covered houses
   (B) Large adobes
   (C) Farm villages
   (D) Special animal-skin tents

6) The word "**sacred**" in Paragraph 3 means
   (A) ancient
   (B) final
   (C) holy
   (D) basic

7) The word "**it**" in Paragraph 3 refers to
   (A) religion
   (B) the Pawnee
   (C) corn
   (D) gift

8) Based on Paragraph 3, what was MOST important to the Pawnee?
   (A) Corn
   (B) Buffalo hunting
   (C) War
   (D) Human sacrifice

9) Why does the author mention "**human sacrifice**" in Paragraph 3?
   (A) To criticize the Pawnee lifestyle
   (B) To show the Pawnee's devotion to religion
   (C) To explain that the Pawnee were harsh
   (D) To contrast the Pawnee with another tribe

10) According to Paragraph 3, preparations for buffalo hunting included
   (A) sharpening arrows
   (B) human sacrifice
   (C) planting and harvesting corn
   (D) days of dancing without stopping

11) Why does the author PROBABLY mention "**forced**" in Paragraph 4?
   (A) To emphasize how strongly the Pawnee tribe resisted U.S. rule
   (B) To show that the Pawnee did not move to Nebraska willingly
   (C) To criticize U.S. intervention in Pawnee ceremonies
   (D) To trace the origins of Native Americans in Nebraska

12) **Directions**: An introductory sentence for a summary of the passage is provided. Complete the summary by selecting the THREE answer choices that are the most important. Some sentences do not belong. **This question is worth 2 points.**

The Pawnee people have a rich history.

-
-
-

Answer Choices
1. They were settled, but took hunting trips.
2. They had ceremonies for good farming and hunting.
3. They lived in diverse, mountainous regions.
4. They thought that the buffalos were a sacred animal.
5. They had good relations with other tribes and colonists.
6. They were forced to move away from their homeland.

Actual Practice

Sunshine Laws

Sunshine laws force federal and local governments to **conduct** their meetings as openly as possible. These laws allow the public to view records and documents and to attend most government meetings. By "**letting the sunshine in**," the laws permitted people to see exactly what elected officials are saying and doing.

Many United States leaders had long felt that government meetings should be closed. However, states gradually began passing laws that required school boards, county boards, and city councils to hold open meetings. **A** **Florida** residents gained "right of access" to meetings in 1905. **Alabama** passed the first full "sunshine law" in 1915. **B** All states eventually followed. **C** Finally, the federal government passed a sunshine law opening federal meetings in 1976, largely because of the government's involvement in the Watergate scandal. **D**

Sunshine laws **vary** greatly. Some allow the public to attend all meetings. Others **authorize** early meetings to be closed as long as the final vote is taken in public. **Many** also allow closed meetings on certain topics, such as personnel matters.

1) The word "**conduct**" in Paragraph 1 means
   (A) put down
   (B) turn on
   (C) carry out
   (D) make up

2) Why does the author put quotes around "**letting the sunshine in**" in Paragraph 1?
   (A) To indicate that the expression is idiomatic
   (B) To indicate that the expression is a metaphor
   (C) To prove that meetings occur in the daytime
   (D) To give an example of a meeting topic

3) Look at the squares [■] that indicate where the sentence below could be added to Paragraph 2.

   The movement started in the South.

   Where would the sentence best fit?
   Circle the square [■] to add the sentence.

4) Why does the author mention "**Florida**" and "**Alabama**" in Paragraph 2?
   (A) To explain why the laws are associated with sunshine
   (B) To point out the least secretive states in the U.S.
   (C) To describe something about where the laws originated
   (D) To help the reader make a mental image of the laws

5) What can be inferred from Paragraph 2?
   (A) Historically, U.S. leaders promoted open meetings.
   (B) Citizens were interested in government activities.
   (C) The U.S. government prevented open federal meetings.
   (D) Local governments had a serious problem with corruption.

6) According to Paragraph 2, what is NOT a reason sunshine laws were created?
(A) Stopping government secrecy
(B) Allowing people to attend government meetings
(C) Preventing scandals like Watergate
(D) Making government officials more efficient

7) What is the primary purpose of Paragraph 2?
(A) To explain the events that led to the spread of sunshine laws
(B) To compare sunshine laws on the state and federal level
(C) To emphasize the impact that sunshine laws have had on government affairs
(D) To prove that meetings have improved since the introduction of sunshine laws

8) The word "**vary**" in Paragraph 3 means
(A) change
(B) differ
(C) improve
(D) move

9) The word "**authorize**" in Paragraph 3 means
(A) oppose
(B) permit
(C) construct
(D) review

10) The word "**Many**" in Paragraph 3 refers to
(A) sunshine laws
(B) all meetings
(C) elected officials
(D) early meetings

11) According to Paragraph 3, for what topic would sunshine laws allow a closed meeting?
(A) Choosing a city mascot
(B) Discussing a freeway expansion
(C) Taking a final vote on an issue
(D) Deciding on employee salaries

12) **Directions**: An introductory sentence for a summary of the passage is provided. Complete the summary by selecting the THREE answer choices that are the most important. Some sentences do not belong. **This question is worth 2 points.**

Sunshine laws require openness but do so using a variety of methods.

●

●

●

Answer Choices
1. Some allow a governing board to have unannounced "study meetings."
2. Some allow councils to discuss issues about their own employees behind closed doors.
3. Some allow governments to have no meetings at all.
4. Some allow politicians to discuss a topic among themselves, yet vote publicly.
5. Some allow the news media to interrupt the meetings.
6. Some allow people to attend any and all meetings of the board.

La Dolce Vita

Time
00:20:00

La Dolce Vita, or "**The Sweet Life**," a 1960 film by Italian director Federico Fellini, became an international success when it was **released**. Since then, the movie has received much criticism and admiration, and has influenced many films as well as popular culture. One character, a photographer named Paparazzo, even inspired the creation of the word *paparazzi*, a term that describes reporters such as Marcello and Paparazzo who follow famous people.

The film shows the moral decay of **members of high society** in 1950s Rome. **A** The main character, Marcello, works as a *gossip columnist*, or a journalist who writes about famous people's lives. **B** He enjoys life at parties, nightclubs, cafes, and castles, but he forms no meaningful relationships. Marcello wants to write important, valuable news, but he also wants to be a part of the empty "sweet life" of the people that he writes about. **C** **The film suggests that most people prefer what is entertaining over what is important. D**

The film drew attention because it was ***nonlinear***, meaning that the scenes appeared to be out of order. However, because the film's characters seem to **mock** religion, some countries banned **it**. For instance, its opening scene has become very famous: two helicopters fly over Rome, one carrying a huge plaster statue of Jesus, the other carrying paparazzi.

1) Why does the author put quotes around "**The Sweet Life**" in Paragraph 1?
(A) To give an example of a film
(B) To praise the meaning of the film
(C) To show that the author spoke the words
(D) To indicate that it is a translation

2) The word "**released**" in Paragraph 1 is closest in meaning to
(A) circulated
(B) overseen
(C) returned
(D) contracted

3) The expression "**members of high society**" in Paragraph 2 is closest in meaning to
(A) the lower class
(B) the middle class
(C) the upper class
(D) the working class

4) Look at the squares [■] that indicate where the sentence below could be added to Paragraph 2.

He meets many glamorous people.

Where would the sentence best fit?
Circle the square [■] to add the sentence.

5) Which of the following best paraphrases the highlighted sentence in Paragraph 2?
(A) The film's theme is that people choose fun over meaningful work.
(B) Fellini says that people tend to put others first.
(C) People are not as important to Fellini as what is real.
(D) Most people prefer reality to scandal in this film.

6) What can be inferred about the filmmaker from Paragraph 2?
    (A) He thinks that most people are sweet.
    (B) He hates journalists and rich people.
    (C) He thinks that fame is actually meaningful.
    (D) He wants to portray a conflicted character.

7) According to Paragraph 2, what is Marcello's job in the movie?
    (A) Filmmaker
    (B) Writer
    (C) Entertainer
    (D) Photographer

8) The author mentions in Paragraph 3 that the film is "*nonlinear*" in order to
    (A) show how the film was too confusing
    (B) illustrate how the film was unusual
    (C) explain why the film was controversial
    (D) criticize the film as poorly made

9) The word "**mock**" in Paragraph 3 means
    (A) make sense of
    (B) make more of
    (C) make use of
    (D) make fun of

10) The word "**it**" in Paragraph 3 refers to
    (A) Italian director
    (B) international success
    (C) the movie
    (D) religion

11) According to the passage, what is NOT true about *La Dolce Vita*?
    (A) It was filmed in nightclubs, cafes, and castles.
    (B) It led to the use of a new word.
    (C) It had many characters that were beautiful, famous, and rich.
    (D) It has been largely ignored by filmmakers and critics.

12) **Directions**: An introductory sentence for a summary of the passage is provided. Complete the summary by selecting the THREE answer choices that are the most important. Some sentences do not belong. **This question is worth 2 points.**

    Fellini criticizes Italian society in *La Dolce Vita*.

    •

    •

    •

    Answer Choices
    1. He shows the media reporting gossip as "news."
    2. He shows the difficulties of being a reporter.
    3. He shows the beauty of the Mediterranean countryside.
    4. He shows characters' disrespect for religious symbols.
    5. He shows fun times but no real personal bonds.
    6. He shows how romantic but boring the city was.

The Laws of the Twelve Tables

The Laws of the Twelve Tables were the first written laws of the Romans. These laws were **inscribed** on 12 bronze tablets. Originally, the tablets were attached to the speaker's stand in the Roman Forum where legal trials were held. These tablets reminded all Roman citizens that their rights were protected under these laws.

The codes of law were based on earlier civil, criminal, and religious customs. They addressed many issues, including legal procedures and the rights of Roman citizens. The laws governed issues such as building codes, marriage, property ownership, and crime.

A The laws were **drawn up** around 450 BCE to **settle** class conflicts. **B** Large parts of the laws were recorded in the works of Roman writers. Like all **Roman boys**, **they** had been required to memorize the laws in their youth. Thus, writers were able to include the text in their works. **C** The laws began to be revised in the 200s BCE. **D**

1) What can be inferred about Roman society from Paragraph 1?
   (A) Romans were fond of arguing and debating.
   (B) Romans valued fair and structured legal proceedings.
   (C) Romans had a total of 12 laws to follow.
   (D) Romans had many large court rooms.

2) The word "**inscribed**" in Paragraph 1 is closest in meaning to
   (A) guarded
   (B) viewed
   (C) written
   (D) spoken

3) According to Paragraph 1, what did the Laws of the Twelve Tables protect?
   (A) Roman citizens' traditions
   (B) Roman citizens' trials
   (C) Roman citizens' rights
   (D) Roman citizens' conflicts

4) According to Paragraph 2, what is NOT discussed by the Twelve Tables?
   (A) Codes for building
   (B) Rules for marriage
   (C) Punishments for crime
   (D) Prices for property

5) The term "**drawn up**" in Paragraph 3 is closest in meaning to
   (A) prepared
   (B) debated
   (C) shown
   (D) known

6) The word "**settle**" in Paragraph 3 is closest in meaning to
   (A) move
   (B) stop
   (C) find
   (D) learn

7) Why are "**Roman boys**" mentioned in Paragraph 3?
  (A) To describe why Rome perished
  (B) To explain who used the laws
  (C) To show how the laws were preserved
  (D) To tell why Romans became writers

8) The word "**they**" in Paragraph 3 refers to
  (A) large parts of the laws
  (B) the works
  (C) Roman writers
  (D) Roman boys

9) Look at the squares [■] that indicate where the sentence below could be added to Paragraph 3.

  They were created by a group of 10 men called *decemvir*.

  Where would the sentence best fit?
  Circle the square [■] to add the sentence.

10) According to Paragraph 3, what PROBABLY happened in the 200s BCE?
  (A) The Twelve Tables were lost.
  (B) Roman society changed.
  (C) Roman boys became writers.
  (D) Laws became unimportant.

11) According to Paragraph 3, the laws were created because
  (A) people wanted to ease social tensions
  (B) people kept forgetting them
  (C) bronze tablets had just been invented
  (D) Roman writers wanted their work preserved

12) **Directions**: An introductory sentence for a summary of the passage is provided. Complete the summary by selecting the THREE answer choices that are the most important. Some sentences do not belong. **This question is worth 2 points.**

  The Laws of the Twelve Tables were important to Romans.

  ●

  ●

  ●

  Answer Choices
  1. They reminded Roman citizens of their legal rights.
  2. They put earlier traditions into writing for everyone.
  3. They reminded Romans to which class they belonged.
  4. They were written on clay tablets.
  5. They gave too much power to the wealthy.
  6. They helped bring peace to Rome.

The Folger Shakespeare Library

The Folger Shakespeare Library, which is located in Washington D.C., has hundreds of thousands of books. It **houses** one of the most important collections of books about British society and culture from about 1485 to 1715. As the name implies, it also owns the world's most important collection of texts by and about William Shakespeare.

A The library's rare books are protected in fire-resistant, air-conditioned **vaults**. **B** It displays many rare books, manuscripts, paintings, and objects of interest from the Elizabethan period of the 16th century. **C** The library also features a theater that **is patterned after** a typical playhouse of the Shakespearian era. **D**

Henry Folger, a successful president of the Standard Oil Company of New York, **founded** the library in 1930. Folger left his fortune for the trustees of Amherst College. He wanted **it** to be used for the development of a great research institution. Nowadays, scholars from all parts of the world come to the Folger Shakespeare Library. They use it for research in history and literature. The library building, a beautiful marble structure, was completed in 1932.

1) The word "**houses**" in Paragraph 1 is closest in meaning to
    (A) is
    (B) has
    (C) does
    (D) makes

2) What can be inferred about British history from Paragraph 1?
    (A) Only the British produced important writing for more than 200 years.
    (B) Shakespeare was the only 16th-century playwright in Britain.
    (C) The library is a popular tourist destination in Great Britain.
    (D) Influential literature was written between the 15th and 18th centuries.

3) Look at the squares [■] that indicate where the sentence below could be added to Paragraph 2.

    Another impressive attraction is the library's exhibition gallery.

    Where would the sentence best fit?
    Circle the square [■] to add the sentence.

4) The word "**vaults**" in Paragraph 2 is closest in meaning to
    (A) covers
    (B) rooms
    (C) galleries
    (D) jobs

5) What can be inferred about the library's rare books in Paragraph 2?
    (A) They are culturally valuable.
    (B) They have pictures and paintings.
    (C) They all belonged to Queen Elizabeth.
    (D) They deal with theater and art history.

6) According to Paragraph 2, what is probably NOT at the Folger Shakespeare Library?
    (A) A photograph of modern London
    (B) A play by William Shakespeare
    (C) A biography of William Shakespeare
    (D) A painting of Queen Elizabeth

7) The term "**is patterned after**" in Paragraph 2 is closest in meaning to
    (A) listens to
    (B) deals with
    (C) looks like
    (D) puts on

8) The word "**founded**" in Paragraph 3 means
    (A) healed
    (B) destroyed
    (C) bought
    (D) established

9) Why is Henry Folger's job mentioned in Paragraph 3?
    (A) To connect the library to New York
    (B) To prove the library's importance
    (C) To explain who worked at the library
    (D) To show how the library was funded

10) The word "**it**" in Paragraph 3 refers to
    (A) Standard Oil Company
    (B) the library
    (C) his fortune
    (D) Amherst College

11) According to Paragraph 3, why did Folger want to build the library?
    (A) He had no use for his fortune.
    (B) He wanted to help Amherst College to expand.
    (C) He wanted to create a facility for research.
    (D) He wished to be a successful scholar.

12) **Directions**: An introductory sentence for a summary of the passage is provided. Complete the summary by selecting the THREE answer choices that are the most important. Some sentences do not belong. **This question is worth 2 points.**

The Folger Shakespeare Library is a cultural treasure.

    ●

    ●

    ●

Answer Choices

1. It includes the most important collection of libraries.
2. It allows visitors to participate in Shakespearian plays.
3. It attracts scholars with its thousands of books and objects.
4. It preserves fragile, old books and manuscripts.
5. It provides a valuable collection of Shakespeare's works.
6. It contains many of the oldest works of English literature.

The Black Forest

Time
00:20:00

The Black Forest is a mountain area in southwestern Germany. **A** It is covered with dense forests of pine trees. **B** Hence, the German name for the area, *Schwarzwald*, means "black forest." **C** The region's highest mountain is Feldberg. The Rhine River flows for 160 kilometers past the edge of the forest. **D**

Besides possessing natural beauty, the forest has long supported many industries. The area is **noted** for its mineral springs. Many health resorts, including the famous city of Baden-Baden, are located near these springs. The forests **yield** a great deal of lumber. New trees are planted to replace those that are harvested. Granite **quarries** are located in the southern part of the Black Forest. Mines located in the northeastern corner of the Black Forest provided a wealth of silver and copper for medieval Germans, allowing towns in the areas to flourish. However, by the 16th century, all these mines had been shut down.

In addition to the Black Forest's natural resources, the area has developed a unique culture. The people of the Black Forest are famous for certain specialty items. For example, they **manufacture** outstanding cuckoo clocks, toys, and musical instruments. **They** are also known for their cherry-covered chocolate cake, and they have kept many other traditions alive, such as seasonal festivals. Moreover, **the castles and villages among the deep dark forest have long been an inspiration for storytellers**. For instance, when the Brothers Grimm wrote *Snow White* and *Hansel and Gretel*, they may have been thinking of the Black Forest.

1) Look at the squares [■] that indicate where the sentence below could be added to Paragraph 1.

   The Danube River also cuts through the area.

   Where would the sentence best fit?
   Circle the square [■] to add the sentence.

2) How is the Black Forest explained in Paragraph 1?
   (A) By giving its history
   (B) By telling a personal story
   (C) By describing it physically
   (D) By showing who lives there

3) The word "**noted**" in Paragraph 2 means
   (A) studied
   (B) sacred
   (C) named
   (D) famed

4) What can be inferred about the Black Forest from Paragraph 2?
   (A) It provides important resources.
   (B) Its residents are healthy.
   (C) It contains many large cities.
   (D) It is known for its unique trees.

5) The word "**yield**" in Paragraph 2 means
   (A) know
   (B) produce
   (C) keep
   (D) wear

6) The word "**quarries**" in Paragraph 2 is closest in meaning to
(A) mines
(B) jobs
(C) people
(D) waterways

7) According to Paragraph 3, for which product is the Black Forest NOT known?
(A) Unique clocks
(B) Toys
(C) Shoes
(D) Special desserts

8) The word "**manufacture**" in Paragraph 3 means
(A) design
(B) steal
(C) copy
(D) make

9) The word "**They**" in Paragraph 3 refers to
(A) the people
(B) toys
(C) cuckoo clocks
(D) musical instruments

10) Which of the following best paraphrases the highlighted phrase in Paragraph 3?
(A) The forest is the imagined setting for many old tales.
(B) People in the forest have dark, centuries-old castles near villages.
(C) The forest is home to many traditional village storytellers.
(D) The story of survival in the forest has long been inspiring.

11) According to Paragraph 3, why was the Black Forest PROBABLY used for German legends?
(A) It is old.
(B) It is large.
(C) It is familiar.
(D) It is mysterious.

12) **Directions**: Select the sentences that most appropriately match the descriptions of each resource or product of the Black Forest. TWO of the answer choices will NOT be used. **This question is worth 3 points.**

Resources of the Black Forest

●

●

●

Products of the Black Forest

●

●

Answer Choices
1. These mineral springs attract tourists.
2. These wooden toys are a specialty.
3. These items lost their uniqueness.
4. These musical instruments are made by crafters.
5. These forests provide wood.
6. These locations have special stone.
7. These castles and villages give tourists a comfortable place to stay.

Phrenology

Time
00:20:00

In 1796, Franz Joseph Gall proposed the theory of phrenology. He said that the human brain is not one organ but 27 **aggregated** organs. He also suggested that each organ had an **intrinsic** role in human behavior. With this information, Gall created a diagram of the organs' locations in the skull. For instance, he said that the organ responsible for a person's level of greed was in front of the ear.

Gall believed that these organs grew to different sizes in different people. **A** A phrenologist would feel a person's head and take notes of the bumps and **contours**. **B** A larger bump meant that a larger organ was underneath. **C** A person could use the trait or ability negatively or positively. **D** For example, someone can be greedy for things and be a thief, or greedy for knowledge and be a scholar.

Phrenology was soon discredited and is no longer considered a science. However, phrenology and similar brain theories had great influence on society well into the 1800s. Many people used the theories to justify **racism, sexism, colonialism, and slavery**. However, many common people liked phrenology because **it** suggested that individuals could control how they used their specific attributes.

1) The word "**aggregated**" in Paragraph 1 is closest in meaning to
    (A) simulated
    (B) divided
    (C) aggravated
    (D) combined

2) What can be inferred about phrenology from Paragraph 1?
    (A) It quickly gained popularity among scientists.
    (B) It made assumptions about the brain.
    (C) It identified important brain cells.
    (D) It was based on ancient medicine.

3) The word "**intrinsic**" in Paragraph 1 is closest in meaning to
    (A) inborn
    (B) instant
    (C) incorrect
    (D) independent

4) According to Paragraph 1, what did Gall map inside the skull?
    (A) Feelings
    (B) Brains
    (C) Roles
    (D) Organs

5) Look at the squares [■] that indicate where the sentence below could be added to Paragraph 2.

    Therefore, the person would display a stronger tendency toward that trait.

    Where would the sentence best fit?
    Circle the square [■] to add the sentence.

6) The word "**contours**" in Paragraph 2 is closest in meaning to
(A) cones
(B) outlines
(C) bones
(D) textures

7) Which of the following best paraphrases the highlighted sentence in Paragraph 3?
(A) People give phrenology credit for being a type of science.
(B) Scientists did not accept phrenology permanently.
(C) Phrenology is now considered the earliest psychology.
(D) People think that phrenology was a way to cheat people.

8) In Paragraph 3, the author mentions "**racism, sexism, colonialism, and slavery**" in order to
(A) illustrate the real purpose of phrenology
(B) criticize the judgment of scientists
(C) explain the complications of phrenology
(D) describe negative consequences of Gall's theory

9) The word "**it**" in Paragraph 3 refers to
(A) science
(B) influence
(C) society
(D) phrenology

10) According to the passage, what is NOT true about phrenology?
(A) It involved the idea that the brain was not one thing.
(B) It involved describing a person's personality.
(C) It involved drawing maps on people's scalps.
(D) It involved looking at the shape of a person's head.

11) What is the primary purpose of the passage?
(A) To explain how phrenology influenced modern cognitive sciences
(B) To describe a medical theory and its impact on 19th-century thinking
(C) To summarize the advancements in brain science during the 18th and 19th centuries
(D) To criticize a practice that justified sexism and the institution of slavery

12) **Directions**: An introductory sentence for a summary of the passage is provided. Complete the summary by selecting the THREE answer choices that are the most important. Some sentences do not belong. **This question is worth 2 points.**

Phrenology was a new way of studying the brain in the early 19th century.

-
-
-

Answer Choices
1. It confirmed European theories that preceded it.
2. It analyzed supposed behavioral tendencies.
3. It formed the basis of modern science.
4. It was popular among common people.
5. It mostly addressed the problem of greediness.
6. It focused on the shape of the skull.

Oracle

In ancient Greece, an oracle was a temple where people went to get **suggestions** from prophets. The word *oracle* also refers to the prophet and to his or her prophecy. Supposedly, prophets had special powers to speak **on behalf of** a god. Thus, people believed that **they** could answer all questions.

The most respected oracle was at the god Apollo's temple in Delphi. **A There, a priestess would sit on a three-legged stool placed over a crack in the side of a mountain, which emitted volcanic gas. B** Because of the **gas**, she would become disoriented* and speak words or syllables that reportedly came straight from Apollo. **C** However, the meaning was usually **puzzling** and unclear. **D** Yet even these interpretations could be mysterious. One prophecy given to a king before battle foretold, "If you cross the river, a great empire will perish." Thus, the oracle predicted that a river crossing during battle would have huge consequences, but it did not state *who* would be affected.

Another famous oracle was Dodona, which is considered the oldest oracle in Greece. It was dedicated to the god Zeus and was located away from any cities. The ancient Greeks believed that the god Zeus spoke through an oak tree when the wind blew through the branches. The priests at Dodona theoretically interpreted these **rustlings**.

Disoriented: mentally and physically confused

1) The word "**suggestions**" in Paragraph 1 is closest in meaning to
   (A) advice
   (B) knowledge
   (C) success
   (D) acceptance

2) In Paragraph 1, *oracle* refers to everything EXCEPT
   (A) a temple
   (B) a prophet
   (C) a prophecy
   (D) a god

3) The term "**on behalf of**" in Paragraph 1 is closest in meaning to
   (A) in
   (B) by
   (C) for
   (D) on

4) The word "**they**" in Paragraph 1 refers to
   (A) suggestions
   (B) prophets
   (C) special powers
   (D) people

5) What can be inferred about ancient Greeks from Paragraph 1?
   (A) They believed that gods knew much more than humans.
   (B) They believed that life was unpredictable and short.
   (C) They built temples for gods to live in.
   (D) They could predict future events.

6) Look at the squares [■] that indicate where the sentence below could be added to Paragraph 2.

Therefore, priests at the temple interpreted it for the public.

Where would the sentence best fit?
Circle the square [■] to add the sentence.

7) Which of the following best paraphrases the highlighted sentence in Paragraph 2?
(A) A priestess at Delphi always sat on a special chair over a volcano.
(B) Delphi priestesses usually enjoyed sitting by a mountain crack that emitted toxic gas.
(C) Its female oracle sat on a tripod over an outlet that vented chemical fumes.
(D) A woman would always place a stool over a hole in the slope of a mountain.

8) Why does the author MOST LIKELY mention "**gas**" in Paragraph 2?
(A) To reveal why oracles were dazed
(B) To question the oracle's societal position
(C) To illustrate why oracles were special
(D) To describe how Apollo communicated

9) The word "**puzzling**" in Paragraph 2 is closest in meaning to
(A) confusing
(B) interesting
(C) correct
(D) dangerous

10) According to Paragraph 3, which of the following is NOT true about Dodona?
(A) People believed that Zeus spoke there.
(B) The oracles there needed to be explained.
(C) It was in a rural setting.
(D) Zeus supposedly lived in an oak tree there.

11) The word "**rustlings**" in Paragraph 3 is closest in meaning to
(A) similarities
(B) sounds
(C) smells
(D) secrets

12) **Directions**: Select the sentences that most appropriately match the descriptions of each oracle. TWO of the answer choices will NOT be used. **This question is worth 3 points.**

Oracle in Delphi
●
●

Oracle in Dodona
●
●
●

Answer Choices
1. This was built to honor Zeus.
2. This contained the largest temple in Greece.
3. This received its prophecies from a sacred tree.
4. This was built on behalf of Apollo.
5. This allowed people to directly communicate with their gods.
6. This had a prophet who used a unique stand.
7. This may have been the first Greek oracle.

Econometrics

Econometrics is a branch of economics that applies mathematics and statistics to economic theory. Thus, businesses and governments use **it** to analyze economic activity.

A Econometrics puts economic relationships into an intricate mathematical form. **B** This application uses statistical **data** to prove that those relationships are **operational**. **C** For example, econometricians might believe that one's income influences how much one spends. In turn, econometricians would state this relationship in a formula. **D** **They might discover that each $10 rise in income brings an $8 increase in spending.**

Econometricians often develop sets of such formulas. These sets are called "models." They establish the relationships among various **factors** of an economy. Models may attempt to describe economic features of a community, a nation, or the world. Econometricians use **computers** to make calculations with the resulting models. The end result may be a prediction about how the economy will respond if certain variables change.

If econometric models predict certain outcomes that do not match real-world results, econometricians may turn to controlled experiments to test aspects of their models. The overall goal is to make sense of how people and resources interact.

1) The word "**it**" in Paragraph 1 refers to
   (A) econometrics
   (B) mathematics
   (C) economic theory
   (D) government

2) Look at the squares [■] that indicate where the sentence below could be added to Paragraph 2.

   Then, they would study data from various groups of people to see how income affects spending.

   Where would the sentence best fit?
   Circle the square [■] to add the sentence.

3) The word "**data**" in Paragraph 2 means
   (A) information
   (B) advice
   (C) time
   (D) motion

4) The word "**operational**" in Paragraph 2 is closest in meaning to
   (A) complex
   (B) influential
   (C) usable
   (D) understandable

5) What can be inferred about economic relationships from Paragraph 2?
   (A) They are descriptive.
   (B) They are increasing.
   (C) They are simple.
   (D) They are complicated.

6) How is econometrics explained in
    Paragraph 2?
    (A) By telling its history
    (B) By showing its use
    (C) By sharing its problems
    (D) By arguing its necessity

7) Which of the following best paraphrases the
    highlighted sentence in Paragraph 2?
    (A) For example, an $8 rise in spending results
        when income increases by $10.
    (B) When people spend $8, they receive $10 for
        every $1 that they spend.
    (C) Generally, a higher income means that
        people will spend less money.
    (D) People tend to spend all of their income as
        they earn it.

8) The word "**factors**" in Paragraph 3 is closest in
    meaning to
    (A) stories
    (B) passages
    (C) people
    (D) parts

9) In Paragraph 3, models describe every economy
    EXCEPT that of
    (A) a small town
    (B) a country
    (C) the global community
    (D) an uninhabited region

10) The author mentions "**computers**" in Paragraph
    3 in order to
    (A) tell when formulas stop
    (B) describe where economies are found
    (C) show how econometricians work
    (D) explain why models are made

11) According to Paragraph 4, controlled
    experiments are used
    (A) when data from real situations is
        unsatisfactory
    (B) every time an econometrician forms a model
    (C) to produce results that contradict other
        models
    (D) only when real-world data cannot be
        obtained

12) **Directions**: An introductory sentence for a
    summary of the passage is provided. Complete
    the summary by selecting the THREE answer
    choices that are the most important. Some
    sentences do not belong. **This question is worth
    2 points.**

    **Econometrics applies mathematics to
    economic theory.**

    ●

    ●

    ●

    Answer Choices
    1. It states economic relationships.
    2. It requires mathematical formulas.
    3. It is primarily used for income-spending
       problems.
    4. It does not make use of real-world
       information.
    5. It does not require a computer.
    6. It is valuable for private and public agencies.

10

Zoning

Time
00:20:00

Actual Practice

Zoning is a method that regulates how land is used. **A** By passing and using specific zoning laws, elected **bodies** divide a city into different areas for different uses. **B** Additionally, these laws may specify how the buildings should look. **C** Rules also may specify requirements for certain building **features** and restrictions on how the building is used. **D**

City planners are the people who carry out zoning. They use zoning as a method to **coordinate** cities' growth and development in an appealing way. For example, they make sure that factories are in one zone, stores in another, and homes in yet another. **City planners make recommendations regarding how or whether the city should approve property owners' construction plans.** When they make their decisions, they have to consider many factors. For example, city planners have to know how to organize the construction of necessary water and power facilities while **they** try to **accommodate** people's needs in the city.

People have regulated land use since ancient times. Zoning became important as population and industry grew in urban areas. In the United States, the first zoning law was passed in New York City in 1916. Today, many cities around the world have zoning laws.

1) Look at the squares [■] that indicate where the sentence below could be added to Paragraph 1.

In some cities, these laws may state how tall buildings can be.

Where would the sentence best fit?
Circle the square [■] to add the sentence.

2) The word "**bodies**" in Paragraph 1 is closest in meaning to
(A) building residents
(B) governing groups
(C) appointed managers
(D) democratic cities

3) The word "**features**" in Paragraph 1 means
(A) characteristics
(B) rooms
(C) changes
(D) windows

4) According to Paragraph 1, what is NOT controlled by zoning?
(A) Building measurements
(B) Building features
(C) Building interiors
(D) Building usage

5) What can be inferred about city planners from Paragraph 2?
(A) They often discourage new businesses.
(B) They own facilities that provide service to people.
(C) They are very important to cities' growth.
(D) They are usually not very organized.

6) The word "**coordinate**" in Paragraph 2 is closest in meaning to
(A) organize
(B) reduce
(C) create
(D) understand

7) Why is the highlighted sentence mentioned in Paragraph 2?
(A) To show that city planners approve most plans
(B) To explain what city planners usually do
(C) To discuss the importance of having zoning laws
(D) To criticize the way that cities are designed

8) The word "**they**" in Paragraph 2 refers to
(A) decisions
(B) factors
(C) city planners
(D) water and power facilities

9) The word "**accommodate**" in Paragraph 2 is closest in meaning to
(A) believe
(B) house
(C) satisfy
(D) restrict

10) What can be inferred about New York City from Paragraph 3?
(A) It had a large population in 1916.
(B) It had few laws before 1916.
(C) Its industry decreased after 1916.
(D) Its residents were upset during 1916.

11) According to Paragraph 3, there are zoning laws
(A) only in large U.S. cities
(B) only in heavily populated cities
(C) in many cities globally
(D) in ancient cities

12) **Directions**: An introductory sentence for a summary of the passage is provided. Complete the summary by selecting the THREE answer choices that are the most important. Some sentences do not belong. **This question is worth 2 points.**

Zoning is a way to control the use of land.

-
-
-

Answer Choices
1. It keeps urban areas attractive.
2. It angers property owners.
3. It has been used since 1916.
4. It is mostly used in New York City.
5. It is decided by elected city councils.
6. It helps cities provide appropriate resources.

The SETI Institute

Actual Practice

Time
00:20:00

A The SETI Institute, established in 1984 in Mountain View, California, is a privately financed research organization. **B** Part of its mission is to determine whether life has developed anywhere other than Earth, although these life forms may or may not be "intelligent." **C** Along with research, the institute provides school curriculum and internships for students, and it hosts radio shows for the interested public audience. **D**

More than 100 different research projects are **occurring** at the SETI Institute at the same time. One of the organization's largest projects was **Project Phoenix**. From 1995 to 2004, this program used some of the world's biggest antennas and tried to **detect** radio signals from intelligent beings that might live around the 800 stars nearest to Earth. However, **none** were found.

In partnership with the University of California, Berkeley (**UC Berkeley**), the institute is building a large **array** of satellite dishes and antennas in northeastern California. These will encompass a square kilometer and greatly increase the institute's ability to search for signals.

1) Look at the squares [■] that indicate where the sentence below could be added to Paragraph 1.

   The term "SETI" stands for the "Search for Extra Terrestrial Intelligence."

   Where would the sentence best fit?
   Circle the square [■] to add the sentence.

2) According to Paragraph 1, what is NOT true of SETI scientists?
   (A) They are eager to seek planets with water.
   (B) They are searching for life forms beyond Earth.
   (C) They are interested in educating the public.
   (D) They are privately funded.

3) What can be inferred about SETI researchers from Paragraph 1?
   (A) They are secretive.
   (B) They are curious.
   (C) They are selective.
   (D) They are foreign.

4) The word "**occurring**" in Paragraph 2 means
   (A) stopping
   (B) resuming
   (C) happening
   (D) succeeding

5) The author MOST LIKELY mentions "**Project Phoenix**" in Paragraph 2 to
   (A) question the reason why SETI Institute exists
   (B) name one of SETI Institute's ongoing projects
   (C) explain what the SETI Institute specializes in
   (D) give an example of an ambitious SETI project

6) What can be inferred about the SETI Institute from Paragraph 2?
   (A) It will be closed at the end of 100 different projects.
   (B) It is eager to conduct many research projects about the unknown.
   (C) It is only aware of 800 stars in the universe.
   (D) It only hires the most intelligent researchers in the world.

7) The word "**detect**" in Paragraph 2 is closest in meaning to
   (A) find
   (B) make
   (C) destroy
   (D) like

8) The word "**none**" in Paragraph 2 refers to
   (A) projects
   (B) antennas
   (C) signals
   (D) stars

9) In Paragraph 3, "**UC Berkeley**" is mentioned because
   (A) SETI employees graduated from there
   (B) a SETI project is located there
   (C) it is sharing a SETI project
   (D) it is opposing SETI projects

10) The word "**array**" in Paragraph 3 is closest in meaning to
    (A) view
    (B) group
    (C) signal
    (D) idea

11) What can be inferred about SETI Institute's new antennas from Paragraph 3?
    (A) They will increase the quantity of data available to SETI Institute.
    (B) They will certainly receive signals from alien life forms.
    (C) They will increase the number of stars in the universe.
    (D) They are being built in a hidden location.

12) **Directions**: An introductory sentence for a summary of the passage is provided. Complete the summary by selecting the THREE answer choices that are the most important. Some sentences do not belong. **This question is worth 2 points.**

Project Phoenix is one of the projects completed by the SETI Institute.

   ●

   ●

   ●

Answer Choices
1. It was done in secret.
2. It searched for radio signals.
3. It was divided into 100 parts.
4. It scanned all the stars.
5. It was one of SETI's largest projects.
6. It found no evidence of life.

Charms

A A charm is usually an object that is believed to give magical or special powers to a person. **B** Some well-known lucky charms are **four-leaf clovers, coins, and horseshoes**. **C** Often, the objects that are **treated** as charms differ from one society to another. **D**

Sometimes, a society considers a **particular** animal to be lucky. For instance, some Native Americans of the Southwest think of the frog as lucky. They have a legend about the frog bringing the people fire by carrying a coal in its mouth. In China, people believe that *Jin Chan*, or a charm in the shape of a "money toad" or "golden toad," **draws wealth to** a home. One story about Jin Chan is that he was originally a greedy monster but later became helpful to people.

Although many people may think of charms as mere superstition, they may value charms more than they admit. For example, an educated person may have a pair of "lucky" socks or a "lucky" necktie. Some people also may use objects such as **dream catchers** because **they** are believed to "catch" nightmares before a person dreams them.

1) Look at the squares [■] that indicate where the sentence below could be added to Paragraph 1.

   One of the most popular types of charm is the lucky charm.

   Where would the sentence best fit?
   Circle the square [■] to add the sentence.

2) Why are "**four-leaf clovers, coins, and horseshoes**" mentioned in Paragraph 1?
   (A) To give common examples of lucky charms
   (B) To criticize the use of such items
   (C) To explain why people value these items
   (D) To illustrate the histories of these lucky charms

3) What is NOT an example of a charm given from Paragraph 1?
   (A) Unusual plant
   (B) Coinage
   (C) Special powers
   (D) U-shaped metal shoes

4) The word "**treated**" in Paragraph 1 is closest in meaning to
   (A) traded
   (B) bought
   (C) written
   (D) considered

5) The word "**particular**" in Paragraph 2 is closest in meaning to
   (A) careful
   (B) specific
   (C) favorite
   (D) common

6) According to Paragraph 2, what animals are considered lucky?
   (A) Greedy monsters
   (B) Specific amphibians
   (C) Imaginary fish
   (D) Furry mammals

7) The phrase "**draws wealth to**" in Paragraph 2 is closest in meaning to
   (A) gets donations for
   (B) builds fortune for
   (C) adds color to
   (D) attracts money to

8) What can be inferred about charms from Paragraph 2?
   (A) They are often drawn from stories and legends.
   (B) They have the purpose of teaching.
   (C) They always bring their owners good fortune.
   (D) They often make people greedy.

9) Which of the following best paraphrases the highlighted sentence in Paragraph 3?
   (A) Some people have superstitious beliefs, and they may carry charms.
   (B) Rejecting the use of lucky charms is wise, but people do not.
   (C) People may say that they do not believe in lucky charms and yet still use them.
   (D) People may think of certain items as "lucky."

10) Why are "**dream catchers**" mentioned in Paragraph 3?
   (A) To explain how charms affect people's minds
   (B) To prove that charms really work
   (C) To give an example of a charm still used
   (D) To illustrate how people interpret dreams

11) The word "**they**" in Paragraph 3 refers to
   (A) charms
   (B) people
   (C) objects
   (D) dream catchers

12) **Directions**: An introductory sentence for a summary of the passage is provided. Complete the summary by selecting the THREE answer choices that are the most important. Some sentences do not belong. **This question is worth 2 points.**

Charms are objects believed to have magical powers.

   -
   -
   -

Answer Choices
1. They are difficult to find in urban life.
2. They differ from culture to culture.
3. They are believed to help their owners.
4. They are always worn on the human body.
5. They are still used today.
6. They provide a solution to people's problems.

Actual Test

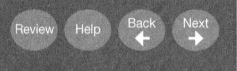

Reading Section Directions

In this section, you will read three passages and answer reading comprehension questions about each passage. Most questions are worth one point, but the last question in each set is worth more than one point. The directions indicate how many points you may receive.

You will have 60 minutes to read all of the passages and answer the questions. Some passages include a word or phrase that is underlined and printed in blue. Click on the word or phrase to see a definition or an explanation.

When you want to move on to the next question, click on **Next**. You can skip questions and go back to them later as long as there is time remaining. If you want to return to previous questions, click on **Back**. You can click on **Review** at any time and the review screen will show you which questions you have answered and which you have not. From this review screen, you may go directly to any question that you have already seen in the reading section.

Confirm later after calculating….

	Very Poor	Poor	Good	Very Good	Excellent
Points	1 - 21	22 - 29	30 - 34	35 - 38	39 - 43
Scale	1 - 14	15 - 19	20 - 23	24 - 26	27 - 30
Your Score					

Time 00:20:00

Questions 1 - 6

Reading 1

1) The word "**disputes**" in Paragraph 1 means
   (A) rituals
   (B) friendships
   (C) treasures
   (D) arguments

2) According to Paragraph 1, which of the following is NOT true about trial by combat?
   (A) It involved two fighters.
   (B) It was used to settle conflicts.
   (C) It was based on religious beliefs.
   (D) It was an illegitimate ancient practice.

3) The word "**appointed**" in Paragraph 1 means
   (A) chose
   (B) knew
   (C) taught
   (D) studied

4) Why is the word "**champions**" italicized in Paragraph 1?
   (A) To emphasize the ability of the fighters
   (B) To show that the word is being defined
   (C) To illustrate the feelings of the nobles, women, and priests
   (D) To honor the skills of trained fighters

5) The word "**them**" in Paragraph 1 refers to
   (A) disputing parties
   (B) nobles, women, and priests
   (C) trained fighters
   (D) *champions*

6) According to Paragraph 1, who often fought in trial by combat?
   (A) Women
   (B) Clergymen
   (C) Experienced fighters
   (D) Socially privileged men

Early Methods of Justice

Trial by combat was a way of deciding legal **disputes** in Europe's Middle Ages. The trial-by-combat method was a *duel* – a legal fight between two people through hand-to-hand combat to resolve accusations and disputes. The belief was that God would help the honest and innocent person win. Nobles, women, and priests often **appointed** trained fighters called *champions* to represent **them** in combat.

A Another method to decide an accused person's guilt or innocence during the Middle Ages was trial by ordeal. B In trial by ordeal, the accused was **subjected to** various types of physical torture. C In some cases, the person was considered innocent if the resulting injuries healed in three days. D Trial by ordeal was less common after 1215 when the church prohibited priests from participating. It was used in later centuries during witch trials.

In England, trial by combat and trial by ordeal **gradually gave way to trial by jury**, in which 12 ordinary men settled cases. In the 1100s, the first juries under King Henry II were groups of 12 neighbors who were invited to help settle questions of land ownership near them.

7) What can be inferred about nobles, women, and priests from Paragraph 1?
(A) They did not think that they should have to fight.
(B) They often enjoyed participating in duels.
(C) They were rarely accused of wrongdoing.
(D) They despised trial by combat.

8) Which of the following best paraphrases the highlighted sentence in Paragraph 2?
(A) Most people accused of crimes were actually innocent.
(B) Trial by ordeal was a medieval way to "discover" guilty individuals.
(C) Trial by ordeal was an additional choice for judges in the Middle Ages.
(D) In the Middle Ages, innocence was determined through torture.

9) Look at the squares [■] that indicate where the following sentence could be added to Paragraph 2.

If the wounds remained, the person was thought to be guilty.

Where would the sentence best fit?
Click on a square [■] to add the sentence.

10) In Paragraph 2, trial by ordeal is explained by
(A) describing how it worked
(B) comparing it to something familiar
(C) examining why it was used
(D) asking questions about it

11) The term "**subjected to**" in Paragraph 2 is closest in meaning to
(A) weakened by
(B) put through
(C) amazed by
(D) found in

Early Methods of Justice

Trial by combat was a way of deciding legal **disputes** in Europe's Middle Ages. The trial-by-combat method was a *duel* – a legal fight between two people through hand-to-hand combat to resolve accusations and disputes. The belief was that God would help the honest and innocent person win. Nobles, women, and priests often **appointed** trained fighters called *champions* to represent **them** in combat.

A **Another method to decide an accused person's guilt or innocence during the Middle Ages was trial by ordeal.** **B** In trial by ordeal, the accused was **subjected to** various types of physical torture. **C** In some cases, the person was considered innocent if the resulting injuries healed in three days. **D** Trial by ordeal was less common after 1215 when the church prohibited priests from participating. It was used in later centuries during witch trials.

In England, trial by combat and trial by ordeal **gradually gave way to trial by jury**, in which 12 ordinary men settled cases. In the 1100s, the first juries under King Henry II were groups of 12 neighbors who were invited to help settle questions of land ownership near them.

Time

00:06:00

Questions 12 - 13

Review Help Back Next

12) Why does the author mention "**gradually gave way to trial by jury**" in Paragraph 3?
   (A) To criticize England for not changing quickly
   (B) To point out something about trials in history
   (C) To describe a slow shift toward a new practice
   (D) To explain a better way of applying justice

13) **Directions**: Select the sentences that most appropriately match the descriptions of each type of trial. TWO of the answer choices will NOT be used. **This question is worth 3 points.**

Trial by combat
-

Trial by ordeal
-
-

Trial by jury
-
-

Answer Choices
1. It assumed that the virtuous person would win a fight.
2. It started as a way to decide rightful ownership of land.
3. It was based on ideas about violence.
4. It involved making the accused suffer.
5. It was unpopular and people demanded change.
6. It was used later for witch trials.
7. It required a dozen citizens.

Early Methods of Justice

Trial by combat was a way of deciding legal **disputes** in Europe's Middle Ages. The trial-by-combat method was a *duel* – a legal fight between two people through hand-to-hand combat to resolve accusations and disputes. The belief was that God would help the honest and innocent person win. Nobles, women, and priests often **appointed** trained fighters called *champions* to represent **them** in combat.

A **Another method to decide an accused person's guilt or innocence during the Middle Ages was trial by ordeal.** **B** In trial by ordeal, the accused was **subjected to** various types of physical torture. **C** In some cases, the person was considered innocent if the resulting injuries healed in three days. **D** Trial by ordeal was less common after 1215 when the church prohibited priests from participating. It was used in later centuries during witch trials.

In England, trial by combat and trial by ordeal **gradually gave way to trial by jury**, in which 12 ordinary men settled cases. In the 1100s, the first juries under King Henry II were groups of 12 neighbors who were invited to help settle questions of land ownership near them.

Review Help Back Next

Questions 14 - 18

14) According to Paragraph 1, Lenny Bruce's shows featured
(A) funny criticisms
(B) history lessons
(C) formal jokes
(D) excessive motion

15) The word "**hypocrisy**" in Paragraph 1 means
(A) mystery
(B) wonder
(C) falseness
(D) truth

16) Which of the following best paraphrases the highlighted information in Paragraph 2?
(A) Many observers praise Bruce for pioneering the use of stand-up comedy to talk about a wide variety of serious issues.
(B) Bruce was criticized for speaking too openly about matters that are usually not discussed in public.
(C) Other stand-up comedians today say that Bruce was their role model because he courageously spoke up.
(D) Bruce always gave his own views on politics and religion, which is something that most comedians do today.

17) The word "**obscene**" in Paragraph 2 means
(A) difficult
(B) important
(C) offensive
(D) proper

18) The word "**Others**" in Paragraph 2 refers to
(A) controversial topics
(B) Yiddish words
(C) his fans
(D) people besides his fans

Lenny Bruce

Lenny Bruce was a controversial American comedian from the 1950s to the 1960s. However, unlike many comedians of the era, Bruce did not seem to tell jokes. Instead, he spoke in an informal way and humorously attacked the **hypocrisy** in society. In other words, he spoke about how people claimed to be good even while their behavior was not.

Bruce is credited with expanding the subject matter discussed by stand-up comedians. He made statements that were considered bold or even outrageous concerning politics, religion, and other controversial topics of the day. Bruce included Yiddish words from his Jewish background, and used many words that are considered **obscene**. His fans thought that he was brilliant for promoting free speech. **Others** were upset by his **subject matter** and "bad" language. Referring to the title of the hugely popular 1936 book by Dale Carnegie, *How to Win Friends and Influence People*, Bruce titled his 1965 autobiography *How to Talk Dirty and Influence People*.

Bruce was born in 1925 in Mineola, New York. **A** In the late 1940s, he began his **career** as a host at adult shows. **B** Bruce performed in nightclubs because his material was too shocking for the television programs of the time. Between 1961 and 1964, he was arrested four times for using indecent language. As a result, many nightclubs would no longer hire him. **C** He was only 40 years old when he died because of an overdose of illegal drugs. **D**

Time

00:12:00

Questions 19 - 23

19) The term "**subject matter**" in Paragraph 2 is closest in meaning to
   (A) speech
   (B) topics
   (C) complaints
   (D) advice

20) According to Paragraph 2, which of the following is NOT true about Lenny Bruce's performance style?
   (A) He drew material from his own ethnic background.
   (B) He tried to set an example of what people should be like.
   (C) He made statements that people might disagree with.
   (D) He used "bad" language, or *profanity*.

21) In Paragraph 2, Bruce's autobiography is PROBABLY mentioned in order to
   (A) summarize everything about Bruce's life
   (B) compare Bruce's book to another book published in the 1930s
   (C) show Bruce's humorous attitude toward his own obscenity
   (D) persuade the reader that Bruce was great

22) Look at the squares [■] that indicate where the following sentence could be added to Paragraph 3.

   His real name was Leonard Alfred Schneider.

   Where would the sentence best fit?
   Click on a square [■] to add the sentence.

23) The word "**career**" in Paragraph 3 means
   (A) course
   (B) profession
   (C) life
   (D) journey

Lenny Bruce

Lenny Bruce was a controversial American comedian from the 1950s to the 1960s. However, unlike many comedians of the era, Bruce did not seem to tell jokes. Instead, he spoke in an informal way and humorously attacked the **hypocrisy** in society. In other words, he spoke about how people claimed to be good even while their behavior was not.

Bruce is credited with expanding the subject matter discussed by stand-up comedians. He made statements that were considered bold or even outrageous concerning politics, religion, and other controversial topics of the day. Bruce included Yiddish words from his Jewish background, and used many words that are considered **obscene**. His fans thought that he was brilliant for promoting free speech. **Others** were upset by his **subject matter** and "bad" language. Referring to the title of the hugely popular 1936 book by Dale Carnegie, *How to Win Friends and Influence People*, Bruce titled his 1965 autobiography *How to Talk Dirty and Influence People*.

Bruce was born in 1925 in Mineola, New York. **A** In the late 1940s, he began his **career** as a host at adult shows. **B** Bruce performed in nightclubs because his material was too shocking for the television programs of the time. Between 1961 and 1964, he was arrested four times for using indecent language. As a result, many nightclubs would no longer hire him. **C** He was only 40 years old when he died because of an overdose of illegal drugs. **D**

24) What can be inferred about television networks in the 1950s and 1960s from Paragraph 3?
(A) They were culturally conservative.
(B) They did not favor comedy.
(C) They were government-sponsored.
(D) They were not broadcasted late at night.

25) According to Paragraph 3, police arrested Lenny Bruce several times for
(A) working as a host at adult shows
(B) writing immoral advice about how to influence others
(C) using an indecent vocabulary onstage
(D) talking about freedom of speech

26) **Directions**: An introductory sentence is written below. Choose the THREE answers from the passage that support the sentence. Some sentences do not belong. **This question is worth 2 points.**

Lenny Bruce was a controversial American comedian.

-
-
-

Answer Choices
1. He was arrested for his comedy.
2. He started out as a musical performer.
3. He took illegal substances.
4. He criticized people's behavior and society.
5. He had an unusual television show.
6. He was disliked by most Americans.

Lenny Bruce

Lenny Bruce was a controversial American comedian from the 1950s to the 1960s. However, unlike many comedians of the era, Bruce did not seem to tell jokes. Instead, he spoke in an informal way and humorously attacked the **hypocrisy** in society. In other words, he spoke about how people claimed to be good even while their behavior was not.

Bruce is credited with expanding the subject matter discussed by stand-up comedians. He made statements that were considered bold or even outrageous concerning politics, religion, and other controversial topics of the day. Bruce included Yiddish words from his Jewish background, and used many words that are considered **obscene**. His fans thought that he was brilliant for promoting free speech. **Others** were upset by his **subject matter** and "bad" language. Referring to the title of the hugely popular 1936 book by Dale Carnegie, *How to Win Friends and Influence People*, Bruce titled his 1965 autobiography *How to Talk Dirty and Influence People*.

Bruce was born in 1925 in Mineola, New York. **A** In the late 1940s, he began his **career** as a host at adult shows. **B** Bruce performed in nightclubs because his material was too shocking for the television programs of the time. Between 1961 and 1964, he was arrested four times for using indecent language. As a result, many nightclubs would no longer hire him. **C** He was only 40 years old when he died because of an overdose of illegal drugs. **D**

Time

00:20:00

Review Help Back Next

Questions 27 - 31

27) What can be inferred from the information in Paragraph 1?
(A) Saola's existence surprised scientists.
(B) Scientists were actively looking for saola.
(C) Saolas were extinct until 1992.
(D) Saolas were captured for research.

28) The word "**remote**" in Paragraph 2 means
(A) celebrated
(B) isolated
(C) remodeled
(D) established

29) Why are antelopes mentioned in Paragraph 3?
(A) To trace the descendants of the saola
(B) To illustrate important behavioral traits that saola may have
(C) To use comparison to describe the saola's appearance
(D) To describe how the saola is a close relative of the antelope

30) The word "**speculate**" in Paragraph 3 means
(A) argue
(B) theorize
(C) imply
(D) emphasize

31) Which of the following best paraphrases the highlighted sentence in Paragraph 3?
(A) Vietnamese spindles give the saola its name because the animal's long horns look like them.
(B) The Vietnamese call the animal *saola*, which means the production of textiles.
(C) The saola's horns often become very long over its lifetime.
(D) In Vietnam, the animal was named at a time when people were still using spindles to make clothing.

Saola

By 1992, it was generally assumed that the world community was aware of all species of large mammals, as no new discoveries had been made in half a century. Then some scientists visiting homes in a village in Vietnam saw several skulls of a deer-like animal with unusually long horns. The skull did not match any known species.

Scientists now know that the spectacular, shy animal, the saola, has until recently lived in the **remote** forests of Vietnam and Laos. Although saolas have been captured by local people and photographed using "camera traps," scientists have never seen saolas in the wild and do not know if they still exist.

Though saolas appear to resemble antelopes, researchers **speculate** that their closest relatives are wild cattle. *Saola* means "spindle horn" in Vietnamese; it was given this name because the animal's long, straight horns growing back over its shoulders resemble *spindles*, or straight sticks used to make yarn. The saola grows about 90 centimeters tall and has a **sturdy** neck, thin snout, and short tail. The body is red-brown, and a black line runs down the back. Various white markings appear on its face, including large white stripes just above each eye. Also, huge scent glands, the largest among mammals, are located on each side of the snout. Saolas can rub **them** on plants and rocks to leave their scent.

A The local villagers believe that the horns of saola can be used for healing or medicinal purposes. As a result, the saola has been illegally hunted or trapped. **B** Also, construction of roads has affected the saola. **C** It is now considered a severely **endangered** species. **D**

Questions 32 - 36

32) The word "**sturdy**" in Paragraph 3 is closest in meaning to
(A) dangerous
(B) long
(C) single
(D) strong

33) According to Paragraph 3, what is NOT a color on the saola?
(A) White
(B) Black
(C) Red-brown
(D) Gray

34) The word "**them**" in Paragraph 3 refers to
(A) stripes
(B) mammals
(C) scent glands
(D) plants

35) According to Paragraph 4, what part of the saola interests hunters?
(A) Its scent gland
(B) Its horns
(C) Its fur
(D) Its neck

36) Which of the following can be inferred about the saola from Paragraph 4?
(A) Saolas are not safe in their current environment.
(B) Local people wish to protect the saolas from hunters.
(C) Saolas are dangerous to other species in the area.
(D) People are building roads in hopes of seeing a saola.

Saola

By 1992, it was generally assumed that the world community was aware of all species of large mammals, as no new discoveries had been made in half a century. Then some scientists visiting homes in a village in Vietnam saw several skulls of a deer-like animal with unusually long horns. The skull did not match any known species.

Scientists now know that the spectacular, shy animal, the saola, has until recently lived in the **remote** forests of Vietnam and Laos. Although saolas have been captured by local people and photographed using "camera traps," scientists have never seen saolas in the wild and do not know if they still exist.

Though saolas appear to resemble antelopes, researchers **speculate** that their closest relatives are wild cattle. *Saola* **means "spindle horn" in Vietnamese; it was given this name because the animal's long, straight horns growing back over its shoulders resemble** *spindles***, or straight sticks used to make yarn.** The saola grows about 90 centimeters tall and has a **sturdy** neck, thin snout, and short tail. The body is red-brown, and a black line runs down the back. Various white markings appear on its face, including large white stripes just above each eye. Also, huge scent glands, the largest among mammals, are located on each side of the snout. Saolas can rub **them** on plants and rocks to leave their scent.

A The local villagers believe that the horns of saola can be used for healing or medicinal purposes. As a result, the saola has been illegally hunted or trapped. **B** Also, construction of roads has affected the saola. **C** It is now considered a severely **endangered** species. **D**

Time

00:06:00

Review   Help   Back   Next

Questions 37 - 39

37) Look at the squares [■] that indicate where the following sentence could be added to Paragraph 4.

This has led to the loss of habitat, which has likely caused a decrease in what remains of the saola population.

Where would the sentence best fit?
Click on a square [■] to add the sentence.

38) The word "**endangered**" in Paragraph 4 is closest in meaning to
(A) attracted
(B) enclosed
(C) threatened
(D) observed

39) **Directions**: An introductory sentence is written below. Choose the THREE answers from the passage that support the sentence. Some sentences do not belong. **This question is worth 2 points.**

The saola is a very rare and unusual animal.

-
-
-

Answer Choices

1. It has horns that are used for weaving in Vietnam.
2. It is now in danger of becoming extinct.
3. It has scent glands that are extremely big in size compared with other mammals.
4. It has special fur that is desired by trappers.
5. It lives only in wilderness areas of Vietnam and Laos.
6. It has some kinship to antelope.

Saola

By 1992, it was generally assumed that the world community was aware of all species of large mammals, as no new discoveries had been made in half a century. Then some scientists visiting homes in a village in Vietnam saw several skulls of a deer-like animal with unusually long horns. The skull did not match any known species.

Scientists now know that the spectacular, shy animal, the saola, has until recently lived in the **remote** forests of Vietnam and Laos. Although saolas have been captured by local people and photographed using "camera traps," scientists have never seen saolas in the wild and do not know if they still exist.

Though saolas appear to resemble antelopes, researchers **speculate** that their closest relatives are wild cattle. *Saola* **means "spindle horn" in Vietnamese; it was given this name because the animal's long, straight horns growing back over its shoulders resemble** *spindles***, or straight sticks used to make yarn.** The saola grows about 90 centimeters tall and has a **sturdy** neck, thin snout, and short tail. The body is red-brown, and a black line runs down the back. Various white markings appear on its face, including large white stripes just above each eye. Also, huge scent glands, the largest among mammals, are located on each side of the snout. Saolas can rub **them** on plants and rocks to leave their scent.

A The local villagers believe that the horns of saola can be used for healing or medicinal purposes. As a result, the saola has been illegally hunted or trapped. **B** Also, construction of roads has affected the saola. **C** It is now considered a severely **endangered** species. **D**

ACTUAL TOEFL
VOCABULARY

Select the vocabulary word or phrase that has the closest meaning.

1. **subsequent**
   A. following
   B. including
   C. generating
   D. preceding

2. **durable**
   A. temporary
   B. doable
   C. short-lived
   D. long-lasting

3. **thus**
   A. consequently
   B. clearly
   C. commonly
   D. obviously

4. **ultimately**
   A. finally
   B. previously
   C. deadly
   D. originally

5. **confines**
   A. boundaries
   B. locations
   C. buildings
   D. conditions

6. **contemporary**
   A. attentive
   B. current
   C. old-fashioned
   D. temporary

7. **disperse**
   A. arrange
   B. disturb
   C. continue
   D. spread

8. **bulk**
   A. majority
   B. priority
   C. minority
   D. loyalty

9. **account for**
   A. complicate
   B. explain
   C. write
   D. confuse

10. **exert**
    A. drop
    B. find
    C. apply
    D. lose

11. **foster**
    A. encourage
    B. discourage
    C. accept
    D. decline

12. **vigor**
    A. variety
    B. difference
    C. attraction
    D. energy

13. **initial**
    A. beginning
    B. final
    C. literate
    D. present

14. **furthermore**
    A. initially
    B. additionally
    C. accordingly
    D. finally

15. **attainment**
    A. failure
    B. acceptance
    C. achievement
    D. rejection

16. **substantial**
    A. unimportant
    B. significant
    C. independent
    D. intelligent

17. **initiate**
    A. increase
    B. finish
    C. free
    D. begin

18. **cope with**
    A. argue with
    B. compare with
    C. deal with
    D. cover with

19. **prevailing**
    A. widespread
    B. minor
    C. unknown
    D. familiar

20. **abruptly**
    A. occasionally
    B. suddenly
    C. steadily
    D. usually

21. **unique**
    A. common
    B. distinct
    C. similar
    D. unclear

22. **intriguing**
    A. inspiring
    B. encouraging
    C. interesting
    D. boring

23. **contend**
    A. honor
    B. retreat
    C. argue
    D. disrespect

24. **confine**
    A. discredit
    B. restrict
    C. confuse
    D. prove

25. **inducement**
    A. introduction
    B. hindrance
    C. incentive
    D. process

26. **potent**
    A. fragile
    B. breakable
    C. powerful
    D. unable

27. **distinction**
    A. difference
    B. obedience
    C. similarity
    D. rebellion

28. **consequent**
    A. original
    B. resultant
    C. conditional
    D. objective

29. **impetus**
    A. challenge
    B. stimulus
    C. collapse
    D. inspiration

30. **impose**
    A. detach
    B. exist
    C. force
    D. relax

31. **alteration**
    A. loss
    B. remain
    C. modification
    D. accident

32. **phenomenal**
    A. normal
    B. refused
    C. extraordinary
    D. approved

33. fragment
A. take up
B. break up
C. bring out
D. pull out

34. massive
A. enormous
B. sensitive
C. cruel
D. minute

35. essential
A. true
B. minor
C. vital
D. false

36. obscure
A. extreme
B. perfect
C. careless
D. unclear

37. consumption
A. completion
B. utilization
C. stability
D. scarcity

38. onset
A. invention
B. attraction
C. interest
D. beginning

39. aggregate
A. collect
B. control
C. plan
D. forget

40. inevitable
A. inexpensive
B. unnecessary
C. unavoidable
D. countable

41. extended
A. reduced
B. experienced
C. affected
D. lengthened

42. refine
A. decline
B. improve
C. learn
D. suggest

43. persist
A. continue
B. leave
C. stop
D. accelerate

44. skeptical
A. believable
B. dishonest
C. dispirited
D. doubtful

45. abound in
A. be plentiful
B. be limited
C. be careful
D. be effective

46. persistent
A. short-lived
B. long-lasting
C. pleasing
D. annoying

47. consent
A. agree
B. disapprove
C. affect
D. contain

48. minute
A. tiny
B. huge
C. great
D. poor

49. inadvertently
A. unintentionally
B. deliberately
C. knowingly
D. identically

50. abundance
A. plenty
B. deficiency
C. absence
D. existence

51. fragmented
A. completed
B. divided
C. weakened
D. strengthened

52. distinct
A. careful
B. distant
C. capable
D. noticeable

53. disseminate
A. disagree
B. collect
C. spread
D. prove

54. modest
A. complex
B. minor
C. simple
D. proud

55. contentious
A. terrible
B. effective
C. argumentative
D. controversial

56. refinement
A. small improvement
B. small invention
C. small argument
D. small interest

57. adjacent
A. neighboring
B. considering
C. conclusive
D. additional

58. embark on
A. discourage
B. start
C. finish
D. challenge

59. imposing
A. impressive
B. attentive
C. unimportant
D. repulsive

60. distinctive
A. influential
B. unique
C. controversial
D. unclear

61. evident
A. apparent
B. uncertain
C. mistaken
D. capable

62. encompass
A. include
B. join
C. exclude
D. direct

63. conspicuous
A. unseen
B. familiar
C. mysterious
D. obvious

64. detect
A. destroy
B. manage
C. discover
D. delete

65. sequentially
A. consecutively
B. secularly
C. suddenly
D. abruptly

66. astonishing
A. boring
B. amazing
C. interesting
D. annoying

67. exhausted
A. taken off
B. used up
C. covered by
D. brought in

68. deliberate
A. harmful
B. unwilling
C. helpful
D. intentional

33B 34A 35C 36D 37B 38D 39A 40C 41D 42B 43A 44D 45A 46B 47A 48A 49A 50A
51B 52D 53C 54C 55C 56A 57A 58B 59A 60B 61A 62A 63D 64C 65A 66B 67B 68D

ACTUAL TOEFL VOCABULARY TEST | 171

69. **exceptionally**
   A. mildly
   B. favorably
   C. excitingly
   D. distinctively

70. **harness**
   A. utilize
   B. produce
   C. complete
   D. harden

71. **offset**
   A. understand
   B. operate
   C. destroy
   D. balance

72. **assume**
   A. know
   B. consume
   C. release
   D. suppose

73. **subsequently**
   A. unfamiliarly
   B. previously
   C. lower
   D. later

74. **prolonged**
   A. reduced
   B. bonded
   C. lengthened
   D. provided

75. **radically**
   A. subsequently
   B. additionally
   C. apparently
   D. drastically

76. **obscured**
   A. exposed
   B. hidden
   C. offensive
   D. obvious

77. **conjecture**
   A. surprise
   B. prove
   C. close
   D. guess

78. **conclusive**
   A. adequate
   B. definitive
   C. unequal
   D. strange

79. **comprise**
   A. include
   B. confirm
   C. destroy
   D. exclude

80. **virtually**
   A. artificially
   B. centrally
   C. differently
   D. importantly

81. **eventually**
   A. in fact
   B. at least
   C. in the end
   D. in the middle

82. **optimize**
   A. make the best use of
   B. make the worst use of
   C. make the least use of
   D. make no use of

83. **uniquely**
   A. commonly
   B. exceptionally
   C. hardly
   D. occasionally

84. **fragmentation**
   A. creation
   B. conclusion
   C. deprivation
   D. disjunction

85. **potential**
   A. probable
   B. unavailable
   C. conceptual
   D. impossible

86. **notable**
   A. insignificant
   B. unable
   C. outstanding
   D. conclusive

87. **prominence**
   A. insignificance
   B. intelligence
   C. ignorance
   D. importance

88. **deliberation**
   A. discussion
   B. destruction
   C. unwillingness
   D. instruction

89. **predominantly**
   A. mainly
   B. certainly
   C. approximately
   D. questionably

90. **integrate**
   A. segregate
   B. switch
   C. divide
   D. combine

91. **contention**
   A. conflict
   B. effect
   C. challenge
   D. disrespect

92. **forage**
   A. search for food
   B. drop food
   C. grow food
   D. eat food

93. **exclusively**
   A. solely
   B. partially
   C. approximately
   D. hardly

94. **ingenious**
   A. very honest
   B. very deceitful
   C. very clever
   D. very awkward

95. **assess**
   A. evaluate
   B. begin
   C. finish
   D. access

96. **intrigue**
   A. bore
   B. warn
   C. reject
   D. fascinate

97. **aggregated**
   A. dispersed
   B. exported
   C. imported
   D. combined

98. **decimate**
   A. rule
   B. destroy
   C. create
   D. yield

99. **entire**
   A. whole
   B. incomplete
   C. halfway
   D. clear

100. **analogous**
   A. passionate
   B. different
   C. analyzed
   D. similar

101. **prevail**
   A. be mature
   B. be dominant
   C. be weak
   D. be afraid

102. **precise**
   A. vague
   B. steep
   C. exact
   D. gradual

103. **intense**
   A. silent
   B. calm
   C. noisy
   D. extreme

104. **roughly**
   A. approximately
   B. greatly
   C. precisely
   D. specifically

105. **inherent**
A. unable
B. capable
C. additional
D. essential

106. **elaborate**
A. immense
B. creative
C. complicated
D. simple

107. **merely**
A. definitely
B. continually
C. completely
D. only

108. **prominent**
A. outstanding
B. alluring
C. different
D. imminent

109. **considerably**
A. calmly
B. greatly
C. lightly
D. unknowingly

110. **notably**
A. particularly
B. approximately
C. generally
D. rarely

111. **readily**
A. narrowly
B. willingly
C. widely
D. fairly

112. **justly**
A. wrongly
B. rightfully
C. unfairly
D. automatically

113. **sustain**
A. take
B. assume
C. support
D. bring

114. **predominant**
A. historic
B. willing
C. principal
D. minor

115. **barely**
A. altogether
B. just
C. always
D. quite

116. **immensely**
A. certainly
B. extremely
C. doubtfully
D. moderately

117. **proliferation**
A. growth
B. reduction
C. excellence
D. production

118. **ample**
A. scarce
B. plentiful
C. incomplete
D. whole

119. **predominated**
A. most controversial
B. most dangerous
C. most helpful
D. most noticeable

120. **configuration**
A. significance
B. arrangement
C. agreement
D. definition

121. **optimum**
A. most current
B. most promising
C. most acceptable
D. most favorable

122. **execute**
A. perform
B. explain
C. exercise
D. blame

123. **consequence**
A. cause
B. trouble
C. agreement
D. outcome

124. **profound**
A. possible
B. impossible
C. significant
D. trivial

125. **proliferate**
A. lessen
B. multiply
C. decrease
D. agree

126. **convention**
A. theory
B. invention
C. exclusive
D. conference

127. **vastly**
A. mildly
B. roughly
C. greatly
D. precisely

128. **ultimate**
A. additional
B. extra
C. final
D. unnecessary

129. **consume**
A. collect from
B. share with
C. use up
D. divide by

130. **vast**
A. narrow
B. enormous
C. insignificant
D. precise

131. **phenomenon**
A. regularity
B. tradition
C. refusal
D. occurrence

132. **modify**
A. change
B. remain
C. design
D. create

133. **accumulate**
A. order
B. correct
C. collect
D. consider

134. **compelling**
A. convincing
B. computing
C. increasing
D. producing

135. **advent**
A. improvement
B. advancement
C. certainty
D. beginning

136. **initially**
A. at last
B. in the end
C. at first
D. in time

137. **consequently**
A. almost
B. therefore
C. always
D. sometimes

138. **striking**
A. typical
B. remarkable
C. influential
D. enormous

139. **marked**
A. vague
B. ambiguous
C. obvious
D. obscure

140. **component**
A. factor
B. potential
C. comfort
D. collection

105D 106C 107D 108A 109B 110A 111B 112B 113C 114C 115B 116B 117A 118B 119D 120B 121D 122A
123D 124C 125B 126D 127C 128C 129C 130B 131D 132A 133C 134A 135D 136C 137B 138B 139C 140A

141. **immense**
    A. large
    B. little
    C. intense
    D. delicate

142. **abundant**
    A. scarce
    B. limited
    C. numerous
    D. unbounded

143. **prolong**
    A. extend
    B. shorten
    C. produce
    D. remove

144. **postulate**
    A. possess
    B. claim
    C. instruct
    D. pretend

145. **potentially**
    A. unlikely
    B. strongly
    C. possibly
    D. greatly

146. **principal**
    A. standard
    B. minor
    C. main
    D. different

147. **pronounced**
    A. indistinct
    B. notable
    C. ordinary
    D. upright

148. **extensive**
    A. widespread
    B. expensive
    C. restricted
    D. precious

149. **plausible**
    A. incredible
    B. believable
    C. unlikely
    D. worthy

150. **severe**
    A. various
    B. extreme
    C. moderate
    D. individual

151. **decimation**
    A. creation
    B. domination
    C. destruction
    D. submission

152. **unprecedented**
    A. new
    B. outdated
    C. common
    D. alternative

153. **amplify**
    A. increase
    B. complete
    C. decrease
    D. empty

154. **intact**
    A. separated
    B. unaffected
    C. combined
    D. damaged

155. **integration**
    A. union
    B. collection
    C. donation
    D. division

156. **pose**
    A. present
    B. gather
    C. reject
    D. accept

157. **considerable**
    A. insignificant
    B. dependent
    C. moderate
    D. significant

158. **conjecture**
    A. fact
    B. doubt
    C. assumption
    D. collection

159. **lucrative**
    A. vague
    B. clear
    C. profitable
    D. unprofessional

160. **significantly**
    A. unwillingly
    B. carefully
    C. considerably
    D. expensively

161. **attain**
    A. assure
    B. lose
    C. retain
    D. reach

162. **flourish**
    A. appear
    B. lose
    C. fail
    D. prosper

163. **remnants**
    A. remains
    B. remembrances
    C. alterations
    D. difficulties

164. **significant**
    A. simple
    B. serious
    C. important
    D. unnecessary

165. **crucial**
    A. effective
    B. insignificant
    C. efficient
    D. important

166. **sequence**
    A. disorder
    B. order
    C. confusion
    D. origin

167. **consensus**
    A. continuity
    B. argument
    C. suspension
    D. agreement

168. **sustained**
    A. abundant
    B. constant
    C. continental
    D. multiple

169. **exploitation**
    A. use
    B. rejection
    C. start
    D. exploration

170. **fragmentary**
    A. forgetful
    B. pleasant
    C. incomplete
    D. conclusive

171. **fluctuation**
    A. change
    B. uniformity
    C. relaxation
    D. easiness

172. **induce**
    A. bring about
    B. focus on
    C. take from
    D. introduce to

173. **critical**
    A. important
    B. unnecessary
    C. possible
    D. clinical

174. **conventional**
    A. traditional
    B. competitive
    C. inconsistent
    D. significant

175. **minutely**
    A. in order
    B. in detail
    C. in absence
    D. in danger

176. **crude**
    A. cruel
    B. primitive
    C. polished
    D. current

141A 142C 143A 144B 145C 146C 147B 148A 149B 150B 151C 152A 153A 154B 155A 156A 157D 158C
159C 160C 161D 162D 163A 164C 165D 166B 167D 168B 169A 170C 171A 172A 173A 174A 175B 176B

177. exceptional
A. effortless
B. widespread
C. reasonable
D. extraordinary

178. lethal
A. dangerous
B. safe
C. harmless
D. reachable

179. inherent in
A. characteristic of
B. knowledge of
C. critical of
D. function of

180. particular
A. public
B. specific
C. general
D. familiar

181. exploit
A. take off
B. take care of
C. take advantage of
D. take away

182. substantially
A. correctly
B. insignificantly
C. inadequately
D. considerably

183. eventual
A. first
B. final
C. early
D. proper

184. intermittently
A. intentionally
B. secretly
C. knowingly
D. periodically

185. simultaneously
A. at different times
B. at the same time
C. at the end
D. at the most

186. stipulate
A. acquire
B. excite
C. imply
D. require

187. account
A. amount
B. report
C. result
D. addition

188. indispensable
A. independent
B. unnecessary
C. essential
D. healthy

189. markedly
A. noticeably
B. slightly
C. extremely
D. mildly

190. mimic
A. control
B. imitate
C. differ
D. oppose

191. radical
A. extreme
B. advanced
C. superficial
D. analytical

192. vigorous
A. various
B. horrible
C. strong
D. weak

193. severity
A. standard
B. seriousness
C. movement
D. fairness

194. albeit
A. while
B. although
C. since
D. whether

195. ingenuity
A. honesty
B. denseness
C. ignorance
D. originality

196. alter
A. change
B. manage
C. turn
D. repair

197. entirely
A. clearly
B. completely
C. separately
D. inadequately

198. optimal
A. flawed
B. absent
C. ideal
D. present

199. advocate
A. oppose
B. compete
C. support
D. clash

200. manipulate
A. generate
B. create
C. control
D. ruin

Answer Keys

Chapter 1 Vocabulary

Warm Up   p. 7
1) bicycle   11) destroyed
2) transport   12) triathlon
3) overworked   13) unique
4) interrupted   14) preview
5) survived   15) hyperactive
6) autonomous   16) misconduct
7) returned   17) extracted
8) nonfiction   18) forecast
9) secured   19) Antarctic
10) engaged   20) unity

Quick Practice   p. 8
1) (A) Any two objects that are *parallel* are similar or alike. Therefore, if New York has no *parallel*, it has no *equal*.

2) (B) *Tradition* describes a characteristic way or style of doing something. Gothic *tradition* is one *style* of building.

3) (C) To *gleam* is to glow or shine, so an object that is *gleaming* is *shiny*.

4) (D) The word *houses* is used here to refer to a publishing firm or business, so the best answer choice is *companies*.

5) (A) *Outstanding* is an adjective that indicates that the orchestras are exceptionally good, or *talented*.

6) (A) To *perform* is to act out or carry out, so the closest answer is to *put on a show*.

7) (B) To *help* is to provide assistance or support, so the best answer is *assist*.

8) (C) In this context, the word *serve* is interchangeable with function or *work*. Thus, dolls "*work* as objects that children can love."

9) (D) *Outlet* means an exit or a way out. As used here, dolls provide a way out or an *opening* for children's emotions.

10) (A) To *reveal* means to make known or to announce, so *shows* is similar in meaning.

11) (C) The word *rehearse* means to *practice*. Thus, "children also *practice* adult roles…by playing with dolls."

12) (B) In acting, *roles* refers to the parts or characters in a play or film. In this passage, *roles* refers to parts or *characters* in a make-believe game.

13) (A) To *absorb* means to *take in*. For example, water is absorbed into, or *taken in*, the paper towel.

14) (D) *Diverse* is an adjective that indicates that there are many kinds of, or *various*, things.

15) (A) To *detect* is to discover something, so the closest answer is *noticed*.

16) (B) To *influence* means to affect or change something or someone. As a noun, *influences* means *effects*.

17) (A) To *retain* is to store or keep something, so if something was *retained* in the rich African music culture, it was stored or *kept* in it.

18) (D) If something is *distinctive*, it has a special or *unique* quality.

19) (C) To *flow* means to run or move through. For instance, water once *moved* on the surface of Mars.

20) (A) *Evidence* includes everything that is used to prove or disprove something. Thus, the valleys may be *proof* that water once flowed on Mars.

21) (B) To *consist of* means to be made up of or *include*. This makes sense: "The evidence *includes* many valleys…."

22) (B) The word *pores* means holes or openings. One important clue provided in the sentence is the phrase "below the surface." Hence, water may be in *holes* below the surface of Mars.

23) (C) We can infer that a space probe *found* "vast amounts of frozen water" because the passage focuses on the *discovery*, or *finding*, of water on Mars.

24) (D) *Vast* is an adjective used to refer to something that is extremely *large* in size.

25) (D) Something *vital* is very *important* to the function of an object. For example, the heart is *vital*

to the body.

26) (C) The noun *resources* refers to tools or materials one can use to do something. In a library, resources are thus the *learning tools* that help people with their work and studies.

27) (A) The word *complete* means to *do* something. The resources in the library help people *do* their work and studies.

28) (B) The word *rank* is used as a verb to indicate that libraries are *placed* or arranged in a particular order, as in first to last.

29) (A) Something that is *necessary* is essential or *needed*. For example, food is *necessary* to the body.

30) (C) *Institutions* often refer to structures for public service, such as schools or hospitals. It is a general term, as is *establishments*.

31) (D) When people are *deprived of* something, they are denied something, so they *lack* it. Thus, "People who are *lacking* sleep cannot concentrate…."

32) (B) To *concentrate* means to think and *focus*. This makes sense because when people lack sleep, they have a hard time *focusing* on what they are doing and they cannot think as well as they want.

33) (C) *Especially* is an adverb that relates to something that is specific or *particular*. Thus, *especially* is similar to *particularly*.

34) (C) If something is *routine*, it is a normal or *regular* procedure.

35) (B) When someone is *distracted*, he or she is not focusing on the main task or purpose but on something else. *Sidetracked* means turned away from a purpose.

36) (D) *Prone* literally means to lean forward or lie face-down. Someone who is prone to something leans toward doing it, or is more *likely to*.

37) (B) The *appeal* of Shakespeare's work is the quality that causes people to like it, or the quality that *attracts* people; or its *attraction*.

38) (A) The adverb *mostly* means for the most or greatest part. *Mainly* also means for the most part, or most importantly.

39) (A) *Deep* refers to something that extends below the surface, as in "a deep hole." Therefore, a *deep* understanding of something would be like a *strong* understanding of it.

40) (C) When it relates to humans, *nature* refers to the character or *characteristics* of an individual.

41) (C) If something is *conventional*, it is usual or expected. *Typical*, or conforming to a certain *type*, is closest in meaning.

42) (D) *Remarkable* refers to something people might *remark* on because it is extreme; *considerably* likewise means to a noticeable extent, or very.

43) (B) *Legitimate* refers to something real and true. If something is true, it follows that it can be trusted, or is *trustworthy*.

44) (C) *Safeguard* is defined as a safety measure or *protection*. Thus, the word *safeguards* means *protections*.

45) (A) If you *tamper with* something, you *change* or alter its function.

46) (B) To *hinder* means to get in the way of something, or to *prevent* something from happening.

47) (D) *Likelihood* means a strong chance or *possibility* for something to occur.

48) (D) If something is *erroneous*, it is wrong. The closest answer is *mistaken*.

49) (A) *Surroundings* refers to the things and conditions around someone or something. Thus, *environment* is the best substitution for *surroundings*.

50) (B) The word *internal* refers to something that is inside, not outside. *Inner* is closest in meaning.

51) (C) To *contain* is to include or *have* something inside. Thus, sharks "have tiny internal ears which *have* cells…."

52) (A) *In addition* is an expres-

sion that shows that you will *add* more information about a topic, as does the adverb *moreover*.

53) Ⓐ The word *trait* means a certain *characteristic*, or a *quality*. This makes sense: Certain *qualities* "help them maneuver through the sea."

54) Ⓑ To *maneuver* is to skillfully steer through an environment. So, if a shark *maneuvers* "through the sea," it *navigates* "through the sea."

55) Ⓓ Because opera houses are *specifically* named and built for "opera performances," we can conclude that opera houses are built uniquely, or *specially*, for a certain type of performance.

56) Ⓐ The word *seat*, used here as a verb, indicates that opera houses *hold* more people (in seats) than do theaters.

57) Ⓑ *Reserved* indicates that something is set aside for a particular use. Therefore, some theaters are set aside or *dedicated* for plays.

58) Ⓐ *Equipment* means tools or gear; such as the *devices* for sound, lighting, effects, and sets needed in an opera house.

59) Ⓐ Something that is *elaborate* is likely to be fancy and complicated in design. Close in meaning to this is *complex*.

60) Ⓑ If something is *required*, one must have it, as it is *needed*.

Chapter 2 Referent

Warm Up   p. 21

1) him	11) he
2) they	12) their
3) its	13) their
4) it	14) a few
5) its	15) others
6) he	16) their
7) it	17) these
8) his	18) your
9) her	19) he
10) their	20) who

Quick Practice   p. 22

1) Ⓑ Because the palace "contained labyrinth-like chambers," it makes sense that the pronoun refers to the *palace*; thus "the *palace* may have been the Cretan Labyrinth."

2) Ⓒ It makes sense to substitute the king's name for the pronoun: "*Minos* supposedly had the labyrinth built…."

3) Ⓐ The referent of *he* is *Schoenberg*, the subject of the passage, as the author continues focusing on him.

4) Ⓒ *It* refers to the singular, neutral noun phrase *atonal music* in the sentence. This makes sense: "*atonal music* did not have any key."

5) Ⓑ The most logical answer is the subject of the preceding clause, *tribes*. Thus, "*tribes* may have been influenced…."

6) Ⓒ The only referent that could be "permanent homes or temporary shelter" is *walled forts*.

7) Ⓐ The purpose of an aquarium is to exhibit sea creatures. Thus, in the clause "*they* started exhibiting more…sea creatures," it makes sense that *they* refers back to the *public aquariums*.

8) Ⓒ *Them* refers to the subject of the preceding sentence, *animal rights groups*. It would make sense to say that keeping animals captive is disturbing to *animal rights groups*.

9) Ⓑ Because the passage focuses on how to be a successful reader, we can infer that *readers* must "relate to the written material," so *they* must refer back to *readers*.

10) Ⓒ The word *it* refers to the *written material* on which readers must concentrate.

11) Ⓐ The referent *wild gerbils* is the only choice that makes sense; the author is describing the environment in which wild gerbils live.

12) Ⓑ Because whatever *These* refers to "are active day and night," we can eliminate *networks* and *holes* as correct answers because neither of those choices can be "active," since they are objects. Thus, the only answer that makes sense is *communities*, as a *community* is a group capable of activity.

13) Ⓑ As the whole passage deals with the nicknames of the city of Chicago, the pronoun *it* should logically refer to the *city of Chicago*.

14) Ⓒ The author mentions four nicknames for the city of Chicago in the preceding sentences. Thus, it is logical to say; "All of these (*nicknames*) are still being used…."

15) Ⓐ *There* is a demonstrative pronoun that refers to the New World, or from the possible choices provided, the *Americas*.

16) Ⓓ *They* logically refers to

the subject of the preceding clause "settlers from Spain and Portugal."

17) Ⓒ The indefinite pronoun refers to *resource*; thus, if "people lack one resource, they can substitute it with another (*resource*)."

18) Ⓓ *Glass* is the referent for *it*. Not only do they agree in number (singular), but *glass* is the only answer choice that makes sense as a type of material that plastic can replace.

19) Ⓒ The pronoun *it* refers to *geometry* discussed in the preceding sentence. Since the passage is about the origin of geometry, it is logical in meaning to read; "*geometry* has been used… since 2000 BCE…."

20) Ⓒ The pronoun *these* refers to *geometric shapes* discussed in the preceding sentence. In turn, the succeeding sentence gives examples of these *geometric shapes* – squares and triangles.

Exercises Ch. 1-2   p. 27

1) Ⓒ The word *goods* refers to things or belongings. Most generically, *goods* means *items*.

2) Ⓓ *Them* is a third-person plural pronoun. All the choices agree in number, but only *animals* fits as the correct referent because a hunter would specifically trade *animals* for other goods and services.

3) Ⓓ *Who* in this sentence refers to *a neighbor* that comes right before the pronoun. This makes sense: *a neighbor* "had made extra pottery" and traded pottery for animals.

4) Ⓑ The word *gradually* means little by little. Therefore, *gradually* in this sentence means *slowly*. "*Slowly*, each person would get better at a chosen task."

5) Ⓓ The word *it* refers to the *skill set* mentioned in the previous sentence. This makes sense: "The *skill set* would be handed down to the next generation."

6) Ⓐ When something is *handed down*, it usually means that it has been passed on to the next generation. The closest in meaning is *taught*. "It would be *taught* to the next generation."

7) Ⓓ The definition of an *elder* is an *older person*. Here it is used in the plural form, so the answer is

older people.

8) Ⓓ The pronoun logically refers to the subject of the preceding sentence. Thus, "When *elders* became sick or died, oral traditions could easily be forgotten," making it difficult for people to share or pass on knowledge.

9) Ⓐ If something is *accessible*, one can reach it easily. That is, it is *available*. It makes sense: "knowledge became more *available*…."

10) Ⓒ The word *minimal* means lowest or *basic*. This makes sense because *basic* unit would mean the lowest unit.

11) Ⓒ The passage focuses on how writing changed learning. Thus, "units of *written expression* allowed people to share knowledge…."

12) Ⓒ The verb *interpret* means to understand, explain, or *translate*. Thus, written symbols "allowed to share knowledge…as long as they could *translate* the symbols."

13) Ⓐ The word *immense* means vast or *large*. The peoples of Africa have created a *large* variety of sculptures.

14) Ⓑ *These* here refers to *sculptures*, the only choice that makes sense if we replace the pronoun: "the materials and meanings of *sculptures*…."

15) Ⓑ To *depend upon* is to *rely on* or need. Thus, "The materials and meanings of these *rely on* the people's way of life."

16) Ⓓ We can deduce that "Settled" people would likely farm most of their food, so *agricultural* must be closest in meaning to *farming*.

17) Ⓒ *Nomadic* comes from the word *nomad*, a person who travels from place to place. Therefore, *nomadic* means *traveling*.

18) Ⓐ The word *ones* is an indefinite pronoun that refers to tribes of settled *peoples* in the preceding sentence compared with the nomadic *peoples* in this sentence.

19) Ⓑ Because "Relatively few" musicians earn success from performing, we can infer that *competition* involves people going against each other, or *rivalry*.

20) **B** If the competition is *keen*, then the competition is *intense*; there are many serious competitors.

21) **D** The word *few* is an indefinite pronoun used in the passage to refer to the *"musicians"* mentioned in the preceding sentence.

22) **A** *Solely* means *only* or entirely. So "few earn a living *only* by performing or composing."

23) **C** The idiom *difficult to come by* means *difficult to find*. Hence, if music jobs are *difficult to come by*, finding such a job would be *difficult to achieve*.

24) **D** Something that is *sudden* occurs *quickly* or unexpectedly. Thus, it makes sense to say that one can *quickly* or unexpectedly become popular.

25) **A** The word *Most* is an indefinite pronoun that refers to *strategy board games* in the first sentence.

26) **C** Here, the word *object* refers to the objective or *goal* of the game.

27) **D** To *capture* means to *take* something by force. So, the purpose of the game Go is to *take* another person's territory.

28) **B** *Territory* is a noun meaning land or region; also a space or an *area*.

29) **D** The word *it* refers to *territory* in the passage because a person captures *territory* by surrounding *it*.

30) **A** The verb *originate* means to start or create; starting a game is like *inventing* it.

Chapter 3 Fact & Detail

Warm Up   p. 35

1) O	6) F	11) O	16) F
2) F	7) O	12) O	17) O
3) O	8) O	13) F	18) O
4) F	9) F	14) O	19) F
5) F	10) O	15) F	20) F

Quick Practice   p. 36

1) **B** *Fluorescent tubes* produce more light per watt, thus use fewer watts, or *save energy*.

2) **B** Because fluorescent tubes last 10,000 hours when incandescent bulbs last 750 hours, we can say that *fluorescent tubes last longer than incandescent bulbs*.

3) **A** The passage indicates that hobbies sometimes develop over time, as people learn (and begin to *study*) more about a particular interest.

4) **B** The passage states that people get information, or *learn*, about their developing hobbies from books and magazines.

5) **C** The passage discusses the features of the Sargasso Sea and that "*different ocean currents*" give the sea its features.

6) **D** The passage states that "the group of seaweeds known as *sargassum*…gives the sea its name." Thus, *specific plants that grow there* give the sea its name.

7) **A** The human eye and a camera both take in light with the consequence of producing a "picture." Since a picture is an outcome or an *image*, [A] is the reasonable answer.

8) **C** The passage tells us that "the camera records pictures," and these "can be seen by many people." In other words, pictures are used for *sharing memories with other people*.

9) **A** The passage states that 1.7 million animal species have been discovered, and 1 million of those are insects, implying that scientists know of *1 million* insects.

10) **D** The passage tells us that scientists discover thousands of insect species every year.

11) **C** According to the second sentence, San Francisco has "some of the steepest streets in the world." So, the streets can be said to be *outstandingly inclined*.

12) **A** The passage states that "cable cars amaze onlookers by resembling elevators," meaning that *they have no trouble climbing hills*.

13) **C** The passage says that hurricanes are most likely to occur "when the weather is warm." So, the *warm weather* contributes.

14) **D** The passage says that "hurricanes can damage buildings, trees, and cars." So, hurricanes cause *property damage*.

15) **B** The passage states that Cleopatra "was known for her intelligence, personality, and ambition." These traits describe *her character*.

16) **D** The word *court* means to try to win a person's love. So, we know from the final sentence that there were some romantic relationships between Cleopatra and the Rome's leaders (e.g., Julius Caesar and Mark Antony).

17) **B** The main idea of the passage is that Clara Barton learned about organizing emergency aid during *two wars*, or the U.S. Civil War (*at home*) and the Franco-Prussian War (*abroad*).

18) **C** The passage states that the Red Cross "meets human needs…to this day." Because this is the only mention of Barton's influence on today's society, we can conclude that *founding the American Red Cross* is her clearest influence on the world today.

19) **D** From the passage, we can see that realistic fiction "aims to provide wisdom or insight into some aspect of life." Thus, readers expect to *learn something about life*.

20) **B** The passage tells us that rather than a focus on character development, "the attention may be on the plot or action." Thus, *what happens in the plot may be more important than the characters' development*.

Chapter 4 Negative Fact

Warm Up   p. 45

1) D	6) A	11) D	16) D
2) C	7) B	12) E	17) C
3) E	8) C	13) C	18) D
4) C	9) D	14) D	19) A
5) E	10) C	15) E	20) D

Quick Practice   p. 46

1) **D** The passage provides examples of resources that are *inexhaustible* – meaning that they will never be used up. However, according to the last sentence, some places already lack "clean, fresh water," or *uncontaminated water*.

2) **C** The passage does not mention anything about increased workers or laborers. The passage tells us that increased productivity has come from fertilizers (*chemicals*), selective breeding (*animal reproduction*), and machines (*motorized devices*).

3) **D** The passage does not

mention anything about rainbows moving.

4) **A** The passage says that the funny bone is "a nerve that runs from the pinky finger through the back of the elbow." Therefore, the funny bone is not found in the brain.

5) **C** The passage tells us that "90 percent of airplanes have only one engine," but not that *90 percent of the people use them*.

6) **B** The passage says that turtles live everywhere except the "Arctic and Antarctic regions," which are *the polar regions of Earth*.

7) **D** The passage does not mention whether or when the Blue Mountains actually *look blue*.

8) **C** The passage states that "To his surprise, he (Cartier) discovered land full of *natural resources and tribes*…." So we know that he was not intentionally looking for those.

9) **C** The passage says that "it was illegal to kill cats" in Egypt, but does not mention anything about *raising cats being illegal*.

10) **D** The passage does not say that Newton invented color, only that he invented the color wheel.

Exercises Ch. 3-4   p. 51

1) **D** Cupid, Amor, and Eros are all different names for the god of love, but Venus is mentioned only as his mother.

2) **C** The passage tells us that the first images of Eros were as a *handsome young man*. It was later that he was pictured as a baby, but the passage does not mention anything about him being *chubby*.

3) **A** The passage states that by the 300s BCE, Eros' appearance was no longer of a "handsome young man," but of a "naked baby with wings." Thus, *his appearance changed*.

4) **B** Those shot with Eros' gold-tipped arrows "fell in love," and those shot with a lead-tipped arrow received "the opposite effect." The opposite of falling in love is *falling out of love*.

5) **B** The passage tells us that "experts still debate what the mind is." Thus, the mind *is not*

well understood.

6) Ⓓ Because animals with a nervous system "react to, and make sense of, their surroundings," we know that they *respond to changes in their environment.*

7) Ⓒ The passage states that only the human mind has "abstract thoughts and feelings." Synonyms for these are *complex ideas* and *emotions.*

8) Ⓒ The passage says that "animals with a nervous system have something like a mind," not that the mind *makes people nervous.*

9) Ⓐ From the passage, we know that the 1890s were associated with an "economic depression" (*bad economy*), "labor unrest" (*workers protesting*), and "the Spanish-American War" (*international conflict*), but not problems with crops.

10) Ⓑ The passage says that "few Americans living in the 1890s ever regarded the period as particularly happy." Readers can infer that they felt *troubled.*

11) Ⓒ The passage mentions that people used the term "Gay Nineties" when they wanted to remember a comfortable past. We can conclude that people at that time wanted to *feel good.*

12) Ⓒ The passage tells us that the 1890s included an economic depression, which clearly is not *great economic success.*

13) Ⓒ The passage describes coriander's leaves as "feathery" rather than as *thick and tough.*

14) Ⓓ Originally the plant "grew wild in the Mediterranean region" but now "is grown and eaten in many cultures." Thus, *its use spread from one area to many areas.*

15) Ⓐ The passage indicates the taste of coriander seeds by saying that they can be made into a "*sweet* spice."

16) Ⓓ Although the passage mentions that ground coriander seeds are sometimes used to spice cakes, there is no mention of the seeds' use as a *grain* or flour.

17) Ⓑ The passage states that paintings are found in caves located in "Australia, France, Italy, Portugal, and Spain." Thus, we can conclude that the paintings are *mostly found in Europe* as well

as Australia.

18) Ⓐ The passage states that paintings can be found in Australia, but does not state anything about *Austria.*

19) Ⓒ The passage tells us that paintings were probably not for decoration because they are located "in dark and isolated parts of caves" (in places that are *hard to find and see*).

20) Ⓓ The second paragraph tells us that early paintings were likely used "for religious purposes" for their animal gods (*ceremonies to honor animals*), "as a communication tool" (*way to interact with others*), and "as a way to measure time" (*method to track time*). However, there is no mention of *predictions of the future.*

Chapter 5 Coherence

Warm Up   p. 59

1) 3-2-1	**6)** 2-3-1
2) 2-1-3	**7)** 1-3-2
3) 1-3-2	**8)** 3-1-2
4) 1-3-2	**9)** 1-3-2
5) 3-1-2	**10)** 3-2-1

Quick Practice   p. 60

1) Ⓐ As is, it is not clear what "this day" is referring to in the passage. So the added sentence has to be placed before the first sentence to give readers more information.

2) Ⓒ It makes sense that "some colonists" would contrast with *others* in the following sentence. Also, the added sentence must precede the last sentence so that readers understand why Native Americans "fought back."

3) Ⓓ Three sentences describe the Moon's so-called "atmosphere"; next should come examples of other space objects that have similar "*atmospheres.*"

4) Ⓑ It makes sense to place information about Walt Disney's childhood after his birth year, but before his high school graduation.

5) Ⓓ The pronoun phrase *these teeth* refers to specific teeth – "the upper teeth" in the third sentence. It is logical to place the pronoun just after the referent.

6) Ⓓ The passage tells us that people "use horses for sport and work." The added sentence provides examples of this, so it should come next.

7) Ⓒ The phrase "these fibers" refers to *plant fibers.* The phrase should follow the referent.

8) Ⓓ The added sentence adds details about vegetables and meat to the main idea of changes to food's structure. It is logical to place the details after the main idea.

9) Ⓒ The pronoun *this* from the added sentence logically refers to "heat" in sentence three. If it is inserted there, we have energy making heat, and heat making steam, which is a logical order.

10) Ⓐ The whole passage contains supporting details of the added sentence, which should be placed at the beginning of the passage as a main idea.

Chapter 6 Inference

Warm Up   p. 69

1) A	**2)** B	**3)** A	**4)** B	**5)** B
6) A	**7)** A	**8)** B	**9)** A	**10)** B

Quick Practice   p. 70

1) Ⓒ The passage says that trucking transports most industrial products and goods, so *Americans rely greatly on trucks.*

2) Ⓐ Since the author mentions that whales look "like fish," we can infer that whales *have been mistaken* for fish.

3) Ⓑ Reintroduction of wolves to Yellowstone Park caused a population increase in young trees, beavers, and dams, "which in turn lead to an increase in fish, frog, and bird populations." Clearly, wolves *create conditions for more types of animals.*

4) Ⓒ The purpose of a census is to count all citizens and residents. So, by not including people from Puerto Rico (who are citizens), the U.S. Census is *not entirely accurate.*

5) Ⓓ If dancing "has been around since before people started recording history" and "helped early people bond, communicate, and thus survive," we can infer that it was probably *important to prehistoric people.*

6) Ⓐ If a group is called "the first group," there is an implication that other groups followed. We can infer that more groups of English settlers arrived in Georgia

after 1733.

7) Ⓓ If "tax rates depend on the role of government," and "the need for taxes has become great," then it is likely that *the role of government is increasing.*

8) Ⓐ The passage tells us that earlier tall buildings were made of only bricks and stone, and did not have elevators. Thus, we can conclude that *new technology was used by the late 19th century* in skyscrapers.

9) Ⓑ From the fact that people traveled, traded, and read more during the Renaissance, we can conclude that *learning about the world was important to many people during this time.*

10) Ⓓ We can deduce that *both living and nonliving things are important* because, in the first sentence, the passage says that they "affect each other in a balanced system."

Exercises Ch. 5-6 p. 74

1) Ⓒ The second sentence mentions two birds that are "flightless." It makes sense to follow with the added sentence about what the birds do "instead of flying…."

2) Ⓔ Paragraph 2 talks about the "special characteristics" of flightless birds. When the added sentence is inserted at the start of Paragraph 2, we can see that it serves both as a transition sentence and a topic sentence.

3) Ⓒ Paragraph 1 indicates that people sometimes mistake hemlock for parsley. So, we can infer that *it looks like parsley.*

4) Ⓑ The passage says that Socrates died from hemlock, which was normally given to criminals condemned to death. Thus, it follows that *Socrates was considered a criminal.*

5) Ⓒ The added sentence begins "But unlike *these grasses…*" so it must follow the mention of several grasses, such as "wheat, oats, and barley."

6) Ⓕ The pronoun "they" is missing a referent, as "tropical countries" cannot "wear bamboo clothing." Thus, the added sentence belongs at [F] because "many people" provides a referent for "they."

7) Ⓑ According to Paragraph

1, vampire bats were named after "an imaginary frightening creature." Therefore, we can assume that vampire bats *scare people*.

8) Ⓐ Paragraph 2 says that vampire bats "can spread diseases through their bites" and "have attacked people who are sleeping." Therefore, we can conclude that *they can be dangerous*.

9) Ⓓ The pronoun phrase *this system* in the added sentence should go right after its logical referent, the "system" of people forming rows and passing buckets of water.

10) Ⓔ The added sentence introduces the first fire-fighting organization. This statement can serve as a topic sentence for Paragraph 2.

11) Ⓒ Paragraph 1 says that the brain is very complex, and that researchers "still have much to discover." Therefore, we can come to a conclusion that the brain *is still not fully understood*.

12) Ⓓ Paragraph 2 says that the brain is "0.5 kilograms at birth" but "increases to 1.4 kilograms" at age six. Therefore, we can conclude that *the brain is not completely formed at birth*.

13) Ⓒ The third sentence supplies additional information ("Also…") about the papers' content (i.e., "less advertising.") Yet, content has not been mentioned. Thus, the added sentence should precede it.

14) Ⓗ Paragraph 2 states that American newspapers were typically sold for about 6 cents a copy. Thus, the statement "This was far more than working people could afford" would logically follow.

15) Ⓒ Because Steinbeck wrote a novel in which workers are starving and brutally controlled, we can clearly assume that he *thought that the California farm economy was unjust*.

16) Ⓑ The passage states that the book was "burned and banned," but it still "won prizes and awards"; thus, most Americans probably *had strong opinions* either for or against it.

17) Ⓓ The phrase "This overall structure" in the added sentence sums up the *effect* of plastics' molecular structure. It

should come just after the description of the structure.

18) Ⓖ The added sentence lists a disadvantage of using plastics for manufactured products. Thus, it should come directly after the sentence stating that plastics "have some disadvantages."

19) Ⓐ Paragraph 1 describes people who are suffering because they have no other choice but to use bacteria-filled water. This demonstrates that as there is less clean water, people will have *to rely on dirtier water*.

20) Ⓑ From Paragraph 2, we know that people are inventing products that produce clean water. It implies that *people are trying to adapt to environmental changes*.

Chapter 7 Purpose

1) PER	6) CR
2) DES	7) DES
3) CR	8) DES
4) PER	9) CR
5) DES	10) PER

1) Ⓓ The second sentence says that "actors wear masks" to show emotions. The author uses ancient Greece as an *example* of a place where theater masks were used for that purpose.

2) Ⓑ The passage says that city planners try to "*predict*" changes "such as" (an example) "changes in population."

3) Ⓓ The main topic is the Moon; the author mentions Earth to *contrast* features of the Moon to features of the Earth.

4) Ⓐ The author is showing that the person he is talking about, Dr. Fitzgerald, called exercise a "cure," but not that the author himself called it that. In other words, it is Dr. Fitzgerald's *opinion*.

5) Ⓒ If Freud's work is both "influential" and "debated," it shows that his work is well known and has prompted people to come to conclusions. This demonstrates that he has affected, or *influenced*, modern psychology.

6) Ⓑ After science is mentioned, the author introduces myths, beginning with the word "But." These are clues that the author is using science *to contrast with myths*.

7) Ⓒ The passage is about the history of domesticating cats, and mentions that Egypt was likely the place of *origin* of this practice, or the place where it first started.

8) Ⓑ Jeans and sneakers are used as an example of clothing more commonly worn in America, in contrast to Arab Americans' homeland. Thus, the wearing of jeans and sneakers supports the claim made in the first sentence.

9) Ⓐ The author mentions Chares because he is the sculptor who "started construction on" the statue, or who *created* it.

10) Ⓐ The first sentence focuses on what "democracy" means, and the author mentions Lincoln because the brief phrase adds details that may *describe democracy in greater detail*.

Chapter 8 Paraphrase

1) A	2) A	3) A	4) B	5) A
6) B	7) B	8) B	9) A	10) B

1) Ⓒ The sentence states that "many schools provide good libraries," while some do not have "adequate" (good enough) ones, so some are better than others.

2) Ⓐ The sentence's main idea is that *many jobs* "require additional schooling," or *education after high school*.

3) Ⓓ The word "although" suggests contradiction, as in a hot place that still gets snow. The answer starts with *despite*, which has the same meaning.

4) Ⓒ The sentence tells us that biographies are supposed to describe "what" the subject did and "why" the person did it – in other words, it *provides the facts of a person's life*.

5) Ⓓ Someone who has "ability and excellence" is *highly talented*, and "many different fields" is similar to *multiple areas*.

6) Ⓐ If the phrase "The only source of knowledge is experience" is reversed, it still has the same meaning, as in "Experience is the only source of knowledge" or "*Experience is the only way to learn*."

7) Ⓒ The passage says that there is a "trend," or direction of change, toward using fewer punctuation

marks. So people are not using the marks as much as they did "in the past" (*used to*).

8) Ⓓ The word "despite" is close in meaning to *no matter what*; and the phrase "struggle to survive" suggests not "financial difficulties."

9) Ⓑ The phrase "once thought to be a worthless desert" suggests that people no longer think that way. As it is now "prosperous," or rich, it is *more valuable than people predicted*.

10) Ⓑ A horse has *a wide vision field* due to the location of its eyes "on the sides of its head," but it does have "blind spots," or *limited vision in some areas* as well.

1) Ⓒ The tone of the passage is neutral – not praising, criticizing, or warning. The passage merely *describes* what the Sioux are known for.

2) Ⓐ Paragraph 2 *introduces* the two Sioux tribes, but does not mention their lifestyles, leaders, or cultures.

3) Ⓒ Paragraph 1 provides examples of fish living in watery environments that are extreme opposites. We can infer from this that fish live in nearly all of Earth's waters.

4) Ⓐ The main point of Paragraph 2 is that fish differ greatly, or *have such variety*.

5) Ⓐ Animals, plants, and people are mentioned to describe how a quilt may be "decorated," or in other words, how it may look or *appear*.

6) Ⓐ Europe is mentioned as the place where immigrants to the American colonies *first learned quilting*.

7) Ⓒ The first sentence of Paragraph 1, which is the main idea, says that "Accidental injuries and deaths in the workplace have gone down within the last century," or *work environments became less risky for laborers*. Although choice [B] may seem like the answer, it is not so because it does not state anything about the workplace.

8) Ⓑ The passage says that "Industries…improved their safety techniques," *an industrial change*, and that "Companies…offer more desk jobs now," an *economic change*. Furthermore, as "there are more deaths from accidents in the home than on the job" these days, we can say that *job safety has improved more than home safety*.

9) Ⓓ The author states that the name "*locoweed*" comes from Spanish, not that the plant comes from Spain. By italicizing the word, the author is indicating that the word is from a foreign language.

10) Ⓐ The final sentence tells us that locoweed's poisonous effect is possibly due to the absorption of selenium. Therefore, selenium is mentioned *to explain why locoweed is poisonous*.

11) Ⓓ The passage says that toys "have played a big role in children's lives," because children can have fun while learning. In other words, *toys have always been beneficial* (good) *learning tools*.

12) Ⓓ Paragraph 2 says that until the early 1900s (20th century), toys were made by parents or crafters. In other words, the *toys were made by hand*, not by factories.

13) Ⓒ By stating "the father of," the author is indicating that Henry Ford started something. In this case, Henry Ford was "the *father* of the American automobile industry," which implies that he *launched* or started the American car industry.

14) Ⓓ In the second paragraph, the author tells us that Ford's views were "inappropriate," meaning improper. The author is giving a negative opinion of Ford, or *criticizing* him.

15) Ⓑ Paragraph 1 says that African Americans who were enslaved developed many songs called spirituals, many of which were about freedom (*religious songs about freedom*).

16) Ⓐ Paragraph 2 says that slaves used stories (*metaphor*) to voice their true feelings (*as a way of their expression*).

17) Ⓑ "Modern lifestyles" refers to nearly every activity we engage in, so the author uses it to show how *important* measuring time is to everything we do.

18) Ⓐ Paragraph 2 says that clocks throughout the world

show different times. The author asks us to imagine the opposite ("Suppose that they all did show the same time") to demonstrate a problem and thus emphasize the need for time zones.

19) Ⓓ Paragraph 1 provides details about a *large continent* existing in the past, which "consisted of land such as Antarctica, Australia, New Zealand…" (*Many continents and islands*).

20) Ⓑ Paragraph 2 gives fossils as evidence that can support the theory discussed in Paragraph 1. It says that a certain type of fossils can be found "not only in Antarctica, but also in India, South America…" (*in different regions of the world*).

Chapter 9 Summary

Warm Up   p. 107
1) 2   **2)** 1   **3)** 3   **4)** 1   **5)** 3
6) 1   **7)** 1   **8)** 2   **9)** 3   **10)** 2

Quick Practice   p. 109
1) 1, 3, 6 The passage indicates that the Europeans came to North America because some did not have "land of their own to farm and lived in poverty" (*few economic opportunities at home*); "some were tired of constant wars" (*wanted to escape conflict*); and "some held religious beliefs that were outlawed" (*wanted religious freedom*).

2) 3, 4, 5 The passage provides reasons that small businesses are beneficial: they allow people to "make more money" (*tend to pay a higher salary*); "may create fewer environmental problems" (*less pollution*); and "give people a sense of control" (*empower people personally*).

3) 1, 2, 5 The passage states that people learn a new language because it "may delay memory loss in old age" (*improves memory among elderly people*); helps "foreign-language learners also acquire more knowledge of their own language" (*improves understanding of a person's native language*); and learning a new language "increases one's opportunity for…communication" (*improves a person's communication abilities with other cultures*).

4) 1, 3, 4 The passage describes

three challenges during adolescence. First, "Many adolescents experiment with alcohol or tobacco" (*start to drink or smoke*). Some violate the law (*commit crimes*). Finally, it is a time to learn "about oneself as a sexual being" (*figure out their sexuality*).

5) 2, 3, 4 The passage gives three examples for why Roosevelt was criticized by some Americans. First, they believed that he "gave the federal government too much power" (*relied too much on the federal government*). Second, they felt that he was "taking over rights belonging to the states" (*disrespected state governments*). And third, they feared that "his… programs would lead to socialism" (*destroying capitalism*).

6) 1, 2, 5 Three examples of current-day effects of colonialism are former colonies still speaking "the language of their former colonizers" (*discourages local languages*); former colonies struggling "because they were less developed economically" (*prevents economic self-sufficiency*); and creation of "borders that are not of their choosing" (*establishes unnatural boundaries of countries*).

7) 2, 3, 6 Some people object to animal experimentation because they "believe that there are more useful research methods" (*they feel that there are better ways to perform laboratory experiments*). They believe that the "benefits gained from it are trivial" (*little can be learned from it*). And they "say that it causes animals to suffer" (*they do not like they way it affects animals*).

8) 1, 3, 5 The passage states that infrared radiation has "a longer wavelength and a lower frequency than" visible radiation, so *it differs from visible light waves*. Using "some goggles, cameras, and telescopes," infrared radiation *can be presented visually*. And infrared radiation emits from "anything that is warmer than its surroundings," so *it radiates from warm objects and people*.

9) 3, 4, 6 According to the passage, crocodilian nests "emit heat as they decompose," so they *warm the eggs by decomposing*. Moreover, "The temperature of the nest determines" *the offspring's gender*,

or "whether the babies will be male or female." Additionally, a nest made from "leaves" produces "males," while one made from "marsh grasses" produces "females," so *nests' materials decay at varying temperatures*.

10) 1, 5, 6 The passage states that drugs used to enhance athletic performance are "illegal" (*are unlawful when used in competitive sports*), and they "can lead to the development of physical characteristics of the opposite sex (*can cause male athletes to develop feminine traits*), as well as life-threatening heart and liver problems (*can lead to severe health problems*)."

Chapter 10 Organization

Warm Up   p. 121
1) Desktop: 1, 6   Laptop: 3, 4
2) Angry: 3, 6   Happy: 2, 5
3) Nose: 2, 3   Eye: 1, 6
4) Car: 2, 6   Motorcycle: 1, 5
5) Trees: 1, 5   Flowers: 2, 4
6) Halloween: 1, 3   Christmas: 4, 5
7) Spring: 1, 4   Winter: 3, 5
8) Skateboard: 1, 4   Snowboard: 2, 6
9) Desert: 1, 4   Forest: 3, 5
10) Rural: 2, 3   Urban: 1, 5

Quick Practice   p. 123
1) Angiosperms: 1, 4
    Gymnosperms: 2, 3, 6
Angiosperms "produce seeds in a protective case" (*shielded seeds*) and "make up the majority of all plants" (*include most plants*). Gymnosperms produce seeds that are "contained in cones" (*cones that have seeds inside*); "usually spread by the wind" (*wind distributes their seeds*); and "unprotected" (*have bare seeds*).

2) Butterflies: 2, 4
    Moths: 1, 6, 7
The passage states that both moths and butterflies have three-part bodies, so choice 5 is incorrect. Butterflies "have thin (*slim*) bodies," "feed during the day" (*eat in the daytime*), and "rest their wings upright" (*standing*). Moths "have thick (*bulky*) bodies," "feed during the night" (*look for food in the darkness*), and "rest their wings outspread" (*extended*).

3) Tragedy: 2, 3
    Comedy: 1, 4, 6
While the passage tells us that

tragedies have imperfect heroes who die, the passage does not mention the opposite for comedies (e.g., a perfect hero who does not die). Tragedy has "an overall somber mood, with some moments of comedy" (*is mostly serious, sometimes funny,*) and has a "flawed" (*imperfect*) hero who dies. Comedy "tries to provoke laughter, but also can have serious moments" (*has the goal of making people chuckle* and is *mostly funny, sometimes serious*) and "ends with a happy resolution" (*has a happy ending*).

4) Trojan horse: 2, 4, 7
   Computer worm: 1, 3
According to the passage, Malware is "harmful." In other words, the programs harm computers, thus they are not useful. A Trojan horse "may present itself as… useful software" (*pretends to be helpful*), but it "may steal, spy, or install other software" (*damage or take personal information* and *set up unwanted programs*). Worms can "duplicate," or *reproduce* themselves, and "clog a network" (*blocks a network with useless material*).

5) Stone Age: 2, 6
   Bronze Age: 1, 5, 7
During the Stone Age, people "pounded stone against stone to make tools" (*relied on hitting rocks to craft things*), and "used wood, bone, shells, plants, deer antlers, and animal skins"(*used bones and other animal parts*). During the Bronze Age, people could "create tough tools and materials in any shape imaginable, such as better axes…buildings" (*able to make a variety of metal tools* and *constructed stronger buildings*) and could "increase economic activity" (*developed more expanded economies*).

6) Brown algae: 2, 5, 6
   Green algae: 3, 4
Brown algae "grow in oceans where there are mild climates" (*relatively warm salt water*); are used to make food and cosmetics (*food and makeup*); and "can grow 60 meters up from the seafloor" (*can be very tall*). Most green algae "live in lakes or streams" (*grow mostly in fresh water*), and can cover an entire (*whole*) lake.

7) Road maps: 4, 5, 7
   Street maps: 2, 6
Road maps "*show* interstate *highways*" and local *highways*." They also show "cities and local attractions connected by these roads," which can show *a larger area in less detail* and *how to get to a town or city*. On the other hand, street maps "show a smaller area in great detail" (*show areas, such as neighborhoods, in detail*) and are used to "find an address" (*used to find specific addresses*).

8) Ethics: 1, 2, 6
   Aesthetics: 3, 4
Ethics deals with "human conduct" (*behavior of people*); asks "What is good and what is bad?" (*makes distinctions between good and bad*); and since ethics looks at ideas of "right and wrong," it *explores the moral aspect of what people should do*. Aesthetics "deals with art" (*painting and music*), and asks "what makes something beautiful" (*why an object is attractive*).

9) Fixed-blade knives: 1, 6
   Folding knives: 3, 4, 7
Fixed means that something *does not move*, so fixed-blade knives *have blades that do not move*. These knives are also "usually carried around in a sheath" (*knife cover*). Folding knives "have blades (i.e., *more than one blade*) that close," or *fold into a handle*, and a pin that "holds the blades to the handle" (*secured with a tiny metal stick*).

10) Tile games: 2, 3, 5
   Target games: 1, 6
Tile games such as dominoes and mahjong "have tiles marked by numbers or patterns" (*use objects with some kind of markings*). Players of tile games also have to *link game pieces together* because the goal is to "earn points by combining tiles" or getting rid of all of their tiles (*may involve winning by having nothing*).Target games require players "to get their object closest to a target" (*require players to aim carefully*), and includes games such as "bowling" that *may require a player to roll a ball at objects*.

Exercises Ch. 9-10   p. 129

1) 1, 3, 6 According to the passage, mammals keep plant-eaters' populations under control (*consume plant-eaters*), fertilize the soil with their bodies and bones (*improve the quality of soil*), and scatter or bury seeds (*move seeds around*).

2) Agricultural fairs: 1, 5, 6
   Trade fairs: 2, 3
The passage says that agricultural fairs are popular in "North America" (including *Canada and the U.S.*); have "rides and games" (*provide entertainment to attendees*); and "have contests for crops, livestock, and home-cooked food" (*focus on cooking and the farming industry*). Trade fairs "focus on a specific product or industry" (*emphasize a particular product or business*), and "limit fair attendance" (*are usually not open to the public*).

3) 3, 4, 5 From the passage, people collect books because "they love them" (*love and enjoy books*), are "interested in a specific type of books" (*have great interest in a particular writer or field*), or "hope their books will increase in value" (*believe that books are good investments*).

4) De Stijl: 5, 7
   Art Deco: 3, 4, 6
The passage says that De Stijl used "rectangular shapes" and "three primary colors" (*was limited in shape and color*), and that it influenced (*affected*) other fashions of the 1900s (*the 20th century*). Art Deco combined (*mixed*) styles from ancient Egypt and Africa (*other cultures*); blended steel, ivory, bronze, and wood (*was made out of many materials*); and used "machine design" (*sometimes looked like machinery*).

5) 2, 3, 4 The passage says that NATO's original purpose was to "discourage (*prevent*) an attack by the Soviet Union" and then to resolve international conflicts (*keeping the peace*) and "developing international security policies" (*create plans for global defense*).

6) Social bees: 1, 5, 7
   Solitary bees: 2, 4
The passage says that social bees "have strict hierarchies" (*are organized into hierarchies*); may have "as many as 80,000 members" (*may have thousands in one colony*); and include "stingless bees and bumblebees." Solitary bees "live alone" (*do not like to live with other bees*), and "there are no special workers" (*they do not have any worker bees*).

7) 1, 3, 5 The passage says that the deep sea waters are "just above freezing" (*always at a very low temperature*), create "enough pressure to crush the bodies of most life forms" (*possesses great crushing pressures*), and its creatures live "in total darkness" (*it is extremely dark all the time*).

8) Alpaca: 2, 4
   Llama: 1, 3, 5
According to the passage, alpacas are "selectively bred" for their fur, so *they are raised mainly for their coat*, and they are "about half the size of llamas, weighing no more than about 84 kilograms," so they *weigh under 100 kilograms*. Llamas, on the other hand, are "tough," or *strong and hardy*, "they make effective guard animals," so they *protect some other animals*, and they are "very intelligent," so they are *especially smart*.

9) 1, 3, 6 The passage says that some scholars "say that the idea for labor unions came from European medieval craft guilds" (*may have originated from groups of people who handcrafted quality goods*). Some feel that labor unions were formed "when market competition caused companies to cut worker pay" (*may have started because of reduced income*). And some think that labor unions were formed because "factory owners had too much power over individual employees" (*may have begun to counter unethical employers*).

10) Warded locks: 2, 5, 7
   Card access locks: 3, 4
The passage says that warded locks have "obstacles called 'wards' that block wrong keys" (*have barriers inside the lock*), are "easy to open" (*not very secure*), and that "the correct key has marks that match the wards in the lock" (*they require keys with patterns*). Card access locks require "a plastic card…that has physical patterns (*a plastic card with marks*) or computerized information…to open the lock (require digital information to operate)."

Chapter 11
Actual Practice

Actual Practice 1   p. 136

1) (A) The first paragraph states that the Pawnee tribe consisted of 12,000 people in the past as compared to 3,240 members now (*once was bigger*) and "lived on rich farmland" (*excellent farmland*).

2) (D) If something is *centered* in an area, it is present in high numbers, or *concentrated*, in that location.

3) (B) The first sentence in Paragraph 2 tells us about the Pawnee houses were made of soil. The added sentence further describes the house, so it should come next.

4) (A) In the second paragraph, the author tells us that "during summer and winter months, the Pawnee left their farms and villages to hunt." We can infer that for the other half of the year, the Pawnee farmed.

5) (B) The passage informs us that the Pawnee lived in houses made of soil (*earth-covered houses*), farms and villages (*farm villages*), and teepees made of buffalo skins (*animal-skin tents*). Adobes are not mentioned.

6) (C) The word *sacred* means *holy* or divine. In Paragraph 3, we see that the Pawnee held "rituals for planting and harvesting" corn, so we can assume that they thought corn was *holy*.

7) (C) The word *it* refers to *corn* discussed in the preceding sentence. This makes sense: "There were rituals for planting and harvesting" *corn*.

8) (A) In Paragraph 3, the author tells us that "corn was a sacred gift" and that "there were rituals for planting and harvesting it." Thus, we can assume that corn was most important to the Pawnee.

9) (B) In Paragraph 3, the author states that the Pawnee "practiced human sacrifice" as one of their many religious ceremonies. This fact shows their strong commitment (*devotion*) to their religion.

10) (D) The last two sentences in Paragraph 3 states that ceremo-

nies for successful buffalo hunting included "*days of nonstop dancing*," or days of dancing without stopping.

11) (B) If something is forced, it is accomplished by coercion. Therefore, the U.S. government moved the Pawnee rather than the Pawnee moving themselves, so they likely *did not move to Nebraska willingly*.

12) 1, 2, 6 According to Paragraph 2, the Pawnee lived in villages and left for hunting (*settled, but took hunting trips*). According to Paragraph 3, they had religious ceremonies for corn and buffalo hunts (*ceremonies for good farming and hunting*). According to paragraph 4, they were forced to move first to Nebraska, and then to Oklahoma (*forced to move away from their homeland*).

Actual Practice 2   p. 138

1) (C) The verb *conduct* means to perform or *carry out* something. So, the federal and local governments must *carry out* their meetings as openly as possible.

2) (B) The laws are not actually about sunshine; the quotation marks indicate that the phrase is a *metaphor* for letting the public see what is happening.

3) (A) In Paragraph 2, the author traces the history of sunshine laws. The added sentence should introduce the specific details about where the laws were first passed.

4) (C) In Paragraph 2, Florida and Alabama are mentioned to *describe* places where the law originated.

5) (C) According to Paragraph 2, "states gradually began passing" open meeting laws, and eventually "All states… followed" Florida's and Alabama's open meeting laws. Thus, we can infer that *citizens were interested in the government activities* discussed at these meetings.

6) (D) From the information provided in the passage, sunshine laws were passed to stop government secrecy, to allow the public to attend government meetings, and to prevent scandals such as Watergate. There is no mention of *making government officials more efficient*.

7) (A) Because Paragraph 2 gives

a chronological progression of sunshine laws in the U.S., we can conclude that it is elaborating upon how the laws gained acceptance (*spread*) over time.

8) (B) The word *vary* means to be different or unlike, or *to differ*. Thus, if sunshine laws *vary*, we can say that they *differ* from one another.

9) (B) The sentence containing *authorize* discusses when a meeting can be closed to the public; thus, it discusses the circumstances that allow, or *permit*, a meeting to be closed.

10) (A) Paragraph 3's main topic is different types of sunshine laws. Each of the supporting sentences describes a type: some do this, others allow that, and "Many also allow…." Thus, *many* refers to *sunshine laws*.

11) (D) In the last sentence of Paragraph 3, the author tells us that sunshine laws allow closed meetings for certain topics such as "personnel matters," or something involving employees. *Employee salaries* would be one example of this.

12) 2, 4, 6 In Paragraph 3, the author tells us that sunshine laws vary. Some "allow the public to attend all meetings" (*attend any and all meetings of the board*), others allow "early meetings to be closed as long as the final vote is taken in public" (*discuss a topic among themselves, yet vote publicly*), and still others "allow closed meetings on certain topics, such as personnel matters" (*discuss issues about their own employees behind closed doors*).

Actual Practice 3   p. 140

1) (D) Quotation marks are used here to provide us with the *translation* of the phrase *La Dolce Vita*, which is the title of the film.

2) (A) If a movie was *released*, it means that the movie was made available for people to see. Closest in meaning is *circulated*.

3) (C) The phrase *upper class*, like the phrase *high society*, is commonly used to refer to rich groups of a society.

4) (B) The referent of the pronoun *he* in the added sentence is "the main character, Marcello" in the

second sentence in Paragraph 2. Logically, it should come next: "The main character, Marcello… writes about famous people's lives. *He (Marcello) meets many glamorous people.*"

5) (A) The film (*film's theme*) suggests that most people prefer (*choose*) what is "entertaining" (*fun*) over what is "important" (*meaningful work*).

6) (D) We can infer that Fellini *wants to portray a conflicted character* based on the information in Paragraph 2, which claims, "Marcello wants to write important… news, but he also wants to be part of the…'sweet life.'" Thus, he is *conflicted* about his goals in life.

7) (B) Paragraph 2 states, "The main character, Marcello, works as a gossip columnist, or a journalist who writes about famous people's lives." From this, we know that he is a *writer*.

8) (B) The author says that the movie drew attention because it was *nonlinear*, that is, the scenes were out of order. From that, we can infer that the author mentioned "nonlinear" to *illustrate how the film was unusual*.

9) (D) According to the passage, the film was banned because it mocked religion. Many countries believe that religion is sacred, and that people should not *make fun of* it, so we can deduce that *mock* means *make fun of*.

10) (C) The word *it* refers to the *movie* discussed in the preceding sentence. This makes sense: "However, because the film's characters seem to mock religion, some countries banned the *movie*."

11) (D) According to Paragraph 2, the movie included famous people in high society and places like nightclubs, cafes, and castles. So, choices [A] and [C] are true. According to Paragraph 3, the word *paparazzi* came from this movie. So, choice [B] is also correct. However, the passage does not say that the movie has been *ignored*, so we can see that choice [D] is the negative fact.

12) 1, 4, 5 The film shows journalists who follow famous people (*the media reporting gossip as "news"*), shows an opening scene which seems to mock religion with

a statue of Jesus (*characters' disrespect for religious symbols*), and shows life at parties and nightclubs without meaningful relationships (*fun times, but no real personal bonds*).

Actual Practice 4   p. 142

1) Ⓑ Because the Twelve Tablets protected the rights of "all Roman citizens," rather than just wealthy or privileged members of society, we can infer that the *Romans valued fair and structured legal proceedings* for all citizens.

2) Ⓒ To *inscribe* means to *write* or carve words on the surface of an object, as in "the laws were *written* on 12 bronze tablets."

3) Ⓒ Paragraph 1 states that the "tablets reminded…citizens that their rights were protected under these laws," so the Twelve Tables protected *Roman citizens' rights*.

4) Ⓓ In Paragraph 2, the author mentions that the Twelve Tables discussed "building codes (*codes for building*), marriage (*rules for marriage*), property ownership, and crime, including murder (*punishments for crimes*)." However, the author does not mention *prices for property*.

5) Ⓐ To *draw up* something as used here means to compose or write it. Close in meaning is to *prepare* it, as in *prepared* it for people to read.

6) Ⓑ One of the meanings of the word *settle* is to resolve, as in ending a conflict. Close in meaning is to *stop*.

7) Ⓒ Paragraph 3 says that writers had memorized laws when they were boys. Thus, *Roman boys* are mentioned to trace *how the laws were preserved* so that we can read about them today.

8) Ⓒ The referent of the pronoun *they* is *Roman writers* from the previous sentence. In other words, the "writers were able to include the text in their works" because the writers had "memorized the laws in their youth."

9) Ⓑ In Paragraph 3, the first sentence informs us *when* and *why* the laws were created. Next should come a description of *who* was in charge of writing them (the *decemvirs*).

10) Ⓑ In Paragraph 3, we learn that the laws changed around 200

BCE ("laws began to be revised"). The passage does not say why, but readers can infer that the laws changed as *Roman society changed*.

11) Ⓐ The author informs us that the laws were created to "settle class conflicts." Thus, we can determine that *people wanted to ease social tension*.

12) 1, 2, 6 The passage says that the Laws of the Twelve Tables were important to Romans because they "established…the rights of Roman citizens" (*reminded Roman citizens of their legal rights*); "were based on earlier civil, criminal, and religious customs" (*put earlier traditions into writing*); and were created "to settle class conflicts" (*they helped bring peace to Rome*).

Actual Practice 5   p. 144

1) Ⓑ When *house* is used as a verb, it means to shelter or *have* something. Thus, the library "has one of the most important collections…."

2) Ⓓ The library's special focus on the years 1485 to 1715 indicates that this era was very important culturally and artistically.

3) Ⓑ In Paragraph 2, first sentence ends with *vaults*, which is plural, and second sentence starts with *It*, which is singular. Adding the new sentence in between these two sentences will provide a singular referent, and makes sense: "It (the exhibition gallery) displays many rare books…."

4) Ⓑ *Vault* here means a safe storage place for valuable things that can have air conditioning. This would be a type of *room*.

5) Ⓐ Paragraph 2 says that the books are rare, and explains how they are carefully protected from fire, other damage, and theft ("protected in fire-resistant, air-conditioned vaults"). We can infer that the books must be very *valuable*.

6) Ⓐ The passage says that the library contains books including those written by and about Shakespeare (Choices [B] and [C]), as well as "paintings" from the Elizabethan period (Choice [D]). There is no mention of material related to modern London or to photography.

7) Ⓒ Being *patterned after* something implies being built from the same plan or pattern, as in copying or imitating something. Therefore, the best choice is *looks like*.

8) Ⓓ The word *founded* means created or e*stablished*. Thus, the library was "established in 1930."

9) Ⓓ The author likely mentions Henry Folger's job as president of a major oil company to explain how he had the money to pay for (to *fund*) such a library.

10) Ⓒ In Sentence 2 of Paragraph 3, the author tells us that "Folger left his fortune," then describes how he wanted *it* spent. Thus, the referent of the pronoun *it* is Folger's (*his*) *fortune*.

11) Ⓒ The paragraph says that Folger wanted his fortune used "for the development of a great research institution" (*facility for research*).

12) 3, 4, 5 The passage says that the Folger Shakespeare Library is amazing because it has hundreds of thousands of books and scholars use it for research (*attracts scholars with its thousands of books and objects*). Also, it has rare books protected in a special way (*preserves fragile, old books and manuscripts*). Finally, it has the world's most important collection of Shakespeare's books (*preserves a valuable collection of Shakespeare's works*).

Actual Practice 6   p. 146

1) Ⓓ The word *also* in the added sentence indicates that the information is *in addition* to what was just mentioned. Thus, after describing the Rhine River, the passage should "also" mention the Danube River.

2) Ⓒ Paragraph 1 tells us that the Black Forest is a mountain area with dark pine trees and rivers. So it describes the Black Forest *physically*.

3) Ⓓ The word *noted* here means known or *famous*. Thus, the area is *famed* for its mineral springs.

4) Ⓐ According to Paragraph 2, the Black Forest "has long supported many industries," which are fueled by natural resources. Included among these are "mineral springs" and "a great deal of lumber." Thus, the Black Forest must *provide important resources*.

5) Ⓑ The word *yield* in this case

means to *produce*. Thus, "the forests *produce* a great deal of lumber."

6) Ⓐ A *quarry* is generally an above-ground site where workers dig out stone and rocks, such as marble or *granite*. The choice that is closest in meaning is *mines*.

7) Ⓒ In Paragraph 3, the author tells us that the people of the Black Forest make cuckoo clocks, toys, musical instruments, and cherry-covered chocolate cake. The only thing not mentioned is *shoes*.

8) Ⓓ To *manufacture* often means to *make* many copies of something. Thus, the people of Black Forest "*make* outstanding cuckoo clocks, toys, and musical instruments."

9) Ⓐ In Paragraph 3, the plural pronoun *they* refers to the subject of the previous sentence, "the people of the Black Forest." Thus, "*The people* also are known for their cherry-covered chocolate cake…."

10) Ⓐ If the forest has "long been an inspiration for storytellers," that means that the forest was used as an *imagined setting* for their works.

11) Ⓓ People have long called the forest "black," so we can infer that the darkness under the dense trees gave it a *mysterious* feel that inspired legends and fairy tales. The passage does not provide any information to support that the forest is funny, cold, or high.

12) Resources: 1, 5, 6
    Products: 2, 4

According to the passage, the Black Forest is noted for its mineral springs (*mineral springs attract tourists*); it yields much lumber (*forests provide wood*); and it has granite quarries (*locations have special stone*). Also, the passage indicates that the people of the Black Forest make *toys* and *musical instruments*.

Actual Practice 7   p. 148

1) Ⓓ To *aggregate* means to accumulate or *combine*. Thus, "human brain is…27 *combined* organs."

2) Ⓑ Paragraph 1 never mentions that phrenology was accurate, or whether any of Gall's theories about the brain were

tested or accurate. Thus, we can infer that phrenology operated based upon *assumptions about the brain.*

3) Ⓐ If a thing is *intrinsic,* it is part of the nature of something. The closest in meaning is *inborn.*

4) Ⓓ According to Paragraph 1, Gall created a diagram of the *organs'* locations in the skull.

5) Ⓒ *That trait* in the added sentence refers to *larger organ* in sentence 3 of Paragraph 2 ("A larger bump meant that a larger organ was underneath"), so it should come next.

6) Ⓑ The word *contour* means the shape, or *outlines* of something.

7) Ⓑ As phrenology was eventually "discredited," it was rejected, or *scientists did not accept* it in the long run.

8) Ⓓ According to Paragraph 3, phrenology was used to justify racism, sexism, and so forth. They are the *negative consequences* of the theory.

9) Ⓓ The word *it* refers to *phrenology* in the same sentence. This makes sense: "many common people liked phrenology because *phrenology* said that individuals could make some choices."

10) Ⓒ The passage says that "Gall created a diagram of the organs' locations," but not that he drew the diagram on people's heads or scalps.

11) Ⓑ The passage primarily discusses "the theory of phrenology," a *medical theory,* and how it "had a great influence on society well into the 1800s," or *its impact on 19th century thinking.*

12) 2, 4, 6 According to the passage, phrenology studied "the organ responsible for a person's level of greed was in front of the ear" (*analyzed supposed behavioral tendencies*), attracted "many common people" (*was popular among common people*); and "created a diagram of the organs' locations in the skull" (*focused on the shape of the skull*).

Actual Practice 8   p. 150

1) Ⓐ Giving *suggestions* means giving someone an idea for consideration; close in meaning is recommendation or *advice.*

2) Ⓓ According to Paragraph

1, an oracle refers to a temple, prophet, or a prophecy. However, the paragraph does not indicate that it refers to *a god.*

3) Ⓒ *On behalf of* means to speak or act *for* someone or something. Thus, "prophets had special powers to speak *for* a god."

4) Ⓑ The plural pronoun *they* is part of a sentence that continues a definition of prophets. If this referent is substituted, it makes sense: "people believed that *prophets* could tell the future."

5) Ⓐ Paragraph 1 tells us that ancient Greeks believed that they could get answers to all questions from prophets. This implies that they believed that the *gods knew much more than humans.*

6) Ⓓ From Paragraph 2, we learn that the meaning of the oracles was unclear, or confusing. Next should come the result: "*So* (as a result of this), *priests at the temple interpreted it....*"

7) Ⓒ The highlighted sentence in Paragraph 2 talks about a priestess (*female oracle*) sitting on a three-legged stool (*sat on a tripod*) over a crack (*an outlet*) that emitted volcanic gases (*that vented chemical fumes*).

8) Ⓐ The passage states that the *gas* caused her to "become dazed" and give "unclear" prophecies. Thus, we can conclude that the *gas* is mentioned to show that she was likely *intoxicated.*

9) Ⓐ If something is *puzzling,* it is like a puzzle; not easy to figure out, or *confusing.* Thus, "the meaning was usually *confusing* and unclear."

10) Ⓓ Although Paragraph 3 talks about how Greeks believed that "the god Zeus spoke through an oak tree," it does not talk about Zeus actually *living* in an oak tree.

11) Ⓑ The noun *rustle* means the slight sound made by movements of leaves, pieces of paper, or the like. Thus, the noun form *rustlings* is closest in meaning to *sounds.*

12) Oracle in Delphi: 4, 6
Oracle in Dodona: 1, 3, 7
According to Paragraph 2, the Oracle in Delphi was "the god Apollo's temple in Delphi" (*built on behalf of Apollo*), and the prophet "would sit on a three-legged stool" (*used a unique stand*). According to Paragraph 3, the Oracle in Dodona

was "dedicated to the god Zeus" (*built to honor Zeus*), the god Zeus "spoke through an oak tree" (*prophecies from a sacred tree*), and "is considered the oldest oracle in Greece" (*may have been the first Greek oracle*).

Actual Practice 9   p. 152

1) Ⓐ The topic of Paragraph 1 is econometrics, and the pronoun *it* refers to this topic. If substituted, this referent makes sense: "Business and government use *econometrics* to analyze economic activity."

2) Ⓓ Paragraph 2 says econometricians might have a belief. Then they would turn it into a formula. Logically, the added sentence should go here, as next they (the econometricians) would study using the formula.

3) Ⓐ The word *data* refers to *information* used for a particular calculation or form of reasoning.

4) Ⓒ If something works or operates, it is *operational.* Thus, it can be used, or is *usable.* This makes sense: Econometrics "uses statistical data to prove that those relationships are *usable.*"

5) Ⓓ Paragraph 2 says that "econometrics puts economic relationships into an intricate mathematical form" and uses data to "prove that those relationships are operational." From this information, we can infer that the relationships are *complicated.*

6) Ⓑ In Paragraph 2, the author explains econometrics by describing *its use.* For example, econometrics could be *used* to predict how much a certain increase in income will affect a person's spending.

7) Ⓐ The correct answer simply switches the order of the phrases in the sentence without changing the sentence's meaning. Choice [A] makes it clear that an increase in income also increases spending without including irrelevant information.

8) Ⓓ A *factor* is one thing that contributes to a result; factors in an economy could include buyers, sellers, employers, and many more *parts* of it.

9) Ⓓ In Paragraph 3, the author tells us that models describe the "economy of a community (*a

small town*), a nation (*a country*), or the world (*the global community*)." However, *an uninhabited region* is not mentioned in the passage.

10) Ⓒ The last sentence in Paragraph 3 tells us that "econometricians use computers to make calculations." Hence, computers are mentioned to *show how econometricians work.*

11) Ⓐ The passage states that "controlled experiments" are used when models "do not match real-world results." In other words, they are used *when data from real situations is unsatisfactory.*

12) 1, 2, 6 Econometrics applies mathematics to economic theory by putting "economic relationships into an intricate mathematical form" (*states economic relationships*), and stating "this relationship in a formula" (*requires mathematical formulas*). Paragraph 1 also says that business and government use it (*valuable for private and public agencies*).

Actual Practice 10   p. 154

1) Ⓑ Sentence 3 in Paragraph 1 elaborates on what the added sentence says, starting with "additionally," so the added sentence should come before that sentence.

2) Ⓑ One of the meanings of a *body* is a group of people organized for some purpose. Groups of people organized to pass and use laws are usually referred to as *governing groups,* or "elected bodies."

3) Ⓐ Building *features* are the ways that structures are designed, such as the height or style. Close in meaning is the word *characteristics.*

4) Ⓒ According to the passage, zoning controls many things such as how tall buildings should be (*building measurements*), how the building should look, and also such things as *building features,* restrictions, and *usage.* However, zoning does not control the inside features, or *building interiors.*

5) Ⓒ According to Paragraph 2, city planners do many things to make cities organized and

ANSWER KEYS | 185

appealing. Therefore, we can assume that they are *very important to cities' growth*.

6) (A) The word *coordinate* means to make things work well as a whole, or *organize*. Thus, city planers organize cities' growth and development.

7) (B) The highlighted part shows *what city planners* exactly *do* for their jobs.

8) (C) The word *they*, which is the subject of this subordinate clause, refers to the subject of the main clause, *city planners*.

9) (C) To *accommodate* a need is to try to fill it, or *satisfy* it. So, city planners "*satisfy* people's needs in the city."

10) (A) Paragraph 3 says that zoning became important as population grew. So, if New York passed its first zoning law in 1916, then we can infer that it *had a large population* at that time.

11) (C) Paragraph 3 says that "many cities around the world (*globally*) have zoning laws."

12) 1, 5, 6 The passage indicates that zoning "coordinates cities in an appealing way" (*keeps urban areas attractive*); that elected bodies pass and use zoning laws (*decided by elected city councils*); and that "city planners have to know how to organize the construction of necessary water and power facilities" (*helps cities provide appropriate resources*).

Actual Practice 11   p. 156

1) (B) The sentence that follows [A] introduces SETI, but does not describe the acronym, and the sentence following [B] contains the pronoun "its," which refers to SETI, the subject of the added sentence. Thus, the added sentence should be placed at [B].

2) (A) According to Paragraph 1, SETI wants "to determine whether life has developed anywhere other than Earth" (*searching for life forms beyond Earth*), and to serve "the interested public audience" (*educating the public*). They are also "privately financed." However, *water* is not mentioned anywhere in Paragraph 1.

3) (B) In Paragraph 1, the author tells us that researchers

at the institute are interested in determining "if life has developed" elsewhere in space. We can conclude that *they are curious*.

4) (C) The word *occur* means to *happen*, as it makes sense that many projects in a research institute would be *happening* "at the same time."

5) (D) Because *Project Phoenix* is described as one of SETI's "largest projects," which lasted nine years, we can conclude that the author mentions the undertaking to *give an example of an ambitious SETI project*, even if it did not succeed in its goal of detecting alien signals.

6) (B) In Paragraph 2, the author tells us that "more than 100 different projects are occurring at the SETI Institute at the same time." From this statement, we can infer that the SETI Institute *is eager to conduct many research projects about the unknown*.

7) (A) To *detect* means to discover or to identify the existence of something. Hence, the correct choice is *find*.

8) (C) Because Project Phoenix "tried to detect," or search for, "signals," we can determine the statement "*none* were found" refers back to the detection of *signals*. Therefore, *none* refers to the radio *signals*.

9) (C) Paragraph 3 says that SETI is "in partnership with" UC Berkeley; thus, the two organizations are *sharing* the project.

10) (B) *Array* means a display or range of things, or a *group* of them.

11) (A) If the new antennas mentioned in Paragraph 3 can "increase the institute's ability to search for signals," we can infer that it will also *increase the quantity of data available to SETI Institute*.

12) 2, 5, 6 According to the passage, Project Phoenix "tried to detect radio signals from intelligent beings" (*searched for radio signals*); was "One of the organization's largest projects" (*was one of SETI's largest projects*); and found "no signals" (*found no evidence of life*).

Actual Practice 12   p. 158

1) (B) The term "lucky charm"

is introduced in the added sentence. So, it should come before the sentence that gives examples of lucky charms.

2) (A) In Paragraph 1, "four-leaf clovers, coins, and horseshoes" are mentioned as examples of well-known (*common*) lucky charms.

3) (C) The author gives us several examples of charms, which include four-leaf clovers (*unusual plant*), coins (*coinage*), and horseshoes (*U-shaped metal shoes*). However, *special powers* is not used as an example.

4) (D) Here, the word *treated* means to act or behave toward something in a certain way. How a person acts toward something shows how he or she thinks about it or *considers* it.

5) (B) The word *particular* is used to emphasize one *specific* thing.

6) (B) A frog is an amphibian, and Paragraph 2 states that "Native Americans…think of the frog as lucky." Thus, *specific amphibians* are considered lucky.

7) (D) The word *draw* here means to pull, or attract. The word *wealth* means fortune, or money. So, the expression *draws wealth* can be substituted with *attracts money*.

8) (A) Paragraph 2 introduces two examples of lucky charms, a frog and Jin Chan, by telling stories about them. From this, we can infer that charms are *often from stories and legends*.

9) (C) "Although many people may think of charms as mere superstition (*People may say they do not believe in lucky charms*), they may value charms more than they realize (*yet still use them*)."

10) (C) In Paragraph 3, the author says that many people value charms "more than they admit" and gives dream catchers as an example.

11) (D) The word *they* refers to *dream catchers*, which precedes *they* in the sentence. This makes sense: "*dream catchers* are believed to "catch" nightmares…."

12) 2, 3, 5 According to the passage, "objects that are treated as charms differ from one society to another" (*differ from culture to culture*); people may "have a

pair of "lucky" socks or a "lucky" necktie" just in case it brings good luck and use "dream catchers because they are believed to "catch" nightmares"(*are believed to help their owners*); and people "may value charms more than they admit" (*are still used today*).

Chapter 12 Actual Test

Reading 1   p. 161

1) (D) To *dispute* something means to question whether something is true, or to disagree with something. However, *dispute* here is used as a noun. Thus, close in meaning to disputes is *arguments*.

2) (D) Because Paragraph 1 states that trial by combat "was a legal fight between two people," we can safely assume that trial by combat was NOT *an illegitimate ancient practice*.

3) (A) If you *appoint* someone, you are selecting or *choosing* that person for a job or task. Thus, "Nobles, women, and priests often *chose* trained fighters…."

4) (B) Since "Nobles, women, and priests often appointed trained fighters…to represent *them*," *them* must refer to *nobles, women, and priests*.

5) (B) Generally, when a word is italicized, it is either being emphasized or defined within the passage. Because "*champions*" follows "trained fighters," we can deduce that *champions* clarifies, or *defines* the previous phrase.

6) (C) The passage says that "Nobles, women, and priests often appointed trained fighters." Thus, the passage states that the ones who mostly participated in trial by combat were the *experienced fighters*.

7) (A) Because "nobles, women, and priests often appointed fighters…to represent them in combat," we can infer that these people *did not think that they should have to fight* if someone else could fight for them instead.

8) (B) The main idea presented in the highlighted portion states that "trial by ordeal" was an alternative judgment system in Europe; in other words, it was a way to *"discover" guilty individuals*.

9) (D) Paragraph 2 describes

trial by ordeal, or torture. The injured person "was considered innocent if the resulting injuries healed in three days." Next should come the other possibility: *If the wounds remained, the person was thought to be guilty.*

10) Ⓐ Paragraph 2 explains trial by ordeal by explaining the process that individuals went through. Because a process is *how something works*, we can determine that [A] is the correct answer.

11) Ⓑ To *subject* someone to something means to *force* him or her to experience it. A similar meaning is the idiom *put through*.

12) Ⓒ When something happens "gradually," it occurs in a *slow shift*. Furthermore, "trial by jury" is described as a *new practice* in medieval Europe.

13) Trial by combat: 1
Trial by ordeal: 4, 6
Trial by jury: 2, 7
Trial by combat described a system in which "God would help the honest and innocent person win," which means the *virtuous person would win*. Trial by ordeal involved "physical torture," or *making the accused suffer*, and was used "during witch trials." Finally, trial by jury involved "12 neighbors (*a dozen citizens*) who were invited to help settle questions of land ownership (*decide rightful ownership of land*)."

Reading 2   p. 164

14) Ⓐ Because Bruce "humorously attacked the hypocrisy in society," we can determine that he used *funny criticisms* of society in his comedy.

15) Ⓒ *Hypocrisy* is a false impression of moral character. The next sentence describes people's false claims to be good. Therefore, *falseness* is closest in meaning.

16) Ⓐ The highlighted portion focuses on Bruce's "expanding the subject matter" of comedy by discussing "politics" and "religion." Thus, he used *comedy to talk about a wide variety of serious issues*.

17) Ⓒ The word *obscene* usually refers to something that offends others or is *offensive*. This makes sense: Lenny Bruce "used many words that are considered *offensive*."

18) Ⓓ The pronoun *others* refers to the subject of the preceding sentence, *His fans*. The two sentences together express the idea that *some* people were admirers (*fans*) of Bruce, while *others* (people besides fans) were not.

19) Ⓑ The term *subject matter* means what is written, discussed, or talked about, as in *topics*.

20) Ⓑ Because Bruce was "arrested four times for using obscene language," we can infer that his stand-up comedy did not provide *an example of what people should be like*.

21) Ⓒ Because Bruce's autobiography modifies the title of a popular book from *How to Win Friends and Influence People* to *How to Talk Dirty and Influence People*, we can infer that he adopted a *humorous attitude toward his own obscenity.*

22) Ⓐ The opening sentence in Paragraph 3 tells us where Bruce was born. A sentence informing us of Bruce's real or birth name would logically follow.

23) Ⓑ The word *career* refers to someone's occupation or *profession*. This makes sense: Bruce "began his *profession*…as a master of ceremonies."

24) Ⓐ If Bruce's "material was too controversial for…television programs," then the programs of the time were likely *culturally conservative* and did not want him using bad language.

25) Ⓒ Paragraph 3 states that Bruce was arrested "for using obscene language." Something that is "obscene" is *indecent*, so Bruce used an *indecent vocabulary onstage*.

26) 1, 3, 4 The passage says Lenny Bruce was "arrested four times for using obscene language" (*was arrested for his comedy*); overdosed "on illegal drugs" (*took illegal substances*); and "attacked the hypocrisy in society" (*criticized people's behavior and society*).

Reading 3   p. 167

27) Ⓐ Paragraph 1 states that "no new [mammal] discoveries had been made in half a century." Because scientists just discovered this mammal recently, it must have been *surprising*.

28) Ⓑ *Remote* here means far away from urban areas; these will be more *isolated* from humans.

29) Ⓒ Paragraph 3 states that "saolas appear to resemble antelopes." Thus, the word *antelope* is used as a *comparison to describe the saola's appearance*.

30) Ⓑ To *speculate* about something means to think deeply about it, or *theorize*. This makes sense because researchers can only *theorize* what they have not discovered through extensive research and experiments.

31) Ⓐ The highlighted portion explains why the saola was given its particular name. Because only [A] accurately summarizes the name's origin, it must be correct.

32) Ⓓ Something that is *sturdy* has a *strong*-looking build. Thus, the saola has a *strong* neck.

33) Ⓓ According to Paragraph 3, the animal has a red-brown body, a black line running down its back, and white markings on its face. The only color that is not mentioned is *gray*.

34) Ⓒ The pronoun *them* refers to the just-mentioned *scent glands* that are located "on each side of the snout." Substituting this referent makes sense: "Saolas can rub *scent glands* on plants and rocks to leave their scent."

35) Ⓑ According to Paragraph 4, the saola has been illegally hunted because of the belief that its horns can be used for healing purposes. Thus, we can assume that hunters want to sell the *horns*.

36) Ⓐ Because Paragraph 3 states that saolas are "now considered a severely endangered species" due to factors such as illegal hunting and road construction, we can deduce that they *are not safe in their current environment*.

37) Ⓒ The expression "This has led to" in the added sentence indicates that there should be a cause before it. So, the added sentence should logically follow the sentences mentioning hunting and road construction.

38) Ⓒ If something is *endangered*, it is in danger of dying out.

Similar in meaning is *threatened*. This makes sense because saolas are *threatened* by illegal hunting and construction.

39) 2, 3, 5 According to the passage, the saola "is now a severely endangered species" (*in danger of becoming extinct*), has "huge scent glands, the largest among mammals" (*has scent glands that are extremely big in size compared with other mammals*), and "lives in the remote forests of Vietnam and Laos" (*lives only in wilderness areas of Vietnam and Laos*).

SIMPLE ANSWERS

Chapter 1
Warm Up
1-5: bicycle, transport, overworked, interrupted, survived

6-10: autonomous, returned, nonfiction, secured, engaged

11-15: destroyed, triathlon, unique, preview, hyperactive

16-20: misconduct, extracted, forecast, Antarctic, unity

Quick Practice
Practice #1 (1-6):
A B C D A A
Practice #2 (7-12):
B C D A C B
Practice #3 (13-18):
A D A B A D
Practice #4 (19-24):
C A B B C D
Practice #5 (25-30):
D C A B A C
Practice #6 (31-36):
D B C C B D
Practice #7 (37-42):
B A A C C D
Practice #8 (43-48):
B C A B D D
Practice #9 (49-54):
A B C A A B
Practice #10 (55-60):
D A B A A B

Chapter 2
Warm Up
1-10: him, they, its, it, its / he, it, his, her, their

11-20: he, their, their, a few, others / their, these, your, he, who

Quick Practice
Practice #1 (1-2): B C
Practice #2 (3-4): A C
Practice #3 (5-6): B C
Practice #4 (7-8): A C
Practice #5 (9-10): B C
Practice #6 (11-12): A B
Practice #7 (13-14): B C
Practice #8 (15-16): A D
Practice #9 (17-18): C D
Practice #10 (19-20): C C

Exercises (Ch. 1-2)
Exercise #1 (1-6):
C D D B D A
Exercise #2 (7-12):
D D A C C C
Exercise #3 (13-18):
A B B D C A
Exercise #4 (19-24):
B B D A C D
Exercise #5 (25-30):
A C D B D A

Chapter 3
Warm Up
1-10:
O F O F F / F O O F O
11-20:
O O F O F / F O O F F

Quick Practice
Practice #1 (1-2): B B
Practice #2 (3-4): A B
Practice #3 (5-6): C D
Practice #4 (7-8): A C
Practice #5 (9-10): A D
Practice #6 (11-12): C A
Practice #7 (13-14): C D
Practice #8 (15-16): B D
Practice #9 (17-18): B C
Practice #10 (19-20): D B

Chapter 4
Warm Up
1-10:
D C E C E / A B C D C
11-20:
D E C D E / D C D A D

Quick Practice
Practice #1: D
Practice #2: C
Practice #3: D
Practice #4: A
Practice #5: C
Practice #6: B
Practice #7: D
Practice #8: C
Practice #9: C
Practice #10: D

Exercises (Ch. 3-4)
Exercise #1 (1-4):
D C A B
Exercise #2 (5-8):
B D C C
Exercise #3 (9-12):
A B C C
Exercise #4 (13-16):
C D A D
Exercise #5 (17-20):
B A C D

Chapter 5
Warm Up
1-5:
3-2-1 / 2-1-3 / 1-3-2 / 1-3-2 / 3-1-2
6-10:
2-3-1 / 1-3-2 / 3-1-2 / 1-3-2 / 3-2-1

Quick Practice
Practice #1: A
Practice #2: C
Practice #3: D
Practice #4: B
Practice #5: D
Practice #6: D
Practice #7: C
Practice #8: D
Practice #9: C
Practice #10: A

Chapter 6
Warm Up
1-10:
A B A B B / A A B A B

Chapter 7
Warm Up
1-10:
PER, DES, CR, PER, DES / CR, DES, DES, CR, PER

Quick Practice
Practice #1: C
Practice #2: A
Practice #3: B
Practice #4: C
Practice #5: D
Practice #6: A
Practice #7: D
Practice #8: A
Practice #9: B
Practice #10: D

Exercises (Ch. 5-6)
Exercise #1 (1-2): C E
Exercise #2 (3-4): C B
Exercise #3 (5-6): C F
Exercise #4 (7-8): B A
Exercise #5 (9-10): D E
Exercise #6 (11-12): C D
Exercise #7 (13-14): C H
Exercise #8 (15-16): C B
Exercise #9 (17-18): D G
Exercise #10 (19-20): A B

Chapter 7
Warm Up
1-10:
PER, DES, CR, PER, DES / CR, DES, DES, CR, PER

Quick Practice
Practice #1: D
Practice #2: B
Practice #3: D
Practice #4: A
Practice #5: C
Practice #6: B
Practice #7: C
Practice #8: B
Practice #9: A
Practice #10: A

Chapter 8
Warm Up
1-10:
A A A B A / B B B A B

Quick Practice
Practice #1: C

Practice #2: A
Practice #3: D
Practice #4: C
Practice #5: D
Practice #6: A
Practice #7: C
Practice #8: D
Practice #9: B
Practice #10: B

Exercises (Ch. 7-8)
Exercise #1 (1-2): C A
Exercise #2 (3-4): C A
Exercise #3 (5-6): A A
Exercise #4 (7-8): C B
Exercise #5 (9-10): D A
Exercise #6 (11-12): D D
Exercise #7 (13-14): C D
Exercise #8 (15-16): B A
Exercise #9 (17-18): B A
Exercise #10 (19-20): D B

Chapter 9
Warm Up
1-10:
2, 1, 3, 1, 3 / 1, 1, 2, 3, 2

Quick Practice
Practice #1: 1, 3, 6
Practice #2: 3, 4, 5
Practice #3: 1, 2, 5
Practice #4: 1, 3, 4
Practice #5: 2, 3, 4
Practice #6: 1, 2, 5
Practice #7: 2, 3, 6
Practice #8: 1, 3, 5
Practice #9: 3, 4, 6
Practice #10: 1, 5, 6

Chapter 10
Warm Up
1) Desktop: 1, 6
   Laptop: 3, 4
2) Angry: 3, 6
   Happy: 2, 5

3) Nose: 2, 3
   Eye: 1, 6
4) Car: 2, 6
   Motorcycle: 1, 5
5) Trees: 1, 5
   Flowers: 2, 4
6) Halloween: 1, 3
   Christmas: 4, 5
7) Spring: 1, 4
   Winter: 3, 5
8) Skateboard: 1, 4
   Snowboard: 2, 6
9) Desert: 1, 4
   Forest: 3, 5
10) Rural: 2, 3
    Urban: 1, 5

Quick Practice
1) Angiosperms: 1, 4
   Gymnosperms: 2, 3, 6
2) Butterflies: 2, 4
   Moths: 1, 6, 7
3) Tragedy: 2, 3
   Comedy: 1, 4, 6
4) Trojan horse: 2, 4, 7
   Computer Worm: 1, 3
5) Stone Age: 2, 6
   Bronze Age: 1, 5, 7
6) Brown algae: 2, 5, 6
   Green algae: 3, 4
7) Road maps: 4, 5, 7
   Street maps: 2, 6
8) Ethics: 1, 2, 6
   Aesthetics: 3, 4
9) Fixed-blade knives: 1, 6
   Folding knives: 3, 4, 7
10) Tile games: 2, 3, 5
    Target games:1, 6

Exercises (Ch. 9-10)
1) 1, 3, 6
2) Agricultural fairs: 1, 5, 6
   Trade fairs: 2, 3
3) 3, 4, 5
4) De Stijl: 5, 7
   Art Deco: 3, 4, 6
5) 2, 3, 4
6) Social bees: 1, 5, 7
   Solitary bees: 2, 4

7) 1, 3, 5
8) Alpaca: 2, 4
   Llama: 1, 3, 5
9) 1, 3, 6
10) Warded locks: 2, 5, 7
    Card access locks: 3, 4

Actual Practice
Actual Practice 1
1-5: A D B A B
6-11: C C A B D / B
12: 1, 2, 6

Actual Practice 2
1-5: C B A C C
6-11: D A B B A / D
12: 2, 4, 6

Actual Practice 3
1-5: D A C B A
6-11: D B B D C / D
12: 1, 4, 5

Actual Practice 4
1-5: B C C D A
6-11: B C C B B / A
12: 1, 2, 6

Actual Practice 5
1-5: B D B B A
6-11: A C D D C / C
12: 3, 4, 5

Actual Practice 6
1-5: D C D A B
6-11: A C D A A / D
12: Resources: 1, 5, 6
    Products: 2, 4

Actual Practice 7
1-5: D B A D C
6-11: B B D D C / B
12: 2, 4, 6

Actual Practice 8
1-5: A D C B A
6-11: D C A A D / B
12: Oracle in Delphi: 4, 6
    Oracle in Dodona: 1, 3, 7

Actual Practice 9
1-5: A D A C D
6-11: B A D D C / A
12: 1, 2, 6

Actual Practice 10
1-5: B B A C C
6-11: A B C C A / C
12: 1, 5, 6

Actual Practice 11
1-5: B A B C D
6-11: B A C C B / A
12: 2, 5, 6

Actual Practice 12
1-5: B A C D B
6-11: B D A C C / D
12: 2, 3, 5

Actual Test
Reading 1
1-5: D D A B B
6-12: C A B D A / B C
13: Trial by combat: 1
Trial by ordeal: 4, 6
Trial by jury: 2, 7

Reading 2
14-18: A C A C D
19-25: B B C A B / A C
26: 1, 3, 4

Reading 3
27-31: A B C B A
32-38: D D C B A / C C
39: 2, 3, 5